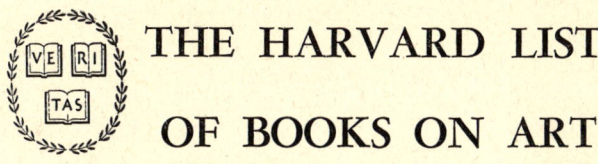

# THE HARVARD LIST OF BOOKS ON ART

*Compiled by E. Louise Lucas*

*Harvard University Press*

Cambridge, Massachusetts

1952

COPYRIGHT, 1952
BY THE PRESIDENT AND FELLOWS OF HARVARD COLLEGE

DISTRIBUTED IN GREAT BRITAIN BY

GEOFFREY CUMBERLEGE

OXFORD UNIVERSITY PRESS

LONDON

LIBRARY OF CONGRESS CATALOG CARD NUMBER: 52–5400

PRINTED IN THE UNITED STATES OF AMERICA

# PREFACE

The attempt to select a few thousand titles basic to the study of art history is as futile as choosing ten books for companionship on a desert island. Nevertheless, here is another such attempt.

Students who have used earlier editions of *Books on Art* will notice many gaps in this one. The omissions result primarily from the desire to publish a shorter list and to emphasize those books that a library may acquire without undue difficulty. Therefore, publications of comparatively recent date have sometimes forced the exclusion of important older titles. Even more than in the past much excellent background material has been omitted, for example, general encyclopedias and histories, museum and private collection catalogues, studies of special sites. Because of these omissions it is incumbent upon all students and librarians who use the list to remember that such catalogues often record the results of some of our most productive scholarship.

Although English texts, and editions still in print, have been chosen when available, language has not been a primary criterion for choice. So far as possible the date of the latest imprint has been used rather than the date of copyright to indicate availability. Truly basic books should remain in print. Good illustrations, regardless of text, have been a determining factor in many instances, for in most libraries published material has to take the place of, or at least to supplement, good photograph collections. In general, books published since 1950 have not been included.

Additional titles will be found in the bibliographies contained in many of the books listed and in the current periodical articles to be found through the *Art Index* or some similar source. Because the *Art Index* is generally available through libraries, no separate listing of periodicals is included here.

The emphasis of *Books on Art* is on architecture, sculpture, painting, and drawing. It deals with books on the history of art; intentionally, the so-called minor arts and the how-to-do-it publications are sketchily treated or conspicuously missing. Classification of titles in such a list is necessarily arbitrary, but the index of authors and artists has been planned to facilitate cross reference.

No two persons will agree on the choice of titles. Therefore this selection—including choices, omissions, and errors—is mine. I have, of course, profited greatly from suggestions and advice from faculty, staff, and students. Miss Helen Styles has prepared the entire manuscript.

Indeed, without the steady assistance of all of the Fogg Museum Library staff the work of compilation could not have been undertaken. I feel deep indebtedness and appreciation for help in the past and shall appreciate corrections in the future.

*Books on Art* is not a blanket order to be given to a book dealer, nor is it a list of the best books in the field of art history. It is a list of suggestions to be used with discretion and imagination by mature students and librarians.

E. L. L.

Fogg Museum of Art
Harvard University
March 1952

# CONTENTS

**REFERENCE HANDBOOKS AND INDEXES**     1

**ICONOGRAPHY AND SYMBOLISM**     3

**HISTORY AND ESTHETICS**     4

    General, 4. Ancient: Assyria, Babylonia, Chaldea, Egypt, Mesopotamia, 6; Crete, Etruria, Greece, Rome, 7; Far East, India, Near East, 10; South and Central America, Mexico, 13. Byzantine, Early Christian, Medieval, 14. Renaissance and Baroque, 17. Nineteenth and Twentieth Centuries, 18. National: France, 19; Germany and Austria, 20; Great Britain and Ireland, 21; Italy, 22; Low Countries, 22; Russia, 23; Scandinavia, 23; Spain, 24; United States and Canada, 25

**ARCHITECTURE**     26

    General, 26. National: France, 27; Germany, Austria, Low Countries, Switzerland, 28; Great Britain, 29; Italy, 30; Scandinavia and Russia, 31; Spain and Portugal, 31; United States, 32; Mexico and Latin America, 32

**SCULPTURE**     34

    General, 34. National: France and Belgium, 35; Germany, Switzerland, Austria, 35; Great Britain, 36; Italy, 37; Spain and Mexico, 37; United States, 38

**PAINTING**     39

    General, 39. National: France, 42; Germany and Austria, 44; Great Britain, 45; Italy, 45; Low Countries, 48; Russia, 49; Scandinavia, 49; Spain, 49; Switzerland, 50; United States and Canada, 50

**GRAPHIC ARTS AND ILLUMINATION** 52

    Drawing and graphic arts, 52. Illuminated manuscripts, 61

**MINOR ARTS** 63

    General, 63. Textiles, tapestries, rugs, 64. Costume, 66. Furniture, 67. Pottery and porcelain, 70. Glass, 72. Enamels, ivories, mosaics, 73. Metalwork, 74

**INDIVIDUAL ARTISTS** 77

**INDEX OF ARTISTS AND AUTHORS** 141

# THE HARVARD LIST
# OF BOOKS ON ART

# REFERENCE HANDBOOKS AND INDEXES

Aeschlimann, Erardo, and Ancona, Paola d'. Dictionnaire des miniaturistes du moyen âge et de la renaissance. 2ª éd. Milan, Hoepli, 1949.

American Art Annual. Washington, American Federation of Arts, 1898–1948. 37 v.

American Art Directory. N. Y., Bowker, 1952 (announced for April; to supersede the American Art Annual).

Art Index, a cumulative author and subject index to a selected list of fine arts periodicals and museum bulletins. N. Y., Wilson, 1930—. v. 1 (1929)—.

Arts, Musées et Curiosité en France. Paris, Ardo, 1946—. v. 1—.

Bénézit, Emmanuel. Dictionnaire critique et documentaire des peintres, sculpteurs, dessinateurs et graveurs. Nouv. éd. Paris, Gründ, 1948—. v. 1— (in progress).

Briquet, Charles M. Les filigranes. Dictionnaire historique des marques du papier, dès leur apparition vers 1282 jusqu'en 1600. 2d ed. Leipzig, Hiersemann, 1923. 4 v.

Bryan, Michael. Bryan's dictionary of painters and engravers. New ed., rev. and enl. by George C. Williamson. N. Y., Macmillan, 1925–27. 5 v.

Édouard-Joseph, René. Dictionnaire biographique des artistes contemporains, 1910–30. Paris, Art et édition, 1930–34. 3 v. Supplement, 1936.

Erréra, Isabelle. Dictionnaire répertoire des peintres depuis l'antiquité jusqu'à nos jours. Paris, Hachette, 1913.

——Répertoire des peintures datées. Bruxelles, Van Oest, 1920–21. 2 v.

Fielding, Mantle. Dictionary of American painters, sculptors, and engravers. N. Y., Struck, 1945.

Hall, H. Van. Repertorium voor de geschiedenis der Nederlandsche schilder-en graveerkunst. The Hague, Nijhoff, 1936–49. 2 v. [continued in Bibliography of the Rijksbureau voor kunsthistorische documentatie].

Holt, Elizabeth B. G., ed. Literary sources of art history. Princeton, Princeton Univ. press, 1947.

Industrial Arts Index. N. Y., Wilson, 1918—. v. 1—.

Internationale Bibliographie der Kunstwissenschaft. Berlin, Behr, 1903–20. 15 v.

Lancour, Adlore Harold. American art auction catalogues, 1785–1942. N. Y., New York Public Library, 1944.

Lugt, Frits. Répertoire des catalogues de ventes publiques. The Hague, Nijhoff, 1938—. v. 1— (in progress).

Mallett, Daniel T. Mallett's index of artists. N. Y., Bowker, 1935. Supplement, 1940 [Reprint ed., N. Y., P. Smith, 1948].

Mireur, Hippolyte. Dictionnaire des ventes d'art. Paris, Vincenti, 1911–12. 7 v.

Müller, Hermann A., and Singer, Hans W. Allgemeines künstler-lexicon. 6$^{te}$ aufl. Frankfurt a/M, Rütten und Loening, 1922. 6 v.

Nagler, George K. Neues allgemeines künstler-lexikon. Vienna, Manz, 1924. 25 v.

Répertoire d'art et d'archéologie. Paris, Bibliothèque d'art et d'archéologie, 1910—. v. 1—.

Rijksbureau voor Kunsthistorische Documentatie. Bibliography. The Hague, Netherlands Institute, 1943—. v. 1—.

Schlosser, Julius. La letteratura artistica. Florence, Nuova Italia, 1935. Appendice di Otto Kurz, 1937.

Thieme, Ulrich, and Becker, Felix. Allgemeines lexikon der bildenden künstler. Leipzig, Seemann, 1908–1947. 36 v.

Who's Who in American Art. Washington, D. C., American Federation of Arts, 1935—. v. 1— [Previously included in American Art Annual].

Who's Who in Art. London, Art trade press, 1927—. v. 1—.

Wurzbach, Alfred. Niederländisches künstler-lexikon. Vienna, Halm, 1906–11. 3 v.

The Year's Art. London, Hutchinson, 1880—. v. 1—.

# ICONOGRAPHY AND SYMBOLISM

Barbier de Montault, Xavier. Traité d'iconographie chrétienne. Paris, Vivès, 1890. 2 v.

Bréhier, Louis. L'art chrétien, son développement iconographique dès origines à nos jours. 2ᵉ éd. Paris, Laurens, 1928.

Cabrol, Fernand. Dictionnaire d'archéologie chrétienne et de liturgie. Paris, Letouzey, 1903—. fasc. 1—.

Didron, Adolphe N. Christian iconography; or, The history of Christian art in the middle ages. Trans. E. G. Millington. London, Bell, 1896. 2 v.

Drake, Maurice. Saints and their emblems. London, Laurie, 1916.

Goldsmith, Elizabeth E. Ancient pagan symbols. N. Y., Putnam, 1929.

——— Sacred symbols in art. 2d ed. N. Y., Putnam, 1912.

Jacobus de Varagine. The golden legend; or, Lives of the saints, as Englished by William Caxton. London, Dent, 1900. 7 v.

Jameson, Anna B. The history of our Lord. 4th ed. London, Longmans, 1881. 2 v.

——— Legends of the Madonna. Boston, Houghton Mifflin, 1911.

——— Legends of the monastic orders. Boston, Houghton Mifflin, 1911.

——— Sacred and legendary art. Boston, Houghton Mifflin, 1911. 2 v.

Künstle, Karl. Ikonographie der christlichen kunst. Freiburg, Herder, 1926–28. 2 v.

Mackenzie, Donald A. The migration of symbols. N. Y., Knopf, 1926.

Mâle, Émile. L'art religieux de la fin du moyen âge en France. 5th éd. Paris, Colin, 1949.

——— L'art religieux du XIIᵉ siècle en France. 5ᵉ éd. Paris, Colin, 1947.

——— L'art religieux du XIIIᵉ siècle en France. 8ᵉ éd. Paris, Colin, 1948.

——— L'art religieux après le Concile de Trente. Paris, Colin, 1932.

——— Religious art from the 12th to the 18th century. N. Y., Pantheon, 1949.

——— Religious art in France, XIII century. Trans. Dora Nussey. N. Y., Dutton, 1913.

Ricci, Elisa. Mille santi nell'arte. Milan, Hoepli, 1931.

Tabor, Margaret E. The saints in art. N. Y., Stokes, 1908.

# HISTORY AND ESTHETICS
## General

Abell, Walter. Representation and form; a study of aesthetic values in representational art. N. Y., Scribner, 1936.

Bell, Clive. Art. New rev. ed. London, Chatto, 1949.

Berenson, Bernhard. Aesthetics and history in the visual arts. N. Y., Pantheon, 1948.

Chambers, Frank P. The history of taste. N. Y., Columbia Univ. press, 1932.

Cheney, Sheldon. A world history of art. N. Y., Viking, 1946.

Croce, Benedetto. Aesthetic as science of expression. Trans. Douglas Ainslie. 2d ed. London, Macmillan, 1922.

Dewey, John. Art as experience. N. Y., Minton, 1935.

Encyclopédie photographique de l'art. Paris, Éditions "Tel," 1936—. v. 1—.

Faure, Élie. History of art. Trans. Walter Pach. N. Y., Dover, 1948. 5 v. in 2.

Focillon, Henri. The life of forms in art. Trans. C. B. Hogan and G. Kubler. 2d English ed. N. Y., Wittenborn, Schultz, 1948.

Fry, Roger E. Transformations. London, Chatto, 1926.

——Vision and design. Harmondsworth, Penguin, 1937.

——French, Flemish and British art. N. Y., Coward-McCann, 1951.

Gardner, Helen. Art through the ages. 3d ed. N. Y., Harcourt, Brace, 1948.

Goldscheider, Ludwig. Art without epoch; works of distant times which still appeal to modern taste. London, Oxford Univ. press, Phaidon ed., 1938.

——Five hundred self portraits from antique times to the present day in sculpture, painting, drawing and engraving. London, Oxford Univ. press, Phaidon ed., 1937.

Goldwater, Robert J., and Treves, Marco, eds. Artists on art, from the XIV to the XX century. 2d ed. N. Y., Pantheon, 1947.

Gombrich, E. H. The story of art. London, Oxford Univ. press, Phaidon ed., 1950.

Greene, Theodore M. The arts and the art of criticism. Princeton, Princeton Univ. press, 1940.

Hagen, Oscar F. L. Art epochs and their leaders. N. Y., Scribner, 1927.

Hauser, Arnold. The social history of art. London, Routledge, 1951. 2 v.

Kallen, Horace M. Art and freedom; a historical and biographical interpretation of the relations between the ideas of beauty, use and freedom in western civilization from the Greeks to the present day. N. Y., Duell, Sloan and Pearce, 1942. 2 v.

Kepes, Gyorgy. Language of vision. Chicago, Theobold, 1944.

Malraux, André. The psychology of art. Trans. Stuart Gilbert. N. Y., Pantheon, 1949–51. 3 v. (Bollingen series, 24).

Michel, André. Histoire de l'art depuis les premiers temps chrétiens jusqu'à nos jours. Paris, Colin, 1905–29. 8 v. in 17.

Munro, Thomas. The arts and their interrelations. N. Y., Liberal arts press, 1949.

Pepper, Stephen C. Principles of art appreciation. N. Y., Harcourt, Brace, 1949.

Pevsner, Nikolaus. Academies of art, past and present. Cambridge [Eng.], University press, 1940.

Pijoán, José. History of art. Trans. R. L. Roys. 2d ed. London, Batsford, 1933. 3 v.

Read, Herbert E. The meaning of art. N. Y., Pitman, 1951 [Rev. ed. of his Anatomy of art].

——Education through art. London, Faber, 1947.

Reinach, Salomon. Apollo. Trans. F. Simmonds. N. Y., Scribner, 1935.

Richardson, Edgar P. The way of western art, 1776–1914. Cambridge, Harvard Univ. press, 1939.

Robb, David M., and Garrison, J. J. Art in the western world. Rev. ed. N. Y., Harper, 1949.

Roos, Frank J. An illustrated handbook of art history. N. Y., Macmillan, 1937.

Ruskin, John. Works. Ed. by E. T. Cook and Alexander Wedderburn. N. Y., Longmans, 1903–12. 39 v.

Scott, Geoffrey. The architecture of humanism. 2d ed. London, Constable, 1924.

Upjohn, Everard M., and others. History of world art. N. Y., Oxford Univ. press, 1949.

Wölfflin, Heinrich. Principles of art history. Trans. M. D. Hottinger. N. Y., Dover, 1949.

# Ancient

ASSYRIA, BABYLONIA, CHALDEA, EGYPT, MESOPOTAMIA

- Aldred, Cyril. Middle kingdom art in ancient Egypt. London, Tiranti, 1950.
- ——New kingdom art in ancient Egypt. N. Y., Transatlantic, 1951.
- ——Old kingdom art in ancient Egypt. London, Tiranti, 1949.
- Boas, Franz. Primitive art. Cambridge, Harvard Univ. press, 1951.
- Capart, Jean. L'art égyptien. Bruxelles, Vromant, 1922–1947. 4 v.
- Childe, Vere G. Progress and archaeology. London, Watts, 1945.
- ——What happened in history. N. Y., Penguin books, 1946.
- Contenau, Georges. Manuel d'archéologie orientale depuis les origines jusqu'à l'époque d'Alexandre. Paris, Picard, 1927–47. 4 v.
- Drioton, Étienne. Egyptian art. Photographs by Étienne Sved. N. Y., Golden Griffin, 1950.
- Gadd, Cyril J. The stones of Assyria. London, Chatto, 1936.
- Handcock, Percy S. P. Mesopotamian archaeology. N. Y., Putnam, 1912.
- Harcourt-Smith, Simon. Babylonian art. London, Benn, 1928.
- Lucas, Alfred. Ancient Egyptian materials and industries. 3d ed. London, Arnold, 1948.
- Maspero, Gaston C. C. Manual of Egyptian archaeology and guide to the study of antiquities in Egypt. Trans. and enl. by A. S. Johns. 6th English ed. N. Y., Putnam, 1914.
- Murray, Margaret A. Egyptian sculpture. N. Y., Scribner, 1930.
- ——Egyptian temples. London, Low, Marston, 1931.
- Peet, Thomas E. The stone and bronze ages in Italy and Sicily. Oxford, Clarendon press, 1909.
- Petrie, William M. F. The arts and crafts of ancient Egypt. Edinburgh, Foulis, 1923.
- Ranke, Hermann. The art of ancient Egypt. Vienna, Phaidon press; London, Allen, 1936.
- Raphael, Max. Prehistoric cave paintings. N. Y., Pantheon, 1945.
- Robinson, David M. Baalbek, Palmyra. Photographs by G. Hoyningen-Huene. N. Y., Augustin, 1946.
- Ross, Edward D. The art of Egypt through the ages. N. Y., Rudge, 1931.

Smith, Earl B. Egyptian architecture as cultural expression. N. Y., Appleton-Century-Crofts, 1938.

Smith, William S. A history of Egyptian sculpture and painting in the old kingdom. 2d ed. Boston, Museum of Fine Arts, 1949.

Steindorff, Georg. Egypt. N. Y., Augustin, 1943.

Swindler, Mary H. Ancient painting, from the earliest times to the period of Christian art. New Haven, Yale Univ. press, 1929.

Sydow, Eckart von. Die kunst der naturvölker und der vorzeit. 2$^e$ aufl. Berlin, Propyläen-verlag, 1927 (Propyläen kunstgeschichte, 1).

Woolley, Charles L. Development of Sumerian art. N. Y., Scribner, 1935.

Worringer, Wilhelm. Egyptian art. Trans. Bernard Rackham. London, Putnam, 1928.

Zervos, Christian. L'art de la Mésopotamie. Paris, Cahiers d'art, 1935.

CRETE, ETRURIA, GREECE, ROME

Anderson, William J. The architecture of ancient Greece. Rev. and enl. by W. B. Dinsmoor. London, Batsford, 1950.

——The architecture of ancient Rome. Rev. by T. Ashby. London, Batsford, 1927.

Baikie, James. The sea-kings of Crete. 4th ed. London, Black, 1926.

Beazley, John D. Attic red-figure vase painters. Oxford, Clarendon press, 1942.

——Etruscan vase-painting. Oxford, Clarendon press, 1947.

——Greek sculpture and painting to the end of the Hellenistic period. Cambridge [Eng.], University press, 1932.

Bossert, Helmuth T. Art of ancient Crete. 3d ed. London, Zwemmer, 1937.

Buschor, Ernst. Greek vase-painting. Trans. G. C. Richards. N. Y., Dutton, 1922.

Carpenter, Rhys. The esthetic basis of Greek art of the fifth and fourth centuries B.C. N. Y., Longmans, Green, 1921.

——The humanistic value of archaeology. Cambrdge, Harvard Univ. press, 1933.

Casson, Stanley. The technique of early Greek sculpture. Oxford, Clarendon press, 1933.

Chisholm, Hugh J. Hellas. Photographs by G. Hoyningen-Huene. N. Y., Augustin, 1943.

913.38 **Daremberg, Charles V., and Saglio, Edmond.** Dictionnaire des anti-
D247 quités grecques et romaines. Paris, Hachette, 1877–1919. 5 v. in 10.

**Daux, Georges.** Les merveilles de l'art antique (Grèce-Rome). Paris, Nathan, 1946.

**Deonna, Waldemar.** Du miracle grec au miracle chrétien. Bâle, Éditions Birkhaeuser, 1945—. v. 1—.

**Dickins, Guy.** Hellenistic sculpture. Oxford, Clarendon press, 1920.

913.38 **Dickinson, Goldsworthy L.** The Greek view of life. 7th ed. Garden
D56a City, N. Y., Doubleday, 1928.

**Ducati, Pericle.** Storia dell'arte etrusca. Firenze, Rinascimento del libro, 1927. 2 v.

913.33 **Fowler, Harold N., and Wheeler, James R.** A handbook of Greek
F829 archaeology. N. Y., American book co., 1909.

**Furtwängler, Adolf, and Urlichs, Heinrich L.** Greek and Roman sculpture. Trans. Horace Taylor. N. Y., Dutton, 1914.

733.3 **Gardner, Ernest A.** A handbook of Greek sculpture. London, Macmil-
G172a lan, 1924.

**Gardner, Percy.** The principles of Greek art. N. Y., Macmillan, 1926.

733.5 **Goldscheider, Ludwig.** Etruscan sculpture. London, Oxford Univ. press,
G572 Phaidon ed., 1941.

——Roman portraits. N. Y., Oxford Univ. press, Phaidon ed., 1940.

**Hall, Harry R. H.** Aegean archaeology; introduction to archaeology of prehistoric Greece. N. Y., Putnam, 1915.

**Head, Barclay V.** Historia numorum; a manual of Greek numismatics. New and enl. ed. Oxford, Clarendon press, 1911.

**Hekler, Antal.** Greek and Roman portraits. London, Heinemann, 1912.

**Hoppin, Joseph C.** A handbook of Attic red-figured vases. Cambridge, Harvard Univ. press, 1919. 2 v.

——A handbook of Greek black-figured vases. Paris, Champion, 1924.

**Huish, Marcus B.** Greek terra-cotta statuettes, their origin, evolution and uses. London, Murray, 1900.

**Lamb, Winifred.** Greek and Roman bronzes. London, Methuen, 1929.

733 **Lawrence, Arnold W.** Classical sculpture. London, Cape, 1929.
L435c
733.3 ——Later Greek sculpture and its influence on East and West. London,
L435 Cape, 1927.

**Macdonald, George.** Coin types, their origin and development. Glasgow, Maclehose, 1905.

**Mattingly, Harold.** Roman coins from the earliest times to the fall of the western empire. N. Y., MacVeagh, 1928.

**Minns, Ellis H.** Scythians and Greeks. Cambridge [Eng.], University press, 1913.

**Pendlebury, John D. S.** The archaeology of Crete. London, Methuen, 1939.

**Pfuhl, Ernst.** Malerei und zeichnung der Griechen. Munich, Bruckmann, 1923. 3 v.

**Picard, Charles.** Manuel d'archéologie grecque. Paris, Picard, 1935–1948. 3 v. (Manuels d'archéologie et d'histoire de l'art).

——La sculpture antique de Phidias à l'ère byzantine. Paris, Laurens, 1926 (Manuels d'histoire de l'art).

——La sculpture antique dès origines à Phidias. Paris, Laurens, 1923 (Manuels d'histoire de l'art).

**Randall-MacIver, David.** The Etruscans. Oxford, Clarendon press, 1927.

——The iron age in Italy. Oxford, Clarendon press, 1927.

——Italy before the Romans. Oxford, Clarendon press, 1928.

——Villanovans and early Etruscans. Oxford, Clarendon press, 1924.

**Reinach, Salomon.** Répertoire de la statuaire grecque et romaine. Paris, Leroux, 1897–1924. 6 v.

——Répertoire de peintures grecques et romaines. Paris, Leroux, 1922.

——Répertoire de reliefs grecs et romains. Paris, Leroux, 1909–12. 3 v.

——Répertoire des vases peints grecs et étrusques. Paris, Leroux, 1899–1900. 2 v.

**Richter, Gisela M. A.** Archaic Greek art against its historical background; a survey. N. Y., Oxford Univ. press, 1949.

——The craft of Athenian pottery. New Haven, Yale Univ. press, 1923.

——The sculpture and sculptors of the Greeks. New rev. ed. New Haven, Yale Univ. press, 1950.

**Rivoira, Giovanni T.** Roman architecture and its principles of construction under the empire. Trans. G. M. Rushforth. Oxford, Clarendon press, 1925.

**Robertson, Donald S.** A handbook of Greek and Roman architecture. 2d ed. Cambridge [Eng.], University press, 1943.

**Rodenwaldt, Gerhart.** Die kunst der antike (Hellas und Rom). Berlin, Propyläen-verlag, 1927 (Propyläen-kunstgeschichte, 3).

**Seltman, Charles T.** Approach to Greek art. N. Y., Studio, 1948.

———Masterpieces of Greek coinage. Oxford, Cassirer, 1949.

**Strong, Eugénie S.** Art in ancient Rome. N. Y., Scribner, 1928. 2 v. (Ars una).

**Tarbell, Frank B.** A history of Greek art. N. Y., Macmillan, 1927.

**Webster, Thomas B. L.** Greek art and literature, 530–400 B.C. Oxford, Clarendon press, 1939.

**Zervos, Christian.** L'art en Grèce des temps préhistoriques au début du XVIIIe siècle. 2e éd. Paris, Cahiers d'art, 1936.

———L'art en Grèce du troisième millénaire au IVe siècle avant notre ère. Paris, Cahiers d'art, 1946.

FAR EAST, INDIA, NEAR EAST

**Arnold, Thomas W.** Painting in Islam; a study of the place of pictorial art in Muslim culture. Oxford, Clarendon press, 1928.

**Ashton, Leigh, and Gray, Basil.** Chinese art. London, Faber, 1935.

**Bachhofer, Ludwig.** Early Indian sculpture. N. Y., Harcourt, Brace, 1929. 2 v.

———A short history of Chinese art. N. Y., Pantheon, 1946.

**Binyon, Laurence.** The flight of the dragon. London, Murray, 1935.

———Japanese colour prints. N. Y., Scribner, 1923.

———Painting in the Far East. 4th ed. London, Arnold, 1934.

———The spirit of man in Asian art. Cambridge, Harvard Univ. press, 1935.

**Binyon, Laurence, and Arnold, Thomas W.** The court painters of the Grand Moguls. London, Oxford Univ. press, 1921.

**Borovka, Grigorii I.** Scythian art. Trans. V. G. Childe. N. Y., Stokes, 1928.

**Brown, Percy.** Indian architecture (Buddhist and Hindu periods). 2d ed. Bombay, Taraporevala, 194–.

———Indian architecture (the Islamic period). Bombay, Taraporevala, 1943.

———Indian painting under the Mughals, A.D. 1550–1750. Oxford, Clarendon press, 1924.

**Bushell, Stephen W.** Chinese art. London, Board of education, 1924. 2 v.

Codrington, Kenneth de B. Ancient India. London, Benn, 1926.

Cohn, William. Chinese painting. N. Y., Oxford Univ. press, Phaidon ed., 1948.

Coomaraswamy, Ananda K. The arts and crafts of India and Ceylon. London, Foulis, 1913.

——Elements of Buddhist iconography. Cambridge, Harvard Univ. press, 1935.

——History of Indian and Indonesian art. N. Y., Weyhe, 1927.

——Rajput painting. N. Y., Oxford Univ. press, 1916. 2 v.

——The transformation of nature in art. Cambridge, Harvard Univ. press, 1934.

Diez, Ernst. Iranische kunst. Wien, Andermann, 1944.

——Die kunst Indiens. Wildpark-Potsdam, Akademische verlagsgesellschaft Athenaion, 1925.

Fenollosa, Ernest F. Epochs of Chinese and Japanese art. N. Y., Stokes, 1913. 2 v.

Ferguson, John C. Chinese painting. Chicago, Univ. of Chicago press, 1927.

Fergusson, James. History of Indian and Eastern architecture. Rev. and ed. by James Burgess and R. P. Spiers. London, Murray, 1910. 2 v.

Fischer, Otto. Die kunst Indiens, Chinas und Japans. Berlin, Propyläen-verlag, 1928 (Propyläen-kunstgeschichte, 4).

Fry, Roger E., ed. Chinese art. New ed. London, Batsford, 1946.

Giles, Herbert A. An introduction to the history of Chinese pictorial art. 2d ed. London, Quaritch, 1918.

Glück, Heinrich, and Diez, Ernst. Die kunst des Islam. Berlin, Propyläen-verlag, 1925 (Propyläen-kunstgeschichte, 5).

Grousset, René. The civilizations of the East. Trans. C. A. Phillips. N. Y., Knopf, 1931-34. 4 v.

Hackin, Joseph, ed. Asiatic mythology. Trans. F. M. Atkinson. London, Harrap, 1932.

Havell, Ernest B. A handbook of Indian art. London, Murray, 1927.

——Indian architecture. 2d ed. London, Murray, 1927.

——Indian sculpture and painting. 2d ed. London, Murray, 1928.

Herzfeld, Ernst E. Iran in the ancient East. N. Y., Oxford Univ. press, 1941.

**Hobson, Robert L.** Chinese art. N. Y., Macmillan, 1927.

——Chinese pottery and porcelain: an account of the potter's art in China from primitive times to the present day. London, Cassell, 1915. 2 v.

**Honey, William B.** The ceramic art of China and other countries of the Far East. London, Faber, 1945.

——Corean pottery. London, Faber, 1947.

**Koop, Albert J.** Early Chinese bronzes. London, Benn, 1924.

**Kramrisch, Stella.** Indian sculpture. London, Oxford Univ. press, 1933.

**Kuo, Hsi.** An essay on landscape painting. Trans. Shio Sakanishi. London, Murray, 1935.

**Laufer, Berthold.** Chinese pottery of the Han dynasty. Leiden, Brill, 1909.

——Jade. 2d ed. South Pasadena, Perkins, 1946.

**Martin, Fredrik R.** The miniature painting and painters of Persia, India and Turkey, from the eighth to the eighteenth century. London, Quaritch, 1912. 2 v.

**Migeon, Gaston, and Saladin, Henri.** Manuel d'art musulman. 2ᵉ éd. Paris, Picard, 1927. 2 v. (v. 1, Saladin: L'architecture; v. 2, Migeon: Les arts plastiques et industriels).

**Minamoto, Hoshu.** An illustrated history of Japanese art. Trans. H. G. Henderson. Kyoto, Hoshino, 1935.

**Mulk-Raj Anand.** The Hindu view of art. London, Allen and Unwin, 1933.

**Okakura Kakuzo.** The book of tea. N. Y., Duffield, 1925.

——The ideals of the East. London, Murray, 1920.

**Pope, Arthur U.** An introduction to Persian art since the seventh century A.D. N.Y., Scribner, 1931.

——Masterpieces of Persian art. N. Y., Dryden press, 1945.

**Rivoira, Giovanni T.** Moslem architecture. Trans. G. M. Rushforth. N. Y., Oxford Univ. press, 1918.

**Rowley, George.** Principles of Chinese painting. Princeton, Princeton Univ. press, 1947 (Princeton monographs in art and archaeology, 24).

**Schäfer, Heinrich, and Andrae, Walter.** Die kunst des alten Orients. Berlin, Propyläen-verlag, 1925 (Propyläen-kunstgeschichte, 2).

**Silcock, Arnold.** Introduction to Chinese art and history. N. Y., Oxford Univ. press, 1948.

Sirén, Osvald. A history of early Chinese painting. London, Medici society, 1933. 2 v.

——A history of later Chinese painting. London, Medici society, 1938. 2 v.

Smith, Vincent A. A history of fine art in India and Ceylon. 2d ed. rev. by Kenneth de B. Codrington. Oxford, Clarendon press, 1930.

Soper, Alexander C. The evolution of Buddhist architecture in Japan. Princeton, Princeton Univ. press, 1942 (Princeton monographs in art and archaeology, 22).

Taki, Sei-Ichi. Three essays on Oriental painting. London, Quaritch, 1910.

Toda, Kenji. Japanese scroll painting. Chicago, Univ. of Chicago press, 1935.

Waley, Arthur. An introduction to the study of Chinese painting. N. Y., Scribner, 1923.

Warner, Langdon. The craft of the Japanese sculptor. N. Y., McFarlane, 1936.

——Japanese sculpture of the Suiko period. New Haven, Yale Univ. press, 1923.

Zimmer, Heinrich. Myths and symbols in Indian art and civilization. N. Y., Pantheon, 1946.

### SOUTH AND CENTRAL AMERICA, MEXICO

Anderson, Lawrence L. The art of the silversmith in Mexico, 1519–1936. N. Y., Oxford Univ. press, 1941. 2 v.

Douglas, Frederic H., and Harnoncourt, René d'. Indian art of the United States. N. Y., Museum of modern art, 1941.

Helm, MacKinley. Modern Mexican painters. N. Y., Harper, 1941.

Joyce, Thomas A. Central American and West Indian archaeology. London, Warner, 1916.

——Maya and Mexican art. London, Studio, 1927.

——Mexican archaeology. London, Warner, 1920.

——South American archaeology. N. Y., Putnam, 1912.

Kelemen, Pál. Baroque and rococo in Latin America. N. Y., Macmillan, 1951.

——Medieval American art. N. Y., Macmillan, 1943. 2 v.

Kidder, Alfred V. An introduction to the study of southwestern archaeology. New Haven, Yale Univ. press, 1924.

709.85 Lehmann, Walter, and Doering, Heinrich. The art of old Peru. Lon-
L528     don, Benn, 1924.

    Morley, Sylvanus G. The ancient Maya. Stanford, Stanford Univ. press, 1946.

    Schmeckebier, Laurence E. Modern Mexican art. Minneapolis, Univ. of Minnesota press, 1939.

    Schmidt, Max. Kunst und kultur von Peru. Berlin, Propyläen-verlag, 1929.

016.7098 Smith, Robert C., and Wilder, Elizabeth. A guide to the art of Latin
Sm64     America. Washington, D. C., Library of Congress, 1948 (Latin American ser., 21).

972.01 Spinden, Herbert J. Ancient civilizations of Mexico and Central Amer-
Sp46     ica. 3d ed. N. Y., Amer. Mus. of Natural History, 1946.

    ——A study of Maya art. Cambridge [Mass.], Peabody museum, 1913.

    Taullard, Alfredo. Platería sudamericana. Buenos Aires, Peuser, 1941.

    Toor, Frances. Mexican popular arts. Mexico, Toor studios, 1939.

    Toscano, Salvador. Arte precolombino de México y de la América central. México, Inst. de investigaciones estéticas, 1944.

    Totten, G. O. Maya architecture. Washington, D. C., Maya press, 1926.

    Toussaint, Manuel. Arte colonial en México. México, Impr. Universitaria, 1948.

    ——Arte mudejar en América. México, Editorial Porrúa, 1946.

972.014 Vaillant, George C. Aztecs of Mexico. Garden City, N. Y., Doubleday,
V194     1941.

    ——Indian arts in North America. N. Y., Harper, 1939.

970.1 Wissler, Clark. The American Indian. N. Y., Oxford Univ. press, 1938.
W765

## Byzantine, Early Christian, Medieval

    Baum, Julius. La sculpture figurale en Europe à l'époque mérovingienne. Paris, Éditions d'art et d'histoire, 1937.

    Bréhier, Louis. L'art byzantin. Paris, Laurens, 1924.

    ——La sculpture et les arts mineurs byzantins. Paris, Éditions d'art et d'histoire, 1936.

    Bunim, Miriam S. Space in medieval painting and the forerunners of perspective. N. Y., Columbia Univ. press, 1940.

    Butler, Howard C. Early Churches in Syria, fourth to seventh centuries. Princeton, Princeton Univ. press, 1929.

Byron, Robert. The birth of western painting. N. Y., Knopf, 1931.
Dalton, Ormonde M. Byzantine art and archaeology. Oxford, Clarendon press, 1911.
——East Christian art. Oxford, Clarendon press, 1925.
Diehl, Charles. Manuel d'art byzantin. 2$^e$ éd. Paris, Picard, 1925–26. 2 v.
——La peinture byzantine. Paris, Van Oest, 1933.
Diez, Ernst, and Demus, Otto. Byzantine mosaics in Greece, Hosios Lucas and Daphni. Cambridge [Mass.], American School of Classical Studies at Athens, 1931.
Ebersolt, Jean. Les églises de Constantinople. Paris, Leroux, 1913.
——Monuments d'architecture byzantine. Paris, Éditions d'art et d'histoire, 1934.
——Orient et occident. Paris, Van Oest, 1928–29. 2 v.
Focillon, Henri. Art d'occident, le moyen âge, roman et gothique. 2$^e$ éd. Paris, Colin, 1947.
——Moyen âge, survivances et reveils. N. Y., Brentano's, 1943.
Grabar, André. L'art byzantin. Paris, Éditions d'art et d'histoire, 1938.
——Martyrium; recherches sur le culte des reliques et l'art chrétien antique. Paris, Collège de France, 1943–46. 2 v.
Harvey, John H. The Gothic world, 1100–1600; a survey of architecture and art. London, Batsford, 1950.
Hauttmann, Max. Die kunst des frühen mittelalters. 2$^e$ aufl. Berlin, Propyläen-verlag, 1937 (Propyläen-kunstgeschichte, 6).
Henry, Françoise. Irish art in the early Christian period. 2d ed. London, Methuen, 1947.
Hinks, Roger P. Carolingian art. London, Sidgwick and Jackson, 1935.
Hubert, Jean. L'art pré-roman. Paris, Éditions d'art et d'histoire, 1938.
Huizinga, Johan. The waning of the middle ages. London, Arnold, 1948.
Jackson, Thomas G. Byzantine and Romanesque architecture. 2d ed. Cambridge [Eng.], University press, 1920. 2 v.
——Gothic architecture in France, England and Italy. Cambridge [Eng.], University press, 1915. 2 v.
Jacobsthal, Paul. Early Celtic art. Oxford, Clarendon press, 1944. 2 v.
Karlinger, Hans. Die kunst der gotik. Berlin, Propyläen-verlag, 1927 (Propyläen-kunstgeschichte, 7).

Kitzinger, Ernst. Early medieval art in the British Museum. London, British museum, 1940. 1964

Kondakov, Nikodim P. Histoire de l'art byzantin considéré principalement dans les miniatures. Paris, Librairie de l'art, 1886–91. 2 v. in 1.

Lethaby, W. R. Mediaeval art, from the peace of the church to the eve of the Renaissance, 312–1350. Rev. by Talbot Rice. N. Y., Philosophical library, 1950.

Lowrie, Walter. Art in the early church. N. Y., Pantheon, 1947.

Mahr, Adolf. Christian art in ancient Ireland. Dublin, Stationery office of Saorstát Eireann, 1932—. v. 1—.

Marle, Raimond van. Iconographie de l'art profane au moyen-âge et à la renaissance, et la décoration des demeures. La Haye, Nijhoff, 1931—. v. 1—.

Millet, Gabriel. L'école grecque dans l'architecture byzantine. Paris, Leroux, 1916.

Morey, Charles R. Early Christian art. Princeton, Princeton Univ. press, 1942.

——— Mediaeval art. N. Y., Norton, 1942.

Moss, Henry St. L. B. The birth of the middle ages, 395–814. Oxford, Clarendon press, 1935.

Muratov, Pavel. La peinture byzantine. Paris, Weber, 1935.

Peirce, Hayford, and Tyler, Royall. L'art byzantin. Paris, Librairie de France, 1932—. v. 1—.

Rey, Raymond. L'art roman et ses origines. Paris, Didier, 1945.

Rice, David T. Byzantine art. Oxford, Clarendon press, 1935.

Rossi, Giovanni B. La Roma sotterranea cristiana. Roma, Cromo-litografia pontificia, 1864–77. 3 v.

Stewart, Cecil. Byzantine legacy. London, Allen, 1947.

Strzygowski, Josef. Die altslavische kunst. Augsburg, Filser, 1929.

——— Die baukunst der Armenier und Europa. Wien, Schroll, 1918. 2 v.

——— Early church art in northern Europe. N. Y., Harper, 1928.

——— Orient oder Rom. Leipzig, Hinrichs, 1901.

——— Origin of Christian church art. Trans. O. M. Dalton and H. J. Braunholtz. Oxford, Clarendon press, 1923.

Taylor, Henry O. The mediaeval mind. 4th ed. Cambridge, Harvard Univ. press, 1949. 2 v.

Van Millingen, Alexander. Byzantine churches in Constantinople. London, Macmillan, 1912.

Volbach, Wolfgang F. Art byzantin. Paris, Levy, 1933.

Whittemore, Thomas. The mosaics of St. Sophia at Istanbul. Paris, Byzantine Institute, 1933—. v. 1—.

Wickhoff, Franz. Roman art. N. Y., Macmillan, 1900.

Wilpert, Josef. Roma sotterranea; le pitture delle catacombe romane. Roma, Desclée, Lefebvre, 1903. 2 v. in 3.

——Die römischen mosaiken und malereien der kirchlichen bauten vom IV. bis XIII. jahrhundert. 2 aufl. Freiburg im Breisgau, Herdersche verlagshandlung, 1917. 4 v.

——I sarcofagi cristiani antichi. Roma, Pontificio istituto di archeologia cristiana, 1929-32. 3 v. (Monumenti dell' antichità cristiana, 1).

Worringer, Wilhelm. Form problems of the Gothic. N. Y., Stechert, 1920.

Wulff, Oskar K. Altchristliche und byzantinische kunst. Berlin-Neubabelsberg, Akademische verlagsgesellschaft Athenaion, 1914-18. 2 v.

——Bibliographisch-kritischer nachtrag zu altchristliche und byzantinische kunst. Potsdam, Akademische verlagsgesellschaft Athenaion, 1935.

## Renaissance and Baroque

Benesch, Otto. The art of the renaissance in northern Europe. Cambridge, Harvard Univ. press, 1945.

Brinckmann, Albert E. Kunst des barocks und rokokos. Berlin-Neubabelsberg, Akademische verlagsgesellschaft Athenaion, 1923.

Clark, George N. The seventeenth century. Oxford, Clarendon press, 1931.

Cox, Trenchard. The renaissance in Europe (1400-1600). London, Methuen, 1933.

Fokker, Timon H. Roman baroque art, the history of a style. London, Oxford Univ. press, 1938. 2 v.

Frey, Dagobert. Gotik und renaissance als grundlagen der modernen weltanschauung. Augsburg, Filser, 1929.

Gengaro, Mario L. Umanesimo e rinascimento. 2 ed. Torina, Unione tipografico-editrice torinese, 1944.

**Glück, Gustav.** Die kunst der renaissance in Deutschland, den Niederlanden, Frankreich. Berlin, Propyläen-verlag, 1928 (Propyläen-kunstgeschichte, 10).

**Kimball, Sidney Fiske.** The creation of the rococo. Philadelphia, Museum of art, 1943.

**Landsberger, Franz.** Die künstlerischen probleme der renaissance. Halle, Niemeyer, 1922.

**Magni, Giulio.** Il barocco a Roma nell'architettura e nella scultura decorativa. Torino, Crudo, 1911–13. 3 v.

**Mahon, Denis.** Studies in seicento art and theory. London, Warburg Inst., 1948.

**Osborn, Max.** Die kunst des rokoko. Berlin, Propyläen-verlag, 1929 (Propyläen-kunstgeschichte, 13).

**Panofsky, Erwin.** Studies in iconology; humanistic themes in the art of the Renaissance. N. Y., Oxford Univ. press, 1939.

**Pater, Walter.** The renaissance. N. Y., Boni and Liveright, 1919.

**Salis, Arnold von.** Antike und renaissance. Erlenbach-Zurich, Rentsch, 1947.

**Sitwell, Sacheverell.** Southern baroque art; a study of painting, architecture and music in Italy and Spain of the 17th and 18th centuries. 3d ed. London, Duckworth, 1931.

**Weisbach, Werner.** Die kunst des barock in Italien, Frankreich, Deutschland und Spanien. Berlin, Propyläen-verlag, 1924 (Propyläen-kunstgeschichte, 11).

## Nineteenth and Twentieth Centuries

**Breton, André.** Le surréalisme et la peinture. N. Y., Brentano's, 1945.

**Brizio, Anna M.** Ottocento, novecento. 2 ed. Torino, Unione tipografico-editrice torinese, 1945.

**Cheney, Sheldon.** The story of modern art. N. Y., Viking, 1941.

**Craven, Thomas.** Modern art; the men, the movement, the meaning. N. Y., Simon and Schuster, 1940.

**Einstein, Carl.** Die kunst des 20. jahrhunderts. 3$^e$ aufl. Berlin, Propyläen-verlag, 1931 (Propyläen-kunstgeschichte, 16).

**Gascoyne, David.** A short survey of surrealism. London, Cobden-Sanderson, 1936.

**Gaunt, William.** The aesthetic adventure. London, Cape, 1945.

**Gleizes, Albert.** Du cubisme. Paris, Arts graphiques, 1947.

Haack, Friedrich. Die kunst des XIX. jahrhunderts und der gegenwart. 6ᵉ aufl. Esslingen, Neff, 1922–25. 2 v.

Huyghe, René. Histoire de l'art contemporain: la peinture. Paris, Alcan, 1934.

Meier-Graefe, Julius. Modern art; being a contribution to a new system of aesthetics. Trans. Florence Simmonds and G. W. Chrystal. N. Y., Putnam, 1908. 2 v.

Moholy-Nagy, László. The new vision. Trans. Daphne M. Hoffman. 4th rev. ed. N. Y., Wittenborn, Schultz, 1949 (Documents of modern art).

——Vision in motion. Chicago, Theobald, 1947.

Pach, Walter. The masters of modern art. N. Y., Viking, 1925.

Pauli, Gustav. Die kunst des klassizismus und der romantik. Berlin, Propyläen-verlag, 1925 (Propyläen-kunstgeschichte, 14).

Read, Herbert E. Art now; an introduction to the theory of modern painting and sculpture. London, Faber, 1948.

Waldmann, Emil. Die kunst des realismus und des impressionismus im 19. jahrhundert. Berlin, Propyläen-verlag, 1927 (Propyläen-kunstgeschichte, 15).

Wilenski, Reginald H. The modern movement in art. New and rev. ed. London, Faber, 1946.

Zervos, Christian. Histoire de l'art contemporain. Paris, Cahiers d'art, 1938.

## National

### FRANCE

Bréhier, Louis. L'art en France dès invasions barbares à l'époque romane. Paris, Renaissance du livre, 1930.

Brownell, William C. French art; classic and contemporary painting and sculpture. New ed. N. Y., Scribner, 1920.

Du Colombier, Pierre. L'art renaissance en France. Paris, Le Prat, 1946 (Nouvelle encyclopédie illustrée de l'art français).

Enlart, Camille. Manuel d'archéologie française depuis les temps Mérovingiens jusqu'à la renaissance. Paris, Picard, 1927. 3 v. in 6.

Evans, Joan. Art in mediaeval France, 987–1498. London, Oxford Univ. press, 1948.

——Cluniac art of the Romanesque period. Cambridge [Eng.], University press, 1950.

Gischia, Léon. Les arts primitifs français. Paris, Éd. arts et métiers graphiques, 1939.

Hourticq, Louis. Art in France. N. Y., Scribner, 1924 (Ars una).

Lantier, Raymond. Les origines de l'art français. Paris, Le Prat, 1947 (Nouvelle encyclopédie illustrée de l'art français).

Lefrançois, Louise P. L'art roman en France, architecture, sculpture, peinture, arts mineurs. Paris, Le Prat, 1943 (Nouvelle encyclopédie illustrée de l'art français).

Lemonnier, Henry. L'art français au temps de Louis XIV (1661–1690). Paris, Hachette, 1911.

——— L'art français au temps de Richelieu et de Mazarin. 2 ed. Paris, Hachette, 1913.

Markham, Violet R. Romanesque France; studies in the archaeology and history of the 12th century. London, Murray, 1929.

Mauricheau-Beaupré, Charles. L'art au XVII$^{me}$ siècle en France. Paris, Le Prat, 1946–47. 2 v. (Nouvelle encyclopédie illustrée de l'art français).

Réau, Louis. L'art gothique en France. Paris, Le Prat, 1945 (Nouvelle encyclopédie illustrée de l'art français).

Rocheblave, Samuel. L'art et le gout en France de 1600 à 1900. 2d ed. Paris, Colin, 1930.

### GERMANY AND AUSTRIA

Beenken, Hermann T. Das neunzehnte jahrhundert in der deutschen kunst. Munich, Bruckmann, 1944.

Benz, Richard E. Die kunst der deutschen romantik. Munich, Piper, 1939.

Christoffel, Ulrich. Die deutsche kunst als form und ausdruck. Augsburg, Filser, 1928.

Clemen, Paul. Die deutsche kunst und die denkmalpflege. Berlin, Deutscher kunstverlag, 1933.

Dehio, Georg G. Geschichte der deutschen kunst. Berlin, De Gruyter, 1921–34. 3 v. in 6.

Doering, Oskar. Deutschlands mittelalterliche kunstdenkmäler als geschichtsquelle. Leipzig, Hiersemann, 1910.

Hagen, Oskar F. L. Deutsches sehen; gestaltungsfragen der deutschen kunst. 2 aufl. Munich, Piper, 1923.

Knackfuss, Hermann. Deutsche kunstgeschichte. Bielefeld, Velhagen und Klasing, 1888. 2 v.

Merin, Peter. Modern German art. Harmondsworth, Penguin books, 1938.

Picton, Harold W. Early German art and its origins, from the beginnings to about 1050. London, Batsford, 1939.

Pinder, Wilhelm. Die deutsche kunst der Dürerzeit. Leipzig, Seemann, 1940.

——Die kunst der deutschen kaiserzeit bis zum ende der staufischen klassik. Leipzig, Seemann, 1935.

——Die kunst der ersten bürgerzeit bis zur mitte des 15. jahrhunderts. Leipzig, Seemann, 1937.

Schmitt, Otto, ed. Reallexikon zur deutschen kunstgeschichte. Stuttgart, Metzler, 1933—. v. 1— (in progress).

Sitwell, Sacheverell. German baroque art. N. Y., Doran, 1928.

Weigert, Hans. Geschichte der deutschen kunst von der vorzeit bis zur gegenwart. Berlin, Propyläen-verlag, 1942.

## GREAT BRITAIN AND IRELAND

Allen, Beverly S. Tides in English taste (1619–1800); a background for the study of literature. Cambridge, Harvard Univ. press, 1937. 2 v.

Brown, Gerard B. The arts in early England. London, Murray, 1903–37. 6 v. in 7.

Evans, Joan. English art, 1307–1461. Oxford, Clarendon press, 1949 (Oxford history of English art, v. 5).

Fry, Roger E., and others. Georgian art, 1760–1820. London, Batsford, 1929 (Burlington magazine monograph, 3).

Kendrick, Thomas D. Anglo-Saxon art to A.D. 900. London, Methuen, 1938.

——Late Saxon and Viking art. London, Methuen, 1949.

London. Royal Academy of Arts. Commemorative catalogue of the exhibition of British art. London, Oxford Univ. press, 1935.

Saunders, O. Elfrida. A history of English art in the middle ages. Oxford, Clarendon press, 1932.

Saxl, Fritz, and Wittkower, Rudolf. British art and the Mediterranean. N. Y., Oxford Univ. press, 1948.

Steegmann, John. The rule of taste from George I to George IV. London, Macmillan, 1936.

Whinney, Margaret D. The interrelation of the fine arts in England in the early middle ages. London, Benn, 1930 (University College monographs in English mediaeval art, 3).

### ITALY

Ancona, Paolo D'. L'arte italiana. Firenze, Bemporad, 1937–47. 3 v.

Blunt, Anthony. Artistic theory in Italy, 1450–1600. Oxford, Clarendon press, 1940.

Bode, Wilhelm von. Die kunst der frührenaissance in Italien. 3 aufl. Berlin, Propyläen-verlag, 1923 (Propyläen-kunstgeschichte, 8).

Burckhardt, Jakob C. Civilization of the renaissance in Italy. Trans. S. G. C. Middlemore. Oxford Univ. press, Phaidon ed, 1945.

Collison-Morley, Lacy. Italy after the renaissance; decadence and display in the 17th century. London, Routledge, 1930.

Costantini, Vincenzo. Storia dell'arte italiana. Milan, Ceschina, 1945–49. 4 v.

Lavagnino, Emilio. Storia dell'arte medioevale italiana. Turin, Unione tip.-edit. torinese, 1936.

London. Royal Academy of Arts. A commemorative catalogue of the exhibition of Italian art. London, Oxford Univ. press, 1931. 2 v.

Muñoz, Antonio. Roma barocca. 2ª ed. Milan, Bestetti e Tumminelli, 1928.

Ricci, Corrado. Art in northern Italy. N. Y., Scribner, 1911 (Ars una).

Schubring, Paul. Die kunst der hochrenaissance in Italien. 2 aufl. Berlin, Propyläen-verlag, 1926 (Propyläen-kunstgeschichte, 9).

Symonds, John A. Renaissance in Italy. N. Y., Modern library, 1945. 2 v.

Venturi, Adolfo. Storia dell'arte italiana. Milan, Hoepli, 1901–39. 11 v.

Wölfflin, Heinrich. The art of the Italian renaissance. Trans. Walter Armstrong. N. Y., Putnam, 1913.

Young, George F. The Medici. N. Y., Modern library, 1933.

### LOW COUNTRIES

Clemen, Paul. Belgische kunstdenkmäler. Munich, Bruckmann, 1923. 2 v.

Fierens, Paul. L'art en Belgique du moyen âge à nos jours. Brussels, Renaissance du livre, 1947.

———L'art flamand. Paris, Larousse, 1945 (Arts, styles et techniques).

Leurs, Stan. Geschiedenis van de vlaamsche kunst. Antwerp, De Sikkel, 1936–40? 2 v.

○ London. Royal Academy of Arts. Commemorative catalogue of the exhibition of Dutch art. London, Oxford Univ. press, 1930.
○ Puyvelde, Leo van. The genius of Flemish art. London, Phaidon press, 1949.
○ Rooses, Max. Art in Flanders. N. Y., Scribner, 1931 (Ars una).
○ Valentiner, Wilhelm R. The art of the Low Countries. Garden City, N. Y., Doubleday, 1914.

### RUSSIA

Alpatov, Mikhail V. Russian impact on art. Ed. by Martin L. Wolf; trans. Ivy Litvinow. N. Y., Philosophical library, 1950.

Alpatov, Mikhail V., and Brunov, Nikolai I. Geschichte der altrussischen kunst. Augsburg, Filser-verlag, 1932. 2 v.

Bunt, Cyril G. E. A history of Russian art. London, Studio, 1946.

Conway, William M. Art treasures in soveit [sic] Russia. London, Arnold, 1925.

Filov, Bogdan D. Geschichte der altbulgarischen kunst. Berlin, De Gruyter, 1932–33. 2 v.

Holme, Geoffrey. Art in the U.S.S.R.: architecture, sculpture, painting, graphic arts, theatre, film, crafts. London, Studio, 1935.

London, Kurt. The seven Soviet arts. New Haven, Yale Univ. press, 1938.

Matthey, Werner von. Russische kunst. Einsiedeln, Benziger, 1948.

Réau, Louis. L'art russe. Paris, Larousse, 1945 (Arts, styles et techniques).

——L'art russe de Pierre le Grand à nos jours. Paris, Laurens, 1922.

——L'art russe dès origines à Pierre le Grand. Paris, Laurens, 1921.

Rice, Tamara A. T. Russian art. West Drayton, Middlesex, Penguin books, 1949 (Pelican books, A182).

Rubissow, Helen. The art of Russia. N. Y., Philosophical library, 1946.

Wulff, Oskar K. Die neurussische kunst im rahmen der kulturentwicklung Russlands von Peter dem Grossen bis zur revolution. Augsburg, Filser-verlag, 1932. 2 v.

### SCANDINAVIA

Hannover, Emil. Dänische kunst des 19. jahrhunderts. Leipzig, Seemann, 1907.

Holme, Charles. Peasant art in Sweden, Lapland and Iceland. London, Studio, 1910.

**Laurin, Carl G. J.** Scandinavian art. Illustrated by Carl Laurin, Emil Hannover, Jens Thiis; with an introduction by Christian Brinton. N. Y., American-Scandinavian foundation, 1922.

**Nørlund, Poul.** Danish art through the ages. Copenhagen, Tidskriftet Danmark, 1948.

**Nordensvan, Georg G.** Schwedische kunst des 19. jahrhunderts. Leipzig, Seemann, 1904.

**Okkonen, Onni.** L'art finlandais aux XIX et XX siècles; traduit du finnois par Arthur Langfors. 2 ed. Helsinki, 1938.

**Roosval, Johnny A. E.** Swedish art. Princeton, Princeton Univ. press, 1932 (Kahn lectures for 1929).

**Tikkanen, Johan J.** Modern art in Finland. Helsinki, Govt. printing office, 1926.

**Wettergren, Erik.** The modern decorative arts in Sweden. N. Y., American-Scandinavian foundation, 1926.

SPAIN

**Dieulafoy, Marcel A.** Art in Spain and Portugal. N. Y., Scribner, 1913 (Ars una).

**Gaya Nuño, Juan A.** Historia del arte español. Madrid, Editorial Plus-ultra, 1946.

**Gudiol i Ricart, Josep.** Ars hispaniae; historia universale del arte hispánico. Madrid, Editorial Plus-ultra, 1947. 6 v.

**Hagen, Oskar F. L.** Patterns and principles of Spanish art. 2d ed. Madison, Univ. of Wisconsin press, 1948.

**Lambert, Élie.** L'art en Espagne et au Portugal. Paris, Larousse, 1945 (Arts, styles et techniques).

**Lozoya, Juan C.** Historia del arte hispánico. Barcelona, Salvat, 1931—. v. 1—.

**Sedgwick, Henry D.** Spain; a short history of its politics, literature, and art from the earliest times to the present. Boston, Little, Brown, 1925.

**Tatlock, Robert R., and others.** Spanish art; an introductory review of architecture, painting, sculpture, textiles, ceramics, woodwork, metalwork. London, Batsford, 1927 (Burlington magazine monograph, 2).

**Tormo y Monzó, Elías.** Pintura, escultura y arquitectura en España; estudios dispersos. Madrid, Inst. Diego Velázquez, 1949.

Tyler, Royall. Spain, a study of her life and arts. N. Y., Kennerley, 1909.

Weisbach, Werner. Spanish baroque art; three lectures delivered at the University of London. Cambridge [Eng.], University press, 1941.

## UNITED STATES AND CANADA

Baur, John I. H. Revolution and tradition in modern American art. Cambridge, Harvard Univ. press, 1951.

Cahill, Holger, and Barr, Alfred H., eds. Art in America; a complete survey. N. Y., Halcyon House, 1939.

Colgate, William G. Canadian art; its origin and development. Toronto, Ryerson, 1943.

Drepperd, Carl W. American pioneer arts and artists. Springfield, Mass., Pond-Ekberg, 1942.

Dunlap, William. A history of the rise and progress of the arts of design in the United States. New ed. Boston, Goodspeed, 1918. 3 v.

Kouwenhoven, John A. Made in America; the arts in modern civilization. Garden City, N. Y., Doubleday, 1948.

La Follette, Suzanne. Art in America. N. Y., Norton, 1939.

Larkin, Oliver W. Art and life in America. N. Y., Rinehart, 1949.

McInnes, Graham. Canadian art. Toronto, Macmillan, 1950.

McMahon, Amos P. Preface to an American philosophy of art. Chicago, Univ. of Chicago press, 1945.

Mather, Frank J., Morey, Charles R., and James, William. The American spirit in art. New Haven, Yale Univ. press, 1927 (Pageant of America, v. 12).

Mellquist, Jerome. The emergence of an American art. N. Y., Scribner, 1942.

Mumford, Lewis. The brown decades; a study of the arts in America, 1865–1895. N. Y., Harcourt, Brace, 1931.

Neuhaus, Eugen. The history and ideals of American art. Stanford, Stanford Univ. press, 1931.

Rourke, Constance M. The roots of American culture and other essays. N. Y., Harcourt, Brace, 1942.

# ARCHITECTURE
## General

Bauer, Catherine. Modern housing. Boston, Houghton Mifflin, 1934.

Behrendt, Walter C. Modern building; its nature, problems and forms. N. Y., Harcourt, Brace, 1937.

Bell, Edward. The origins of architecture. London, Bell, 1915–26. 4 v.

Briggs, Martin S. Baroque architecture. N. Y., McBride, 1914.

Brownell, Baker. Architecture and modern life. N. Y., Harper, 1937.

Cheney, Sheldon. The new world architecture. London, Longmans, 1930.

Clapham, Alfred W. Romanesque architecture in western Europe. Oxford, Clarendon press, 1936.

Clark, Kenneth M. The Gothic revival; an essay in the history of taste. Rev. ed. N. Y., Scribner, 1950.

Fletcher, Banister F. A history of architecture on the comparative method. 15th ed., rev. N. Y., Scribner, 1950.

Giedion, Sigfried. Space, time and architecture; the growth of a new tradition. Cambridge, Harvard Univ. press, 1949.

Hamlin, Talbot F. Architecture, an art for all men. N. Y., Columbia Univ. press, 1947.

——Architecture through the ages. N. Y., Putnam, 1940.

Hitchcock, Henry-Russell. The international style: architecture since 1922. N. Y., Norton, 1932.

——Modern architecture, romanticism and reintegration. N. Y., Payson, 1929.

Hudnut, Joseph. Architecture and the spirit of man. Cambridge, Harvard Univ. press, 1949.

Kimball, Sidney Fiske, and Edgell, George H. A history of architecture. 2d ed. N. Y., Harper, 1946.

Moore, Charles H. Character of renaissance architecture. N. Y., Macmillan, 1905.

——Development and character of Gothic architecture. 2d ed. N. Y., Macmillan, 1899.

New York. Museum of Modern Art. What is modern architecture? N. Y., distributed by Simon and Schuster, 1946.

Newcomb, Rexford. History of modern architecture. Scranton, Pa., International textbook co., 1942.

Pevsner, Nikolaus. An outline of European architecture. 3d ed. Harmondsworth, Penguin, 1951 (Pelican A109).

—— Pioneers of modern design from William Morris to Walter Gropius. 2d ed. N. Y., Museum of modern art, 1949.

Porter, Arthur K. Medieval architecture, its origins and development; with lists of monuments and bibliographies. N. Y., Baker and Taylor, 1912. 2 v.

Richards, James M. An introduction to modern architecture. N. Y., Penguin, 1947 (Pelican P20).

Simpson, Frederick M. A history of architectural development. N. Y., Longmans, Green, 1905–11. 3 v.

Statham, Henry H. A history of architecture. 3d rev. ed. N. Y., Batsford, 1950.

Sturgis, Russell. A dictionary of architecture and building, biographical, historical and descriptive. N. Y., Macmillan, 1901–02. 3 v.

Taut, Bruno. Modern architecture. N. Y., Boni, 1929.

Vignola (Giacomo Barozzi). Five orders of architecture. Trans. A. L. Tuckermann. N. Y., Comstock, 1891.

Viollet-le-Duc, Eugène E. Discourses on architecture. Trans. Henry Van Brunt. Boston, Osgood, 1875.

Vitruvius Pollio. On architecture; edited from the Harleian manuscript 2767 and translated into English by Frank Granger. Cambridge, Harvard Univ. press, 1945 (Loeb classical library).

Wasmuths Lexikon der Baukunst. Berlin, Wasmuth, 1929–32. 5 v. [v. 5 = nachtrag].

Whittick, Arnold. European architecture in the twentieth century. London, Lockwood, 1950—. v. 1—.

Yorke, Francis R. S. The modern house. 5th ed. London, Architectural press, 1944.

## National

### FRANCE

Adams, Henry. Mont-Saint-Michel and Chartres. Boston, Houghton Mifflin, 1937.

Aubert, Marcel. L'architecture cistercienne en France. Paris. Éditions d'art et d'histoire, 1943. 2 v.

—— L'architecture française à l'époque gothique. Paris, Éditions d'art et d'histoire, 1943.

**Baum, Julius.** Romanesque architecture in France. 2d ed. London, Country life, 1928.

**Blomfield, Reginald T.** A history of French architecture from the reign of Charles VIII till the death of Mazarin. London, Bell, 1911. 2 v.

——A history of French architecture from the death of Mazarin till the death of Louis XV, 1661-1774. London, Bell, 1921. 2 v.

——Three hundred years of French architecture, 1494-1794. N. Y., Macmillan, 1936.

**Colas, René.** Le style gothique en France dans l'architecture et la décoration des monuments. Paris, Colas, 1926.

——Le style roman en France dans l'architecture et la décoration des monuments. Paris, Colas, 1927.

**Deshoulières, François.** Au début de l'art roman, les églises de l'onzième siècle en France. 2 éd. Paris, Éditions d'art et d'histoire, 1943.

**Evans, Joan.** The romanesque architecture of the order of Cluny. Cambridge [Eng.], University press, 1938.

**Gardner, Arthur.** An introduction to French church architecture. N. Y., Macmillan, 1938.

**Hautecoeur, Louis.** Histoire de l'architecture classique en France. Paris, Picard, 1943—. v. 1—.

**Lasteyrie du Saillant, Robert C.** L'architecture religieuse en France à l'époque gothique. Paris, Picard, 1926-27. 2 v.

——L'architecture religieuse en France à l'époque romane. 2 éd. Paris, Picard, 1929.

**Lavedan, Pierre.** L'architecture française. Paris, Larousse, 1944 (Arts, styles et techniques).

**Viollet-le-Duc, Eugène E.** Dictionnaire raisonné de l'architecture française du XI$^e$ au XVI$^e$ siècle. Paris, Morel, 1867-1873. 10 v.

**Ward, William H.** The architecture of the renaissance in France. 2d ed. N. Y., Scribner, 1926. 2 v.

GERMANY, AUSTRIA, LOW COUNTRIES, SWITZERLAND

**Dehio, George G., and Bezold, Gustav von.** Die kirchliche baukunst des abendlandes. Stuttgart, Cotta, 1887-1901. 2 v.

**Hempel, Eberhard.** Geschichte der deutschen baukunst. Munich, Bruckmann, 1949.

**Pinder, Wilhelm.** Deutsche dome des mittelalters. Königstein im Taunus, Langewiesche, 1941.

——Deutscher barock; die grossen baumeister des 18. jahrhunderts. Königstein im Taunus, Langewiesche, 1940.

Platz, Gustav A. Die baukunst der neuestein zeit. Berlin, Propyläenverlag, 1927.

Popp, Hermann. Die architektur der Barock- und Rokokozeit im Deutschland und der Schweiz. Stuttgart, Hoffmann, 1913.

Rittich, Werner. Architektur und bauplastik der gegenwart. 3 aufl. Berlin, Rembrandt-verlag, 1944.

Smith, George E. K. Switzerland builds; its native and modern architecture. N. Y., Bonnier, 1950.

Stange, Alfred. Die deutsche baukunst der renaissance. Munich, Schmidt, 1926.

Wackernagel, Martin. Baukunst des 17. und 18. jahrhunderts in den germanischen ländern. Berlin-Neubabelsberg, Akademische verlagsgesellschaft Athenaion, 1915 (Handbuch der kunstwissenschaft).

GREAT BRITAIN

Blomfield, Reginald T. A history of renaissance architecture in England, 1500–1800. London, Bell, 1897. 2 v.

Bond, Francis. An introduction to English church architecture from the eleventh to the sixteenth century. London, H. Milford, 1913. 2 v.

Clapham, Alfred W. English romanesque architecture after the conquest. Oxford, Clarendon press, 1934.

——English romanesque architecture before the conquest. Oxford, Clarendon press, 1930.

Cox, John C. The parish churches of England. N. Y., Scribner, 1935.

Gardner, Alfred H. Outline of English architecture; an account for the general reader of its development from early times to the present day. 2d ed. London, Batsford, 1946.

Garner, Thomas, and Stratton, Arthur. The domestic architecture of England during the Tudor period. 2d ed. N. Y., Scribner, 1929. 2 v.

Godfrey, Walter H. The story of architecture in England. N. Y., Harper, 1931. 2 v. in 1.

Gotch, John A. Early renaissance architecture in England. 2d ed. London, Batsford, 1914.

Harvey, John D. M. An introduction to Tudor architecture. London, Art and Technics, 1949.

Lloyd, Nathaniel. A history of the English house from primitive times to the Victorian period. New ed. London, Architectural press, 1949.

Pilcher, Donald. The Regency style, 1800 to 1830. London, Batsford, 1947.

Prior, Edward S. A history of Gothic art in England. London, Bell, 1900.

Reilly, Paul. An introduction to regency architecture. N. Y., Pellegrini, 1948.

Richardson, Albert E. An introduction to Georgian architecture. London, Art and Technics, 1949 (Introductions to architecture).

Sitwell, Sacheverell. British architects and craftsmen; a survey of taste, design, and style during three centuries, 1600 to 1830. 4th ed. London, Batsford, 1948.

Summerson, John N. Georgian London. N. Y., Scribner, 1946.

Tallmadge, Thomas E. The story of England's architecture. N. Y., Norton, 1934.

ITALY

Anderson, William J. The architecture of the renaissance in Italy. 5th ed. London, Batsford, 1927.

Baum, Julius. Baukunst und dekorative plastik der frührenaissance in Italien. Stuttgart, Hoffmann, 1920.

Brinckmann, Albert E. Die baukunst des 17. und 18. jahrhunderts in den romanischen ländern. Berlin-Neubabelsberg, Akademische verlagsgesellschaft Athenaion, 1919–22. 2 v.

Cummings, Charles A. A history of architecture in Italy from the time of Constantine to the dawn of the renaissance. New ed. Boston, Houghton, 1927. 2 v.

Delogu, Giuseppe. Italienische baukunst; eine anthologie vom 11. bis 19. jahrhundert. Zürich, Fretz und Wasmuth, 1947.

Frey, Dabobert. Architecture of the renaissance from Brunelleschi to Michaelangelo. The Hague, G. Naeff, 1925.

Gromort, Georges. Italian renaissance architecture. Trans. George F. Waters. Paris, Vincent, 1922.

Porter, Arthur K. Lombard architecture. New Haven, Yale Univ. press, 1915–17. 4 v.

Ricci, Corrado. Architecture and decorative sculpture of the high and late renaissance in Italy. N. Y., Brentano's, 1923.

———Baroque architecture and sculpture in Italy. Stuttgart, Hoffmann, 1926.

———Romanesque architecture in Italy. N. Y., Brentano's, 1925.

Rivoira, Giovanni T. Lombardic architecture. Trans. G. M. Rushforth. London, Heinemann, 1910. 2 v.

Schubring, Paul. Die architektur der italienischen frührenaissance. Munich, Schmidt, 1923.

———Die architektur der italienischen hochrenaissance. Munich, Schmidt, 1924.

Willich, Hans. Die baukunst der renaissance in Italien bis zum tode Michelangelos. Berlin-Neubabelsberg, Akademische verlagsgesellschaft Athenaion, 1914–29. 2 v.

Wittkower, Rudolf. Architectural principles in the age of humanism. London, Warburg inst., Univ. of London, 1949.

### SCANDINAVIA AND RUSSIA

Buxton, David R. Russian mediaeval architecture; with an account of the Transcaucasian styles and their influence in the West. Cambridge [Eng.], University press, 1934.

Redslob, Edwin. Alt-Dänemark. 3 aufl. Munich, Delphin-verlag, 1922.

Smith, George E. K. Sweden builds; its modern architecture and land policy, background, development and contribution. N. Y., Bonnier, 1950.

Voyce, Arthur. Russian architecture, trends in nationalism and modernism. N. Y., Philosophical library, 1948.

### SPAIN AND PORTUGAL

Bevan, Bernard. History of Spanish architecture. N. Y., Scribner, 1939.

Gómez-Moreno, Manuel. Iglesias mozárabes; arte español de los siglos IX à XI. Madrid, Centro de estudios históricos, 1919. 2 v.

Lampérez y Romea, Vicente. Arquitectura civil española de los siglos I al XVIII. Madrid, Saturnino Calleja, 1922. 2 v.

———Historia de la arquitectura cristiana española en la edad media según el estudio de los elementos y los monumentos. 2 ed. Madrid, Espasa-Calpe, 1930. 3 v.

Puig y Cadafalch, José. L'arquitectura romanica a Catalunya. Barcelona, Inst. d'estudis catalans, 1909–18. 3 v.

Reis Santos, Luiz. Monuments of Portugal. Lisbon, National Secretariat of Information, 194–.

Weise, Georg. Studien zur spanischen architektur der spätgotik. Reutlingen, Gryphius-verlag, 1933.

Whitehill, Walter M. Spanish romanesque architecture of the eleventh century. London, Oxford Univ. press, 1941.

UNITED STATES

Eberlein, Harold D. The architecture of colonial America. Boston, Little, Brown, 1927.

Edgell, George H. The American architecture of to-day. N. Y., Scribner, 1928.

Hamlin, Talbot F. The American spirit in architecture. New Haven, Yale Univ. press, 1926 (Pageant of America, v. 13).

———Greek revival architecture in America. London, Oxford Univ. press, 1944.

Hitchcock, Henry-Russell. American architectural books; a list of books, portfolios and pamphlets on architecture and related subjects. 3d ed. Minneapolis, Univ. of Minnesota press, 1946.

Kimball, Sidney Fiske. American architecture. Indianapolis, Bobbs-Merrill, 1928.

———Domestic architecture of the American colonies and of the early republic. N. Y., Scribner, 1927.

Major, Howard. The domestic architecture of the early American republic, the Greek revival. Philadelphia, Lippincott, 1926.

Mock, Elizabeth B. Built in U. S. A., 1932–1944. N. Y., Museum of modern art, 1944.

Mumford, Lewis. The South in architecture. N. Y., Harcourt, Brace, 1941.

———Sticks and stones; a study of American architecture and civilization. N. Y., Boni and Liveright, 1926.

Roos, Frank J. Writings on early American architecture; an annotated list of books and articles on architecture constructed before 1860 in the eastern half of the U. S. Columbus, Ohio State Univ. press, 1943.

Tallmadge, Thomas E. The story of architecture in America. New ed. N. Y., Norton, 1936.

MEXICO AND LATIN AMERICA

Baxter, Sylvester. La arquitectura hispano colonial en México. México, D. F., 1934.

**Benavides Rodríguez, Alfredo.** La arquitectura en el virreinato del Perú y en la capitanía general de Chile. Santiago de Chile, Ediciones Ercilla, 1941.

**Buschiazzo, Mario J.** Estudios de arquitectura colonial hispano america. Buenos Aires, Kraft, 1944.

**Camón Aznar, José.** La arquitectura plateresca. Madrid, Aguirre, 1945. 2 v.

**Costa Torres, Raul.** A arquitectura dos descobrimentos e o renascimento ibérico. Braga, Livraria Cruz, 1943.

**Goodwin, Philip L.** Brazil builds; architecture new and old, 1652–1942. N. Y., Museum of modern art, 1943.

**Kilham, Walter H.** Mexican architecture of the vice-regal period. N. Y., Longmans, Green, 1927.

**Kubler, George.** Mexican architecture of the sixteenth century. New Haven, Yale Univ. press, 1948. 2 v.

**Sanford, Trent E.** The story of architecture in Mexico. N. Y., Norton, 1947.

**Wethey, Harold E.** Colonial architecture and sculpture in Peru. Cambridge, Harvard Univ. press, 1949.

# SCULPTURE
## General

**Agard, Walter R.** The new architectural sculpture. N. Y., Oxford Univ. press, 1935.

**Brinckmann, Albert E.** Barock-bozzetti. English-German edition. Frankfurt am Main, Frankfurter verlagsanstalt, 1923–25. 4 v.

——Barockskulptur. 3 aufl. Potsdam, Akademische verlagsgesellschaft Athenaion, 1932.

**Casson, Stanley.** Some modern sculptors. London, Oxford Univ. press, 1929.

——XXth century sculptors. London, Oxford Univ. press, 1930.

**Chase, George H., and Post, Chandler R.** A history of sculpture. N. Y., Harper, 1925.

**Focillon, Henri.** L'art des sculpteurs romans; recherches sur l'histoire des formes. Paris, Leroux, 1931.

**Giedion-Welcker, C.** Modern plastic art, elements of reality, volume and disintegration. English version by P. Morton Shand. Zürich, Girsberger, 1937.

**Kowalczyk, Georg.** Decorative sculpture. N. Y., Weyhe, 1927.

**Kuhn, Alfred.** Die neuere plastik von achtzehnhundert bis zur gegenwart. 2 aufl. Munich, Delphin-verlag, 1922.

**Maryon, Herbert.** Modern sculpture, its methods and ideals. London, Pitman, 1933.

**Maskell, Alfred.** Wood sculpture. N. Y., Putnam, 1911 (The connoisseur's library).

**Miller, Alec.** Tradition in sculpture. N. Y., Studio, 1949.

**Porter, Arthur K.** Romanesque sculpture of the pilgrimage roads. Boston, Marshall Jones, 1923. 10 v.

**Post, Chandler R.** A history of European and American sculpture from the early Christian period to the present day. Cambridge, Harvard Univ. press, 1921. 2 v.

**Rich, Jack C.** The materials and methods of sculpture. N. Y., Oxford Univ. press, 1947.

**Rothschild, Lincoln.** Sculpture through the ages. N. Y., Whittlesey house, 1942.

**Seymour, Charles.** Tradition and experiment in modern sculpture. Washington, D. C., American Univ. press, 1949.

Sobotka, Georg. Die bildhauerei der barockzeit. Vienna, Schroll, 1927.

Taft, Lorado. Modern tendencies in sculpture. Chicago, Univ. of Chicago press, 1921 (Scammon lectures for 1917).

○ Toft, Albert. Modelling and sculpture; a full account of the various methods and processes employed in these arts. Rev. ed. N. Y., Macmillan, 1950.

Valentiner, Wilhelm R. Origins of modern sculpture. N. Y., Wittenborn, Schultz, 1946.

Wilenski, Reginald H. The meaning of modern sculpture; an essay on some original sculpture of the present day. London, Faber, 1932.

## National

### FRANCE AND BELGIUM

Aubert, Marcel. French sculpture at the beginning of the Gothic period, 1140–1225. N. Y., Harcourt, Brace, 1929.

———La sculpture française au moyen-âge. Paris, Flammarion, 1947.

Benoist, Luc. La sculpture française. Paris, Larousse, 1945 (Arts, styles et techniques).

Deschamps, Paul. French sculpture of the Romanesque period, eleventh and twelfth centuries. N. Y., Harcourt, Brace, 1930.

———La sculpture française, époque romane. Paris, Éditions du Chêne, 1947.

Gardner, Arthur. Medieval sculpture in France. Cambridge [Eng.], University press, 1931.

Lefrançois, Louise P. Les sculpteurs français du XII siècle. Paris, Plon, 1931.

———Les sculpteurs français du XIII siècle. Paris, Plon, 1931.

Rousseau, Henry. La sculpture aux XVII$^e$ et XVIII$^e$ siècles. Brussels, Van Oest, 1911.

Vitry, Paul. French sculpture during the reign of Saint-Louis, 1226–1270. N. Y., Harcourt, Brace, 1929.

Vitry, Paul, and Brière, Gaston. Documents de sculpture française. Paris, Longuet, 1906–11. 3 v.

### GERMANY, SWITZERLAND, AUSTRIA

Beenken, Hermann T. Romanische skulptur in Deutschland (11. und 12. jahrhundert). Leipzig, Klinkhardt und Biermann, 1924.

**Deonna, Waldemar.** La sculpture suisse dès origines à la fin du XVI siècle. Bale, Birkhaeuser, 1946 (Art suisse, 1).

**Feulner, Adolf.** Die deutsche plastik des sechzehnten jahrhunderts. Florence, Pantheon, 1926.

——Die deutsche plastik des siebzehnten jahrhunderts. Florence, Pantheon, 1926.

——Skulptur und malerei des 18. jahrhunderts in Deutschland. Wildpark-Potsdam, Akademische verlagsgesellschaft Athenaion, 1929.

**Halm, Philipp M.** Studien zur süddeutschen plastik; Altbayern und Schwaben, Tirol und Salzberg. Augsburg, Filser, 1926–27. 2 v.

**Jantzen, Hans.** Deutsche plastik des 13. jahrhunderts. 2 aufl. Munich, Bruckmann, 1944.

**Lüthgen, Eugen.** Romanische plastik in Deutschland. Bonn, Schroeder, 1923.

**Panofsky, Erwin.** Die deutsche plastik des elften bis dreizehnten jahrhunderts. Munich, Wolff, 1924. 2 v.

**Pinder, Wilhelm.** Deutsche barockplastik. Königstein im Taunus, Langewiesche verlag, 1933.

——Die deutsche plastik des fuenfzehnten jahrhunderts. Munich, Wolff, 1924.

——Die deutsche plastik vom ausgehenden mittelalter bis zum ende der renaissance. Wildpark-Potsdam, Akademische verlagsgesellschaft Athenaion, 1924–29. 2 v.

**Tietze-Conrat, Erika.** Österreichische barockplastik. Vienna, Schroll, 1920.

GREAT BRITAIN

**Crossley, Frederick H.** English church monuments A.D. 1150–1550; an introduction to the study of tombs and effigies of the mediaeval period. N. Y., Scribner, 1921.

**Esdaile, Katharine A. M.** English church monuments, 1510 to 1840. London, Batsford, 1946.

——English monumental sculpture since the renaissance. N. Y., Macmillan, 1927.

**Gardner, Arthur.** English medieval sculpture. Cambridge [Eng.], University press, 1951.

**Prior, Edward S., and Gardner, Arthur.** An account of medieval figure-sculpture in England. Cambridge [Eng.], University press, 1912.

## ITALY

**Baroni, Costantino.** Sculptura gotica lombarda. Milan, Bestetti, 1944.

**Biehl, Walther.** Toskanische plastik des frühen und hohen mittelalters. Leipzig, Seemann, 1926.

**Bode, Wilhelm von.** Florentine sculptors of the renaissance. 2 ed., rev. by F. L. R. Brown. London, Methuen, 1928.

**Crawford, David A. E. L. (Lord Balcarres).** The evolution of Italian sculpture. N. Y., Dutton, 1910.

**Delogu, Giuseppe.** Italienische bildhauerei; eine anthologie vom 12. bis 19. jahrhundert. Zürich, Fretz und Wasmuth, 1942.

**Galassi, Giuseppe.** La scultura fiorentina del quattrocento. Milan, Hoepli, 1949 (Valori plastici).

**Haseloff, Arthur E. G.** Pre-Romanesque sculpture in Italy. N. Y., Harcourt, Brace, 1931.

**Jullian, René.** L'éveil de la sculpture italienne. Paris, Van Oest, 1945–1950. 2 v.

**Maclagan, Eric R. D.** Italian sculpture of the renaissance. Cambridge, Harvard Univ. press, 1935.

**Mayer, August L.** Mittelalterliche plastik in Italien. Munich, Delphinverlag, 1923.

**Planiscig, Leo.** Venezianische bildhauer der renaissance. Vienna, Schroll, 1921.

**Reymond, Marcel.** La sculpture florentine. Florence, Alinari, 1897–1900. 4 v.

**Salmi, Mario.** Romanesque sculpture in Tuscany. Florence, Rinascimento del libro, 1928.

**Waters, William G.** Italian sculptors. 2d ed. London, Methuen, 1926.

**Wiles, Bertha H.** The fountains of Florentine sculptors and their followers, from Donatello to Bernini. Cambridge, Harvard Univ. press, 1933.

## SPAIN AND MEXICO

**Gaillard, Georges.** Les débuts de la sculpture romane espagnole; Leon, Jaca, Compostelle. Paris, Hartmann, 1938.

**Mayer, August L.** Mittelalterliche plastik in Spanien. Munich, Delphinverlag, 1922.

——Spanische barock-plastik. Munich, Riehn und Reusch, 1923.

**Pillement, Georges.** La sculpture baroque espagnole. Paris, Michel, 1945.

**Porter, Arthur K.** Spanish romanesque sculpture. Florence, Pantheon, 1928. 2 v.

**Weise, George.** Spanische plastik aus sieben jahrhunderten. Reutlingen, Gryphius-verlag, 1925–1939. 4 v. in 6.

**Weismann, Elizabeth W.** Mexico in sculpture, 1521–1821. Cambridge, Harvard Univ. press, 1950.

UNITED STATES

735.73 Sch 59 **Schnier, Jacques P.** Sculpture in modern America. Berkeley, Univ. of Calif. press, 1948.

735.73 T125a **Taft, Lorado.** The history of American sculpture. New ed. N. Y., Macmillan, 1930.

# PAINTING
## General

Abbot, Edith R. The great painters in relation to the European tradition. N. Y., Harcourt, Brace, 1927.

Barr, Alfred H. Cubism and abstract art. N. Y., Museum of modern art, 1936.

——Fantastic art, Dada, Surrealism; essays by George Hugnet. N. Y., Museum of modern art, 1947.

——What is modern painting? N. Y., Museum of modern art, 1947.

Bell, Clive. Landmarks in nineteenth-century painting. N. Y., Harcourt, Brace, 1927.

——Since Cézanne. N. Y., Harcourt, Brace, 1923.

Boehn, Max von. Miniaturen und silhouetten, ein kapitel aus kulturgeschichte und kunst. 3 aufl. Munich, Bruckmann, 1917.

Bradley, Morton C. The treatment of pictures. Cambridge [Mass.], Art Technology, 1950.

Cennini, Cennino. Il libro dell'arte. New Haven, Yale Univ. press, 1932–33. 2 v. (v.2, The craftsman's handbook, trans. D. V. Thompson).

Cheney, Sheldon. Expressionism in art. Rev. ed. N. Y., Tudor, 1948.

Clark, Kenneth M. Landscape painting. N. Y., Scribner, 1950 (published in London under the title, Landscape into art).

Craven, Thomas. A treasury of art masterpieces, from the renaissance to the present day. N. Y., Simon and Schuster, 1939.

Davenport, Cyril J. H. Miniatures, ancient and modern. Chicago, McClurg, 1908.

Dörner, Max. The materials of the artist and their use in painting, with notes on the techniques of the old masters. Trans. Eugen Neuhaus. Rev. ed. N. Y., Harcourt, Brace, 1949.

Eastlake, Charles L. Materials for a history of oil painting. London, Longmans, Green, 1847–1869. 2 v.

Evans, Ralph M. An introduction to color. N. Y., Wiley, 1948.

Foster, Joshua J. A dictionary of painters of miniatures, 1525–1850, with some account of exhibitions, collections, sales, etc., pertaining to them. London, Allan, 1926.

Friedländer, Max J. Landscape, portrait, still-life; their origin and development. Trans. R. F. C. Hull. N. Y., Philosophical library, 1950.

Gettens, Rutherford J., and Stout, George L. Painting materials, a short encyclopaedia. N. Y., Van Nostrand, 1942.

Goldwater, Robert J. Primitivism in modern painting. N. Y., Harper, 1938.

Heath, Dudley. Miniatures. N. Y., Putnam, 1905.

Holmes, Charles J. Notes on the science of picture-making. N. Y., Stokes, 1928.

——Old masters and modern art; the National gallery. N. Y., Harcourt, Brace, 1924–27, 3 v.

Hubbard, Eric H. Materia pictoria; an encyclopaedia of methods in painting and the graphic arts. 2d ed. London, Pitman, 1948—. v. 1—.

Johnson, Charles. The language of painting. Cambridge [Eng.], University press, 1949.

Kahnweiler, Daniel H. The rise of cubism. Trans. Henry Aronson. N. Y., Wittenborn, Schultz, 1949.

Laurie, Arthur P. The materials of the painter's craft in Europe and Egypt from earliest times to the end of the XVIIth century. Philadelphia, Lippincott, 1911.

——The painter's methods and materials; the handling of pigments in oil, tempera, water-colour and in mural painting. Philadelphia, Lippincott, 1926.

——The technique of the great painters. London, Carroll and Nicholson, 1949.

Luckiesh, Matthew. Color and its applications. N. Y., Van Nostrand, 1927.

Mather, Frank J. Modern painting. Garden City, N. Y., Garden City pub. co., 1934.

——Western European painting of the Renaissance. N. Y., Tudor, 1948.

Mayer, Ralph. The artist's handbook of materials and techniques. N. Y., Viking, 1940.

——The painter's craft; an introduction to artists' materials. N. Y., Van Nostrand, 1948.

Merrifield, Mary P. Original treatises, dating from the XIIth to XVIIIth centuries on the arts of painting, in oil, miniature, mosaic, and on glass. London, Murray, 1849. 2 v.

**Munsell, Albert H.** A color notation; an illustrated system defining all colors and their relations by measured scales of hue, value, and chroma. 10th ed. Baltimore, Munsell color co., 1946. 535. 6 M

**Myers, Bernard.** Modern art in the making. N. Y., Whittlesey, 1950.

**Newton, Eric.** An introduction to European painting. N. Y., Longmans, Green, 1949 ("A revision of the author's European painting and sculpture, 1941").

O **Ostwald, Wilhelm.** Colour science; a handbook for advanced students in schools, colleges, and the various arts, crafts, and industries depending on the use of colour. London, Winsor and Newton, 1931–33. 2 v.

**Pevsner, Nikolaus.** Barockmalerei in den romanischen ländern. Wildpark-Potsdam, Akademische verlagsgesellschaft Athenaion, 1928.

O**Pope, Arthur.** The language of drawing and painting. Cambridge, Harvard Univ. press, 1949.

**Rathbun, Mary C., and Hayes, Bartlett H.** Layman's guide to modern art; painting for a scientific age. N. Y., Oxford Univ. press, 1949.

**Raynal, Maurice.** History of modern painting. Trans. Gilbert Stuart. Geneva, Skira, 1949–50. 3 v. (v.1, From Baudelaire to Bonnard; v.2, Matisse, Munch, Rouault; Fauvism, Expressionism; v.3, From Picasso to Surrealism).

**Read, Herbert E.** Surrealism. N. Y., Harcourt, Brace, 1936.

**Reinach, Salomon.** Répertoire de peintures du moyen âge et de la renaissance, 1280–1580. Paris, Leroux, 1905–1923. 6 v.

**Ritchie, Andrew C.** Abstract painting and sculpture in America. N. Y., Museum of modern art, 1951.

**Robb, David M.** The Harper history of painting: the occidental tradition. N. Y., Harper, 1951.

O**Ross, Denman W.** On drawing and painting. Boston, Houghton Mifflin, 1912.

——The painter's palette; a theory of tone relations, an instrument of expression. Boston, Houghton Mifflin, 1919.

——A theory of pure design; harmony, balance, rhythm. Boston, Houghton Mifflin, 1907.

**Soby, James T.** After Picasso. N. Y., Dodd, Mead, 1935.

——Contemporary painters. N. Y., Museum of modern art, 1948.

? **Thompson, Daniel V.** The materials of medieval painting. New Haven, Yale Univ. press, 1936.

**Thompson, Daniel V.** (continued)
——The practice of tempera painting. New Haven, Yale Univ. press, 1936.

**Toch, Maximilian.** The chemistry and technology of paintings. 3d ed. N. Y., Van Nostrand, 1925.

——Paint, paintings and restoration. 2d ed. N. Y., Van Nostrand, 1945.

**Uhde, Wilhelm.** The impressionists. Vienna, Phaidon press, 1937.

**Venturi, Lionello.** Les archives de l'impressionnisme. N. Y., Durand-Ruel, 1939. 2 v.

——Impressionists and symbolists. Trans. Francis Steegmuller. N. Y., Scribner, 1950.

——Modern painters. N. Y., Scribner, 1947.

——Painting and painters; how to look at a picture, from Giotto to Chagall. N. Y., Scribner, 1945.

**Wild, Angenitus M. de.** The scientific examination of pictures; an investigation of the pigments used by the Dutch and Flemish masters. Trans. L. C. Jackson. London, Bell, 1929.

**Zucker, Paul.** Styles in painting, a comparative study. N. Y., Viking, 1950.

## National

### FRANCE

**Apollinaire, Guillaume.** The cubist painters; aesthetic meditations, 1913. Trans. Lionel Abel. 2d ed. N. Y., Wittenborn, Schultz, 1949 (Documents of modern art, 1).

**Bell, Clive.** An account of French painting. London, Chatto and Windus, 1931.

**Dimier, Louis.** French painting in the sixteenth century. N. Y., Scribner, 1911.

——Histoire de la peinture française au XIX$^e$ siècle, 1793–1890; avec un epilogue allant jusqu'à nos jours. 2$^e$ éd. Paris, Delagrave, 1926.

——Les peintres français du XVIII$^e$ siècle; histoire des vies et catalogue des oeuvres. Paris, Van Oest, 1928–30. 2 v.

**Dimier, Louis, and Réau, Louis.** L'histoire de la peinture française depuis les origines jusqu'à David. Paris, Van Oest, 1925–27. 5 v. (v.1, Dimier: Histoire ... Dès origines au retour de Vouet, 1300–1627; v.2–3, Dimier: Histoire ... Du retour de Vouet à la mort de Lebrun, 1627–1690; v.4–5, Réau: Histoire ... Au XVIII$^e$ siècle).

**Dorival, Bernard.** Les étapes de la peinture française contemporaine. Paris, Gallimard, 1943–. v. 1— (v.1, De l'impressionnisme au fauvisme, 1883–1905; v.2, Le fauvisme et le cubisme, 1905–1911; v.3, Depuis le cubisme, 1911–1944).

——La peinture française. Paris, Larousse, 1942. 2 v. (Arts, styles et techniques).

**Escholier, Raymond.** La peinture française, XIX$^e$ siècle. Paris, Floury, 1941–1943. 2 v.

——La peinture française, XX$^e$ siècle. Paris, Floury, 1937.

**Florisoone, Michel.** Le dix-huitième siècle: la peinture française. Paris, Tisné, 1948.

**Focillon, Henri.** La peinture aux XIX$^e$ et XX$^e$ siècles du réalisme à nos jours. Paris, Renouard, 1928.

——La peinture au XIX$^e$ siècle; le retour à l'antique, le romantisme. Paris, Laurens, 1927.

**Gauss, Charles E.** The aesthetic theories of French artists, 1855 to the present. Baltimore, Johns Hopkins press, 1949.

**Goncourt, Edmond L. A. H. de.** French XVIII century painters. Trans. Robin Ironside. London, Oxford Univ. press, Phaidon ed., 1948.

**Huyghe, René.** Les contemporains. Notices biographiques, par Germain Bazin. Nouv. éd. Paris, Tisné, 1949.

**Jamot, Paul.** La peinture en France. Paris, Plon, 1934.

**Jewell, Edward A.** French impressionists and their contemporaries represented in American collections. N. Y., Hyperion press, 1944.

**Lemoisne, Paul A.** Gothic painting in France, fourteenth and fifteenth centuries. N. Y., Harcourt, Brace, 1931.

**Leroy, Alfred.** Évolution de la peinture française dès origines à nos jours. Paris, Horizons de France, 1943.

——Histoire de la peinture française (1800–1933), son évolution et ses maîtres. Paris, Michel, 1934.

——Histoire de la peinture française au XVIII$^e$ siècle (1700–1800), son évolution et ses maîtres. Paris, Michel, 1934.

——Histoire de la peinture française au moyen âge et à la renaissance, son évolution et ses maîtres. Paris, Michel, 1937.

**Michel, Paul H.** Romanesque wall paintings in France. Paris, Éditions du Chêne, 1949.

**Réau, Louis.** French painting in the XIVth, XVth, and XVIth centuries. Trans. Mary Chamot. London, Hyperion press, 1939.

**Rewald, John.** The history of impressionism. N. Y., Museum of modern art, 1946.

**Ring, Grete.** A century of French painting, 1400–1500. London, Oxford Univ. press, Phaidon ed., 1949.

**Rocheblave, Samuel.** French painting in the XVIIIth century. Trans. G. F. Lees. London, Commodore press, 1937.

——French painting of the nineteenth century. Trans. Douglas Lord. London, Commodore press, 1936.

**Sterling, Charles.** Les peintres primitifs. Paris, Nathan, 1949.

——La peinture française; les peintres du moyen âge. Paris, Tisné, 1942.

**Terrasse, Charles.** French painting in the XXth century. Trans. Eveline Byam Shaw. N. Y., Hyperion press, 1939.

**Wilenski, Reginald H.** French painting. Rev. ed. Boston, Branford, 1949.

——Modern French painters. N. Y., Harcourt, Brace, 1949.

GERMANY AND AUSTRIA

**Burger, Fritz.** Die deutsche malerei vom ausgehenden mittelalter bis zum ende der renaissance. Berlin, Akademische verlagsgesellschaft Athenaion, 1913–22. 3 v. (Handbuch der kunstwissenschaft).

**Dickinson, Helena A. S.** German masters of art. N. Y., Stokes, 1914.

**Drost, Willi.** Barockmalerei in den germanischen ländern. Wildpark-Potsdam, Akademische verlagsgesellschaft Athenaion, 1927 (Handbuch der kunstwissenschaft).

**Fischer, Otto.** Geschichte der deutschen malerei. Munich, Bruckmann, 1943.

**Glaser, Curt.** Die altdeutsche malerei. Munich, Bruckmann, 1924.

——Les peintres primitifs allemands du milieu du XIV$^e$ siècle à la fin du XV$^e$. Paris, Van Oest, 1931.

**Goering, Max.** Deutsche malerei des siebzehnten und achtzehnten jahrhunderts, von dem manieristen bis zum klassizismus. Berlin, Genius verlag, 1940.

**Hamann, Richard.** Die deutsche malerei im 19. jahrhundert. Leipzig, Teubner, 1914.

——Die deutsche malerei vom rokoko bis zum expressionismus. Leipzig, Teubner, 1925.

**Rave, Paul O.** Deutsche malerei des 19. jahrhunderts. Berlin, Mann, 1949.

**Stange, Alfred.** Deutsche malerei der gotik. Berlin, Deutscher kunstverlag, 1934–51. 4 v.

——German painting; XIV–XVI centuries. N. Y., Macmillan, 1950.

Winkler, Friedrich. Altdeutsche tafelmalerei. Munich, Bruckmann, 1941.

Worringer, Wilhelm. Die anfänge der tafel-malerei. Leipzig, Inselverlag, 1924.

GREAT BRITAIN

Baker, Charles H. C. British painting. London, Medici society, 1933.

Baker, Charles H. C. and Constable, William G. English painting of the sixteenth and seventeenth centuries. N. Y., Harcourt, Brace, 1930.

Binyon, Laurence. English water-colours. 2d ed. London, Black, 1944.

Borenius, Tancred. English painting in the XVIIIth century. Paris, Hyperion press, 1938.

Borenius, Tancred, and Tristram, Ernest W. English medieval painting. N. Y., Harcourt, Brace, 1929.

Cursiter, Stanley. Scottish art to the close of the nineteenth century. N. Y., Chanticleer press, 1949.

Fergusson, John D. Modern Scottish painting. Glasgow, MacLellan, 1943.

Johnson, Charles. English painting from the seventh century to the present day. London, Bell, 1932.

Oakeshott, Walter F. The sequence of English medieval art, illustrated chiefly from illuminated mss., 650–1450. London, Faber, 1950.

Redgrave, Richard. A century of British painters. New ed. London, Oxford Univ. press, Phaidon ed., 1947. 759.2 R249

Walpole, Horace. Anecdotes of painting in England, 1760–1795, with some account of the principal artists. New Haven, Yale Univ. press, 1937.

Whitley, William T. Art in England, 1800–1820. N. Y., Macmillan, 1928.

——Art in England, 1821–1837. Cambridge [Eng.], University press, 1930.

——Artists and their friends in England, 1700–1799. Boston, Medici society, 1928. 2 v.

Wilenski, Reginald H. English painting. London, Faber, 1943.

ITALY

Ancona, Paolo d'. Les primitifs italiens du XI$^e$ au XIII$^e$ siècle. Paris, Éditions d'art et d'histoire, 1935.

45

**Antal, Frederick.** Florentine painting and its social background; the bourgeois republic before Cosimo de' Medici's advent to power: XIV and early XV centuries. London, Kegan Paul, 1948.

**Berenson, Bernhard.** The Italian painters of the renaissance. London, Oxford Univ. press, 1932.

——Italian pictures of the renaissance; a list of the principal artists and their works. Oxford, Clarendon press, 1932.

——The study and criticism of Italian art. London, Bell, 1901–1916. 3 v.

——Three essays in method. Oxford, Clarendon press, 1927.

**Borenius, Tancred.** Florentine frescoes. London, T. C. Jack, 1930.

**Brandi, Cesare.** Quattrocentisti senesi. Milan, Hoepli, 1949 (Valori plastici).

**Cecchi, Emilio.** The Sienese painters of the trecento. Trans. Leonard Penlock. London, Warne, 1931.

**Crowe, Joseph A., and Cavalcaselle, Giovanni B.** A history of painting in Italy, Umbria, Florence and Siena from the second to the sixteenth century. 2d ed. N. Y., Scribner, 1903–14. 6 v.

——A history of painting in north Italy, Venice, Padua, Vicenza, Verona, Ferrara, Milan, Friuli, Brescia, from the fourteenth to the sixteenth century. 2d ed. N. Y., Scribner, 1913. 3 v.

**Delogu, Giuseppe.** Antologia della pittura italiana dal XIII al XIX secolo. 2 ed. Bergamo, Istituto italiano d'arti grafiche, 1947.

——Italienische malerei, eine anthologie vom 14. bis 19. jahrhundert. Zürich, Fretz und Wasmuth, 1939.

**Edgell, George H.** A history of Sienese painting. N. Y., Dial press, 1932.

**Fiocco, Giuseppe.** Venetian painting of the seicento and the settecento. N. Y., Harcourt, Brace, 1929.

**Garrison, Edward B.** Italian Romanesque panel painting; an illustrated index. Florence, Olschki, 1949.

**Goering, Max.** Italian painting of the sixteenth century. London, Zwemmer, 1936.

——Italienische malerei des siebzehnten und achtzehnten jahrhunderts. Berlin, Wolff, 1936.

**Longhi, Roberto.** Proporzioni; studi di storia dell'arte. Florence, Sansoni, 1943—. v. 1—.

**McComb, Arthur K.** The baroque painters of Italy; an introductory historical survey. Cambridge, Harvard Univ. press, 1934.

Marle, Raimond van. The development of the Italian schools of painting. The Hague, Nijhoff, 1923-1938. 19 v. 759.5 M

Mather, Frank J. A history of Italian painting. N. Y., Holt, 1927. 759.5 M43

Ojetti, Ugo. La pittura italiana del seicento e del settecento alla Mostra di palazzo Pitti. Milan, Bestetti e Tumminelli, 1924.

——La pittura italiana dell'ottocento. Milano, Casa ed. d'arte, 1929.

Pallucchini, Rudolfo. La pittura veneziana del cinquecento. Novara, Inst. geografico De Agostini, 1944. 2 v. (Storia della pittura italiana).

Pope-Hennessy, John. Sienese quattrocento painting. London, Oxford Univ. press, Phaidon ed., 1947.

Ricci, Corrado. North Italian painting of the cinquecento; Piedmont, Liguria, Lombardy, Emilia. N. Y., Harcourt, Brace, 1929.

Rinaldis, Aldo de. Neapolitan painting of the seicento. N. Y., Harcourt, Brace, 1929.

Schmeckebier, Laurence E. A handbook of Italian renaissance painting. N. Y., Putnam, 1938.

Schubring, Paul. Cassoni; truhen und truhenbilder der italienischen frührenaissance. Leipzig, Hiersemann, 1915. 2 v.

Soby, James T., and Barr, Alfred H. Twentieth-century Italian art. N. Y., Museum of modern art, 1949.

Toesca, Pietro. Florentine painting of the trecento. N. Y., Harcourt, Brace, 1929.

Vasari, Giorgio. Lives of seventy of the most eminent painters, sculptors and architects. Trans. Mrs. Jonathan Foster; ed. by E. H. and E. W. Blashfield. N. Y., Scribner, 1909. 4 v.

Vavalà, Evelyn S. Uffizi studies; the development of the Florentine school of painting. Florence, Olschki, 1948.

Venturi, Adolfo. North Italian painting of the quattrocento; Emilia. N. Y., Harcourt, Brace, 1931.

——North Italian painting of the quattrocento; Lombardy, Piedmont, Liguria. N. Y., Harcourt, Brace, 1931.

——Italian painting, the creators of the Renaissance; critical studies. Geneva, Skira, 1950 (Painting, colour, history).

Voss, Hermann G. A. Die malerei des barock in Rom. Berlin, Propyläenverlag, 1924.

——Die malerei der spätrenaissance in Rom und Florenz. Berlin, Grote, 1920. 2 v.

**Waterhouse, Ellis K.** Baroque painting in Rome, the seventeenth century. London, Macmillan, 1937.

**Weigelt, Curt H.** Sienese painting of the trecento. N. Y., Harcourt, Brace, 1930.

LOW COUNTRIES

**Baker, Charles H. C.** Dutch painting of the seventeenth century. London, Studio, 1926.

**Bode, Wilhelm von.** Great masters of Dutch and Flemish painting. Trans. Margaret L. Clarke. N. Y., Scribner, 1909.

**Cornette, Arthur J. H.** The art of painting in the Low Countries. Amsterdam, Veen, 1947.

**Elst, Joseph J. M. I. van der.** The last flowering of the middle ages. N. Y., Doubleday, Doran, 1944.

**Fierens, Paul.** La peinture flamande de Bruegel au XVIII$^e$ siècle. Paris, Éditions d'art et d'histoire, 1942.

——La peinture flamande dès origines à Quentin Metsys. Paris, Éditions d'art et d'histoire, 1938.

**Fierens-Gevaert, Hippolyte.** Histoire de la peinture flamande dès origines à la fin du XV siècle. Paris, Van Oest, 1927-29. 3 v.

**Friedländer, Max J.** Die altniederländische malerei. Berlin, Cassirer, 1924-37. 14 v.

——Die niederländischen maler des 17. jahrhunderts. Berlin, Propyläen-verlag, 1923 (Propyläen-kunstgeschichte, 12).

**Fromentin, Eugène.** The Masters of past time; Dutch and Flemish painting from Van Eyck to Rembrandt. Trans. Andrew Boyle. London, Oxford Univ. press, Phaidon ed. 1948.

**Hofstede de Groot, Cornelis.** Beschreibendes und kritisches verzeichnis der werke der hervorragendsten holländischen maler des XVII. jahrhunderts. Esslingen, Neff, 1907-1928. 10 v.

**Lambotte, Paul.** Flemish painting before the eighteenth century. Trans. H. B. Grimsditch. London, Studio, 1927.

**Mander, Carel van.** Dutch and Flemish painters. Trans. Constant Van de Wall. N. Y., McFarlane, 1936.

**Puyvelde, Leo van.** La peinture flamande à Rome. Brussels, Librairie encyclopédique, 1950.

**Tovell, Ruth M.** Flemish artists of the Valois courts; a survey of the fourteenth and early fifteenth century development of book illumination and panel painting at the courts of the princes of the House of Valois. Toronto, Toronto Univ. press, 1950.

**Wilenski, Reginald H.** An introduction to Dutch art. London, Faber and Gwyer, 1929.

**Winkler, Friedrich.** Die altniederländische malerei; die malerei in Belgien und Holland von 1400–1600. Berlin, Propyläen-verlag, 1924.

RUSSIA

**Farbman, Michael S., ed.** Masterpieces of Russian painting; reproductions of Russian icons and frescoes from the XI to the XVIII centuries. London, Europa, 1930.

**Kondakov, Nikodim P.** The Russian icon. Trans. Ellis H. Minns. Oxford, Clarendon press, 1927.

**Lukomskii, Georgii K.** History of modern Russian painting (1840–1940). Trans. "G. K." London, Hutchinson, 1945.

SCANDINAVIA

**Lindblom, Andreas A. F.** La peinture gothique en Suède et en Norvège; étude sur les relations entre l'Europe occidentale et les pays scandinaves. Trans. Stéphane Harel. Stockholm, Wahlström, 1916.

**Østby, Leif.** Modern Norwegian painting. Trans. Christopher Norman. Oslo, Mittet, 1949.

SPAIN

**Beruete y Moret, Aureliano de.** Historia de la pintura española en el siglo XIX; elementos nacionales y extranjeros que han influido en ella. Madrid, Ruiz, 1926.

———Spanish painting. Trans. Lewis Spence. London, Studio, 1921.

**Harris, Enriqueta.** Spanish painting. N. Y., French and European publications, 1937.

**Lafuente Ferrari, Enrique.** Breve historia de la pintura española. 3 ed. Madrid, Dossat, 1946.

**Mayer, August L.** Historia de la pintura española. 2 ed. Madrid, Espasa-Calpe, 1942.

**Post, Chandler R.** A history of Spanish painting. Cambridge, Harvard Univ. press, 1930—. v. 1—.

## SWITZERLAND

**Bovy, Adrien.** La peinture suisse de 1600 à 1900. Bâle, Birkhaeuser, 1948.

**Gradmann, Erwin.** Schweizer malerei und zeichnung im 17. und 18. jahrhundert. Basel, Holbein, 1944.

**Jedlicka, Gotthard.** Zur schweizerischen malerei der gegenwart. Erlenbach-Zürich, Rentsch, 1947.

**Neuweiler, Arnold.** La peinture à Genève de 1700 à 1900. Genève, Jullien, 1945.

**Schmidt, George.** Schweizer malerei und zeichnung im 15. und 16. jahrhundert. Basel, Holbein, 1940.

**Wescher, Paul R.** Die romantik in der schweizer malerei. Frauenfeld, Huber, 1947.

## UNITED STATES AND CANADA

759.1
B245a

**Barker, Virgil.** American painting, history and interpretation. N. Y., Macmillan, 1950.

**Born, Wolfgang.** American landscape painting; an interpretation. New Haven, Yale Univ. press, 1948.

758.4
B645

———Still-life painting in America. N. Y., Oxford Univ. press, 1947.

**Buchanan, Donald W.** Canadian painters, from Paul Kane to the group of seven. London, Oxford Univ. press, Phaidon ed., 1945.

———The growth of Canadian painting. London, Collins, 1950.

759.1
B94

**Burroughs, Alan.** Limners and likenesses; three centuries of American painting. Cambridge, Harvard Univ. press, 1936.

**Cheney, Martha C.** Modern art in America. N. Y., Whittlesey house, 1939.

**Flexner, James T.** America's old masters; first artists of the new world. N. Y., Viking, 1939.

———First flowers of our wilderness, American painting. Boston, Houghton Mifflin, 1947.

**Hagen, Oskar F. L.** The birth of the American tradition in art. N. Y., Scribner, 1940.

759.1
Is3

**Isham, Samuel.** The history of American painting. New ed., with supplementary chapters by Royal Cortissoz. N. Y., Macmillan, 1936.

759.1
J256

**Janis, Sidney.** They taught themselves; American primitive painters of the 20th century. N. Y., Dial press, 1942.

Kimball, Sidney Fiske, and Venturi, Lionello. Great paintings in America. N. Y., Coward-McCann, 1948.
Lipman, Jean H. American primitive painting. London, Oxford Univ. press, 1942.
Lipman, Jean H., and Winchester, Alice, comps. Primitive painters in America, 1750-1950; an anthology. N. Y., Dodd, Mead, 1950.
Richardson, E. P. American romantic painting. N. Y., Weyhe, 1944.
Sherman, Frederic F. American painters of yesterday and today. N. Y., priv. pr., 1919.
Soby, James T., and Miller, Dorothy C. Romantic painting in America. N. Y., Museum of modern art, 1943.
Walker, John, and James, Macgill. Great American paintings from Smibert to Bellows, 1729-1924. N. Y., Oxford Univ. press, 1943.
Wight, Frederick. Milestones of American painting in our century. N. Y., Chanticleer, 1949.

# GRAPHIC ARTS AND ILLUMINATION
## Drawing and Graphic Arts

**Arms, John T.** Handbook of print making and print makers. N. Y., Macmillan, 1934.

——Handbook illustrations. N. Y., Knoedler, 1934. 2 v.

**Bartsch, Adam von.** Le peintre graveur. Nouv. éd. Würzburg, Verlagsdruckerei Würzburg, 1920. 21 v. in 18.

**Baudi di Vesme, Alessandro.** Le peintre-graveur italien; ouvrage faisant suite au peintre-graveur de Bartsch. Milan, Hoepli, 1906.

**Becker, Felix.** Handzeichnungen alter meister in privatsammlungen. Leipzig, Tauchnitz, 1922.

**Behne, Adolf B.** Alte deutsche zeichner; meisterwerke deutscher graphik von den Karolingern bis zum barock. Berlin, Deutsche Buch-Gemeinschaft, 1943.

**Benesch, Otto.** Oesterreichische handzeichnungen des XV. und XVI. jahrhunderts. Freiburg im Breisgau, Urban-verlag, 1936 (Meisterzeichnung, 5).

——Venetian drawings of the eighteenth century in America. N. Y., Bittner, 1947.

**Berenson, Bernhard.** The drawings of the Florentine painters. Amplified ed. Chicago, Univ. of Chicago press, 1938. 3 v.

**Berger, Klaus.** French master drawings of the nineteenth century. Trans. Robert Allen. N. Y., Harper, 1950.

**Bersier, Jean E.** La gravure; les procédés, l'histoire. Paris, Table ronde, 1948 (Techniques et histoire des arts).

○ **Blake, Vernon.** The art and craft of drawing. London, Oxford Univ. press, 1927.

**Bliss, Douglas P.** A history of wood-engraving. N. Y., Dutton, 1928.

**Blum, André.** La gravure en Angleterre au XVIII$^e$ siècle. Paris, Van Oest, 1930.

——The origins of printing and engraving. Trans. H. M. Lydenberg. N. Y., Scribner, 1940.

**Blunt, Anthony.** The French drawings in the collection of His Majesty the King at Windsor castle. London, Oxford Univ. press, Phaidon ed., 1945.

**Bock, Elfried.** Die deutsche graphik. Munich, Hanfstängl, 1922.

―――Geschichte der graphischen kunst von ihren anfängen bis zur gegenwart. Berlin, Propyläen-verlag, 1930 (Propyläen-kunstgeschichte).

**Brown, Bolton.** Lithography. N. Y., Carrington, 1923.

**Calabi, Augusto.** L'incisione italiana. Milan, Fratelli Treves, 1931.

**Carrington, Fitz Roy.** Prints and their makers; essays on engravers and etchers old and modern. N. Y., Century, 1912.

**Cogniat, Raymond.** Le dessin français au XVIII<sup>e</sup> siècle. Monaco, 1943 (Documents d'art).

O **Colin, Paul.** La gravure et les graveurs. Bruxelles, Van Oest, 1916–18. 2 v.

O **Courboin, François.** La gravure française; essai de bibliographie. Paris, Le Garrec, 1927–28. 3 v.

―――Histoire illustrée de la gravure en France. Paris, Le Garrec, 1923–28. 4 v.

**Craven, Thomas.** A treasury of American prints; a selection of one hundred etchings and lithographs by the foremost living American artists. N. Y., Simon and Schuster, 1939.

**Cumming, David.** Handbook of lithography; a practical treatise for all who are interested in the process. London, Black, 1904.

**Cundall, Joseph.** A brief history of wood-engraving from its invention. London, Low, Marston, 1895.

**Dacier, Émile.** La gravure française. Paris, Larousse, 1945 (Arts, styles et techniques).

**Davenport, Cyril J. H.** Mezzotints. N. Y., Putnam, 1903.

O **Degenhart, Bernhard.** Europäische handzeichnungen aus fünf jahrhunderten. Berlin, Atlantis, 1943.

O **Delacre, Maurice, and Lavallée, Pierre.** Dessins de maîtres anciens. Paris, Van Oest, 1927.

**Delen, Adrien J. J.** Flemish master drawings of the seventeenth century. Trans. Robert Allen. N. Y., Harper, 1950 (Master drawings).

―――Histoire de la gravure dans les anciens Pays-Bas et dans les provinces belges des origines jusqu'à la fin du XVIII siècle. Paris, Van Oest, 1924–35. 2 pts.

**Delogu, Giuseppe.** Venezianische zeichnungen aus dem 18. jahrhundert. Zürich, Fretz und Wasmuth, 1947.

**Delteil, Loÿs.** Manuel de l'amateur d'estampes des XIX<sup>e</sup> et XX<sup>e</sup> siècles. (1801–1924). Paris, Dorbon aîné, 1925. 2 v. Complement: 700 reproductions. Paris, Dorbon aîné, n. d. 2 v.

**Delteil, Loÿs** (continued)

———Manuel de l'amateur d'estampes du XVIII siècle. Paris, Dorbon aîné, 1910.

**De Tolnay, Charles.** History and technique of old master drawings; a handbook. N. Y., Bittner, 1943.

**Dilke, Emilia F. S.** French engravers and draughtsmen of the XVIIIth century. London, Bell, 1902.

**Dimier, Louis.** Dessins français du XVIe siècle. Paris, Encyclopédie Alpina, 1937.

○ **Dodgson, Campbell.** Modern drawings. London, Studio, 1933.

○ **Dörries, Bernhard.** Deutsche zeichnungen des 18. jahrhunderts. Munich, Bruckmann, 1943.

**Donati, Lamberto.** Incisioni fiorentine del quattrocento. Bergamo, Istituto italiano d'arti grafiche, 1944.

**Dussler, Luitpold.** Italienische meisterzeichnungen. Frankfurt a/M, Prestel, 1938.

**Ede, Harold S.** Florentine drawings of the quattrocento. N. Y., McBride, 1926 (Drawings of the great masters).

**Fielding, Mantle.** American engravers upon copper and steel. Philadelphia, priv. pr., 1917.

**Fischel, Oskar.** Die zeichnungen der Umbrer. Berlin, Grote, 1917.

**Friedländer, Max J.** Der holzschnitt. 2 aufl. Berlin, Vereinigung wissenschaftlicher verleger, 1921.

○ **Friedländer, Max J., and Bock, Elfried.** Handzeichnungen deutscher meister des 15. und 16. jahrhunderts. Berlin, Propyläen-verlag, 1921.

**Furst, Herbert.** The modern woodcut; a study of the evolution of the craft. N. Y., Dodd, Mead, 1924.

———Original engraving and etching, an appreciation. London, Nelson, 1931.

**Ganz, Paul.** Handzeichnungen schweizerischer meister des XV.–XVIII. jahrhunderts. 1–3 serie. Basel, Helbing und Lichtenhahn, 1904–08. 3 v.

○ **Garzarolli-Thurnlackh, Karl.** Die barocke handzeichnung in Österreich. Zürich, Amalthea-verlag, 1928.

○ **Geiger, Benno.** Handzeichnungen alter meister. Zürich, Amalthea-verlag, 1948.

**Geisberg, Max.** Geschichte der deutschen graphik vor Dürer. Berlin, Deutscher verein für kunstwissenschaft, 1939 (Forschungen zur deutschen kunstgeschichte, 32).

**George, Waldemar.** Le dessin français de David à Cézanne et l'esprit de la tradition baroque. Paris, Éditions chroniques du jour, 1929.

**Glaser, Curt.** Gotische holzschnitte. Berlin, Propyläen-verlag, 1923.

——Die graphik der neuzeit vom anfang des XIX. jahrhunderts bis zur gegenwart. Berlin, Cassirer, 1922.

**Gómez Sicre, José.** Spanish drawings, XV–XIX centuries. N. Y., Hyperion, 1950 (Hyperion drawings series).

**Gradmann, Erwin.** Dessins de maîtres espagnols. Trans. S. Stelling-Michaud. Bâle, Éditions Holbein, 1944.

——French master drawings of the eighteenth century. Trans. Robert Allen. N. Y., Harper, 1949 (Harper's art library).

**Gray, Basil.** The English print. London, Black, 1937.

**Hadeln, Detlev von.** Venezianische zeichnungen der hochrenaissance. Berlin, Cassirer, 1925.

——Venezianische zeichnungen der spätrenaissance. Berlin, Cassirer, 1926.

——Venezianische zeichnungen des quattrocento. Berlin, Cassirer, 1925.

**Hagen, Oskar F. L.** Deutsche zeichner von der gotik bis zum rokoko. Munich, Piper, 1921.

**Hamerton, Philip G.** Etching and etchers. Boston, Little, Brown, 1916.

**Hayden, Arthur.** Chats on old prints. 2d ed. London, Unwin, 1913.

**Hayter, Stanley W.** New ways of gravure. N. Y., Pantheon, 1949.

**Henkel, Max D.** Le dessin hollandais des origines au XVII$^e$ siècle. Paris, Van Oest, 1931.

**Hind, Arthur M.** Guide to the processes and schools of engraving represented in the exhibition of select prints. London, British Museum, 1933.

——A history of engraving and etching from the 15th century to the year 1914. 3d ed. London, Constable, 1927.

——An introduction to a history of woodcut, with a detailed survey of work done in the fifteenth century. London, Constable, 1935. 2 v.

**Hollstein, F. W. H.** Dutch and Flemish etchings, engravings and woodcuts, ca. 1450–1700. Amsterdam, Hertzberger, 1949—. v. 1—.

**Holman, Louis A.** The graphic processes: intaglio, relief and planographic. Boston, Goodspeed, 1929.

**Holme, Bryan.** Master drawings. London, Studio, 1943.
**Holme, Charles.** Modern etching and engraving. London, Studio, 1902.
——Modern etchings, mezzotints and dry-points. London, Studio, 1913.
——Old English mezzotints. London, Studio, 1910.
**Holme, Geoffrey.** Etchings of today. London, Studio, 1949.
——Modern woodcuts and lithographs by British and French artists. London, Studio, 1919.
**Hubbard, Eric H.** On making and collecting etchings; a handbook for etchers, students and collectors. London, Ringwood, 1920 (Print Soc. publ., 1).
——Some Victorian draughtsmen. Cambridge [Eng.], University press, 1944.
O **Hugelshofer, Walter.** Dessins et aquarelles de maîtres français du XIX$^e$ siècle. Trans. S. Stelling-Michaud. Bâle, Holbein, 1947.
——Schweizer handzeichnungen des XV. und XVI. jahrhunderts. Freiburg im Breisgau, Urban-verlag, 1928 (Meisterzeichnung, 1).
O **Huyghe, René.** Le dessin français au XIX$^e$ siècle. Lausanne, Mermod, 1948.
**Ivins, William M.** How prints look; photographs with a commentary. N. Y., Metropolitan Museum, 1943.
——Prints and books; informal papers. Cambridge, Harvard Univ. press, 1926.
**Kent, Norman.** Drawings by American artists. N. Y., Watson-Guptill, 1947.
**Kristeller, Paul.** Early Florentine woodcuts. London, Kegan Paul, 1897.
——Kupferstich und holzschnitt in vier jahrhunderten. 4$^e$ aufl. Berlin, Cassirer, 1922.
**Lavallée, Pierre.** Le dessin français. Paris, Larousse, 1948 (Arts, styles et techniques).
O ——Le dessin français du XIII$^e$ au XVI$^e$ siècle. Paris, Van Oest, 1930.
O ——Les techniques du dessin, leur évolution dans les différents écoles de l'Europe. Paris, Van Oest, 1943.
**Laver, James.** A history of British and American etching. London, Benn, 1929.
**Lehrs, Max.** Geschichte und kritischer katalog des deutschen, niederländischen und französischen kupferstichs im XV. jahrhundert. Vienna, Gesellschaft für vervielfältigende kunst, 1908–1934. 9 v.

**Leipnik, F. L.** A history of French etching from the sixteenth century to the present day. London, Lane, 1924.

O **Leporini, Heinrich.** Die künstlerzeichnung; ein handbuch für liebhaber und sammler. Berlin, Schmidt, 1928.

O ——Der kupferstichsammler; ein hand- und nachschlagebuch samt künstlerverzeichnis für den sammler druckgraphischer kunst. Berlin, Schmidt, 1924.

O ——Die stilentwicklung der handzeichnung, XIV. bis XVIII. jahrhundert. Vienna, Manz, 1925.

**Lippmann, Friedrich.** Engraving and etching; a handbook for the use of students and print collectors. 3d ed. London, Grevel, 1906.

**Lozowick, Louis.** A treasury of drawings, from pre-history to the present. N. Y., Lear, 1948.

**Lugt, Frits.** Les marques de collections de dessins et d'estampes; marques estampillées et écrites de collections particulières et publiques. Amsterdam, Vereenigde drukkerijen, 1921.

**Lumsden, Ernest S.** The art of etching; a complete and fully illustrated description of etching, drypoint, soft-ground etching, aquatint, and their allied arts. Philadelphia, Lippincott, 1925.

**Mayer, August L.** Dibujos originales de maestros españoles. N. Y., Hispanic society, 1928. 2 v.

**Meder, Joseph.** Die handzeichnung; ihre technik und entwicklung. 2 aufl. Vienna, Schroll, 1923. 740 M468

**Mellaart, J. H. J.** Dutch drawings of the seventeenth century. N. Y., McBride, 1926 (Drawings of the great masters).

**Mongan, Agnes.** Master drawings, selected from the museums and private collections of America. Buffalo, Albright art gallery, 1934.

O ——One hundred master drawings. Cambridge, Harvard Univ. press, 1949.

**Mongan, Agnes, and Sachs, Paul J.** Drawings in the Fogg museum of art. 2d ed. Cambridge, Harvard Univ. press, 1946. 2 v.

**Muchall-Viebrook, Thomas W.** Deutsche barockzeichnungen. Munich, Delphin-verlag, 1925.

——Flemish drawings of the seventeenth century. N. Y., McBride, 1926 (Drawings of the great masters).

**Old Master Drawings;** a quarterly magazine for students and collectors. London, Batsford, 1926–1940. 14 v.

**Oppé, Adolf P.** English drawings, Stuart and Georgian periods, in the collection of His Majesty the King at Windsor Castle. London, Oxford Univ. press, Phaidon ed., 1950.

**Osborn, Max.** Der Holzschnitt. Bielefeld, Velhagen und Klasing, 1905.

**Parker, Karl T.** Drawings of the early German schools. N. Y., McBride, 1926 (Drawings of the great masters).

——Elsässische handzeichnungen des XV. und XVI. jahrhunderts. Freiburg am Breisgau, Urban-verlag, 1928. (Meisterzeichnung, 2).

——North Italian drawings of the quattrocento. London, Benn, 1927 (Drawings of the great masters).

**Passavant, Johann D.** Le peintre-graveur; contenant l'histoire de la gravure sur bois, sur métal et au burin jusque vers la fin du XVI. siècle. Leipsic, Weigel, 1860–64. 6 v. in 3.

**Pennell, Elizabeth R.** Lithography and lithographers. N. Y., Macmillan, 1915.

**Pittaluga, Mary.** L'incisione italiana nel cinquecento. Milan, Hoepli, 1930.

**Plenderleith, Harold J.** The conservation of prints, drawings and manuscripts. London, Oxford Univ. press, 1937.

**Popham, Arthur E.** Drawings of the early Flemish school. N. Y., McBride, 1926 (Drawings of the great masters).

——A handbook to the drawings and watercolours in the Department of Prints and Drawings, British museum. London, The Trustees, 1939.

——The Italian drawings of the XV and XVI centuries in the collection of His Majesty the King at Windsor Castle. London, Oxford Univ. press, Phaidon ed., 1949.

——Italian drawings in the Department of prints and drawings in the British museum, the fourteenth and fifteenth centuries. London, The Trustees, 1950. 2 v.

**Prideaux, Sarah T.** Aquatint engraving. London, Duckworth, 1909.

**Puyvelde, Leo van.** The Dutch drawings in the collection of His Majesty the King at Windsor castle. London, Oxford Univ. press, Phaidon ed., 1944.

——The Flemish drawings in the collection of His Majesty the King at Windsor Castle. London, Oxford Univ. press, Phaidon ed., 1942.

**Ratouis de Limay, Paul.** Le pastel en France au XVIII$^e$ siècle. Paris, Éditions Baudinière, 1946.

Regteren Altena, Johan Q. van. Holländische meisterzeichnungen des siebzehnten jahrhunderts. Basel, Holbein-verlag, 1949.

Reitlinger, Henry S. Old master drawings; a handbook for amateurs and collectors. N. Y., Moffat, Yard, 1923.

Reynolds, Graham. Nineteenth century drawings, 1850–1900. London, Pleiades books, 1949.

——Twentieth century drawings. London, Pleiades books, 1946.

Robert-Dumesnil, A. P. F. Le peintre-graveur français; ou catalogue raisonné des estampes gravées par les peintres et les dessinateurs de l'école française. Paris, Warée, 1835–71. 11 v.

Rosenthal, Leon. La gravure. Paris, Laurens, 1909 (Manuels d'histoire de l'art).

Sachs, Paul J. The pocket book of great drawings. N. Y., Pocket books, 1951 (Pocket book, 765).

Salaman, Malcolm C. The great painter-etchers from Rembrandt to Whistler. N. Y., Studio, 1914.

——The new woodcut. London, Studio, 1930.

——Old English colour prints. N. Y., Studio, 1909.

——Old English mezzotints. London, Studio, 1910.

Schendel, Arthur F. E. van. Le dessin en Lombardie jusqu'à la fin du XVe siècle. Bruxelles, Éditions de la Connaissance, 1938.

Schilling, Edmund. Altdeutsche meisterzeichnungen. Frankfurt a/M, Prestel-verlag, 1934.

——Deutsche romantiker-zeichnungen. Frankfurt a/M, Prestel-verlag, 1935.

——Nürnberger handzeichnungen des XV. und XVI. jahrhunderts. Freiburg im Breisgau, Urban-verlag, 1929 (Meisterzeichnung, 3).

Shoolman, Regina L., and Slatkin, Charles E. Six centuries of French master drawings in America. N. Y., Oxford Univ. press, 1950.

Silsby, Wilson. Etching methods and materials; a new and simplified technique. N. Y., Dodd, Mead, 1943.

Singer, Hans W. Handbuch für kupferstichsammler; technische erklärungen ratschläge für das sammeln und das aufbewahren. 2 aufl. Leipzig, Hiersemann, 1922.

Slatkin, Charles E., and Shoolman, Regina. Treasury of American drawings. N. Y., Oxford Univ. press, 1947.

**Soares, Ernesto.** História da gravura artística em Portugal os artistas e as suas obras. Lisboa, Santelmo, 1940–41. 2 v.

**Stauffer, David M.** American engravers upon copper and steel. N. Y., Grolier club, 1907. 2 v.

**Sternberg, Harry.** Modern methods and materials of etching. N. Y., McGraw-Hill, 1949.

**Stix, Alfred.** Meisterwerke der graphik im XVIII. jahrhundert. Vienna, Wolf, 1920–21.

**Sullivan, Edward.** The book of Kells. 4th ed. London, Studio, 1933.

**Sutton, Denys.** French drawings of the eighteenth century. London, Pleiades books, 1949.

**Swarzenski, Georg, and Schilling, Edmund.** Handzeichnungen alter meister aus deutschem privatbesitz. Frankfurt a/M, Frankfurter verlags-anstalt, 1924.

**Tietze, Hans.** European master drawings in the United States. N. Y., Augustin, 1947.

**Tietze, Hans, and Tietze-Conrat, Erika.** The drawings of the Venetian painters in the 15th and 16th centuries. N. Y., Augustin, 1944.

**Updike, Daniel B.** Printing types, their history, forms and use; a study in survivals. Cambridge, Harvard Univ. press, 1951. 2 v.

**Vasari Society.** Reproductions of drawings by old masters. N. Y., Oxford Univ. press, 1905–1935. Series I, pts. 1–10; Series II, pts. 1–16.

**Voss, Hermann G. A.** Zeichnungen der italienischen spätrenaissance. Munich, Delphin-verlag, 1928.

**Wedmore, Frederick.** Etchings. 2d ed. London, Methuen, 1912 (Connoisseur's library).

——Fine prints. New and enl. ed. Edinburgh, Grant, 1905 (The collector series).

**Weinberger, Martin.** Deutsche rokokozeichnungen. Munich, Delphin-verlag, 1923.

**Weitenkampf, Frank.** American graphic art. New ed. rev., enl. N. Y., Macmillan, 1924.

——How to appreciate prints. 4th rev. ed. N. Y., Scribner, 1942.

**Wheeler, Monroe.** Modern drawings. N. Y., Museum of modern art, 1944.

**Whitman, Alfred.** Print-collector's handbook. 6th ed. London, Bell, 1912.

Winkler, Friedrich. Mittel-, niederrheinische und westfälische handzeichnungen des XV. und XVI. jahrhunderts. Freiburg im Breisgau, Urban-verlag, 1932 (Meisterzeichnung, 4).

Winzinger, Franz. Deutsche meisterzeichnungen der gotik. Munich, Prestel-verlag, 1949.

Zigrosser, Carl. The book of fine prints; an anthology of printed pictures and introduction to the study of graphic art in the west and the east. N. Y., Crown, 1948 [1st ed. titled: Six centuries of fine prints].

## Illuminated Manuscripts

Ancona, Paolo d'. La miniature italienne du X$^e$ au XVI$^e$ siècle. Trans. P. Poirier. Paris, Van Oest, 1925.

Blum, André, and Lauer, Philippe. La miniature francaise au XV$^e$ et XVI$^e$ siècles. Paris, Van Oest, 1930.

Boinet, Amédée. La miniature carolingienne, ses origines, son développement. Paris, Picard, 1913.

Domínguez Bordona, Jesús. Spanish illumination. N. Y., Harcourt, Brace, 1930. 2 v.

Durrieu, Paul. La miniature flamande au temps de la cour de Bourgogne, 1415–1530. Brussels, Van Oest, 1921.

Ebersolt, Jean. La miniature byzantine. Paris, Van Oest, 1926.

Gerstinger, Hans. Die griechische buchmalerei. Vienna, Druck und verlag der Österreichischen staatsdruckerei, 1926. 2 v.

Goldschmidt, Adolph. German illumination. N. Y., Harcourt, Brace, 1928. 2 v.

Herbert, John A. Illuminated manuscripts. 2d ed. London, Methuen, 1912 (Connoisseur's library).

Johnston, Edward. Writing and illuminating, and lettering. London, Pitman, 1948.

Köhler, Wilhelm R. W. Die karolingischen miniaturen. Berlin, Cassirer, 1930–33. 2 v.

Martin, Henry M. R. La miniature française du XIII$^e$ au XV$^e$ siècle. 2 éd. rev. Paris, Van Oest, 1924.

Masai, François. Essai sur les origines de la miniature dite irlandaise. Bruxelles, Erasme, 1947.

Micheli, Geneviève. L'enluminure du haut moyen âge et les influences irlandaises. Bruxelles, Éditions de la Connaissance, 1939.

**Millar, Eric G.** English illuminated manuscripts from the Xth to the XIIIth century. Paris, Van Oest, 1926.

——English illuminated manuscripts of the XIVth and XVth centuries. Paris, Van Oest, 1928.

**Omont, Henri A.** Miniatures de plus anciens manuscrits grecs de la Bibliothèque nationale du VI$^e$ au XIV$^e$ siècle. Paris, Champion, 1929.

**Réau, Louis.** Histoire de la peinture au moyen-âge. Melun, Librairie d'Argences, 1946—. v. 1— [La miniature].

**Saunders, O. Elfrida.** English illumination. Florence, Pantheon, 1928. 2 v.

**Swarzenski, Hanns.** Vorgotische miniaturen, die ersten jahrhunderte deutscher malerei. 2., umgearb. aufl. Königstein in Taunus, Langewiesche, 1931.

**Weitzmann, Kurt.** Illustrations in roll and codex, a study of the origin and method of text illustration. Princeton, Princeton Univ. press, 1947 (Studies in manuscript illumination, 2).

**Winkler, Friedrich.** Die flämische buchmalerei des XV. und XVI. jahrhunderts; künstler und werke von den brüdern van Eyck bis zu Simon Bening. Leipzig, Seemann, 1925.

**Zimmermann, Ernst H.** Vorkarolingische miniaturen. Berlin, Deutscher verein für kunstwissenschaft, 1916. 5 v.

# MINOR ARTS
## General

**Berliner, Rudolf.** Ornamentale vorlage-blätter des 15. bis 18. jahrhunderts. Leipzig, Klinkhardt und Biermann, 1925–26. 3 v.

**Bossert, Helmuth T.** An encyclopaedia of colour decoration from the earliest times to the middle of the XIX century. N. Y., Weyhe, 1928.

———Geschichte des kunstgewerbes aller zeiten und völker, in verbindung mit zahlreichen fachgelehrten. Berlin, Wasmuth, 1928–35. 6 v.

———Ornament in applied art, 122 color plates reproducing over 2000 decorative motives from the arts of Asia, primitive Europe, North, Central and South America, Africa, Oceania and from the peasant arts of Europe. N. Y., Weyhe, 1924.

**Christie, Archibald H.** Traditional methods of pattern designing; an introduction to the study of formal ornament. 2d ed. Oxford, Clarendon press, 1929.

**Evans, Joan.** Pattern, a study of ornament in western Europe from 1180 to 1900. Oxford, Clarendon press, 1931. 2 v.

———Style in ornament. London, Oxford Univ. press, 1950.

**Glazier, Richard.** Manual of historic ornament. 6th ed. rev. N. Y., Scribner, 1948.

**Hamlin, Alfred D. F.** A history of ornament, renaissance and modern. N. Y., Century, 1916–23. 2 v.

**Jones, Owen.** The grammar of ornament. London, Quaritch, 1910.

**Lehnert, Georg H.** Illustrierte geschichte des kunstgewerbes. Berlin, Oldenbourg, 1907–09. 2 v.

**Meyer, Franz S.** A handbook of ornament. Chicago, Wilcox and Follett, 1945.

**Molinier, Émile.** Histoire générale des arts appliqués à l'industrie du V$^e$ à la fin du XVIII$^e$ siècle. Paris, Lévy, 1896–1910. 6 v.

**Ostwald, Wilhelm.** Die welt der formen. Leipzig, Unesma, 1922–25. 4 v.

**Racinet, Auguste.** L'ornement polychrome. Paris, Firmin-Didot, 1885–87. 10 pts.

**Scott, Robert G.** Design fundamentals. N. Y., McGraw-Hill, 1951.

**Speltz, Alexander.** Styles of ornament, exhibited in designs, and arranged in historical order, with descriptive text. Trans. David O'Conor. N. Y., Grosset and Dunlap, 1936.

## Textiles, Tapestries, Rugs

**Ackerman, Phyllis.** Tapestry, the mirror of civilization. N. Y., Oxford Univ. press, 1933.

**Algoud, Henri.** La soie, art et histoire. Paris, Payot, 1928.

**Baschet, Jacques.** Tapisseries de France. Paris, Nouvelles éditions françaises, 1947.

**Christie, Grace.** Embroidery and tapestry weaving. N. Y., Macmillan, 1906.

——English medieval embroidery; a brief survey of English embroidery dating from the beginning of the tenth century until the end of the fourteenth. Oxford, Clarendon press, 1938.

**Clouzot, Henri.** Painted and printed fabrics; a history of the manufactory at Jouy and other ateliers in France, 1760–1815. New Haven, Yale Univ. press, 1927.

**Demotte, G. J.** La tapisserie gothique. N. Y., Demotte, 1924.

**Dilley, Arthur U.** Oriental rugs and carpets; a comprehensive study. N. Y., Scribner, 1931.

**Falke, Otto von.** Decorative silks. New ed. N. Y., Helburn, 1922.

**Fenaille, Maurice.** État général des tapisseries de la manufacture des Gobelins depuis son origine jusqu'à nos jours, 1600–1900. Paris, Hachette, 1903–23. 5 v.

**Flemming, Ernst R.** An encyclopaedia of textiles from the earliest times to the beginning of the 19th century. N. Y., Weyhe, 1927.

**Glazier, Richard.** Historic textile fabrics; a short history of the tradition and development of pattern in woven and printed stuffs. London, Batsford, 1923.

**Göbel, Heinrich.** Wandteppiche. Leipzig, Klinkhardt und Biermann, 1923–24. 3 v. in 6.

**Guiffrey, Jules M. J., and others.** Histoire générale de la tapisseries. Paris, Société anonyme de publ. périodiques, 1875–85. 25 pts. (classed in 3 parts: 1, Guiffrey: Tapisseries françaises; 2, Eugéne Müntz: Tapisseries italiennes, allemandes, anglaises, danoises, espagnoles, russes, etc.; 3, Alexander Pinchart: Tapisseries flamandes).

——Les manufactures nationales de tapisseries; les Gobelins et Beauvais. Paris, Laurens, 1907.

——La tapisserie. Paris, Picard, 1904.

Hawley, Walter A. Oriental rugs, antique and modern. N. Y., Tudor, 1937.

Holt, Rosa B. Oriental and occidental rugs, antique and modern. New rev. ed. Garden City, N. Y., Garden City pub. co., 1937.

Hunter, George L. The practical book of tapestries. Philadelphia, Lippincott, 1925.

——Tapestries, their origin, history and renaissance. N. Y., Lane, 1913.

Kendrick, Albert F. Catalogue of tapestries. London, Victoria and Albert Museum, 1924.

——English decorative fabrics of the sixteenth to eighteenth centuries. Benfleet [Eng.], Lewis, 1934.

Kendrick, Albert F., and Tattersall, C. E. C. Handwoven carpets, Oriental and European. London, Benn, 1922. 2 v.

Kurth, Betty. Die deutschen bildteppiche des mittelalters. Wien, Schroll, 1926. 3 v.

——Gotische bildteppiche aus Frankreich und Flandern. Munich, Riehn und Reusch, 1923.

Lejard, André. French tapestry. London, Elek, 1946.

——La tapisserie de Bayeux, accompagnée de la conquête de l'Angleterre par Guillaume le Conquérant; texte extrait de "La chronique de Normandie." Paris, Éditions du Chêne, 1946.

Lewis, George G. The practical book of oriental rugs. 5th ed. Philadelphia, Lippincott, 1920.

Little, Frances. Early American textiles. N. Y., Century, 1931.

Lurçat, Jean. Tapisserie française. Paris, Bordas, 1947.

Marquet de Vasselot, Jean J. Bibliographie de la tapisserie, des tapis et de la broderie en France. Paris, Colin, 1935 (Archives de l'art français, nouv. per. t. XVIII).

Martin, Fredrik R. A history of oriental carpets before 1800. Vienna, I. and R. State and court printing office, 1908.

Migeon, Gaston. Les arts du tissu. Paris, Laurens, 1909.

Moore, Hannah H. The lace book. N. Y., Tudor, 1937.

Müntz, Eugène. La tapisserie. 5$^e$ éd. Paris, Picard, 1903.

Mumford, John K. Oriental rugs. N. Y., Scribner, 1923.

Neugebauer, Rudolf. Handbuch der orientalischen teppichkunde. Leipzig, Hiersemann, 1930.

**Palliser, Fanny M.** History of lace. 4th ed. N. Y., Scribner, 1902.
**Pethebridge, Jeanette E.** A manual of lace. London, Cassell, 1947.
**Podreider, Fanny.** Storia dei tessuti d'arte in Italia, secolo XII–XVIII. Bergamo, Istituto italiano d'arti grafiche, 1928.
**Priest, Alan, and Simmons, Pauline.** Chinese textiles; an introduction to the study of their history, sources, techniques, symbolism, and use occasioned by the exhibition of Chinese court robes and accessories. N. Y., Metropolitan museum of art, 1931.
**Reath, Nancy A., and Sachs, Eleanor B.** Persian textiles and their technique from the sixth to the eighteenth centuries, including a system for general textile classification. New Haven, Yale Univ. press, 1937.
—— The weaves of hand-loom fabrics; a classification with historical notes. Philadelphia, Pennsylvania museum, 1927.
**Ricci, Elisa.** Old Italian lace. Philadelphia, Lippincott, 1913. 2 v.
**Sangiorgi, Giorgio.** Contributi allo studio dell'arte tessile. Milan, Bestetti e Tumminelli, 1919.
**Schmitz, Hermann.** Bildteppiche, geschichte der Gobelinwirkerei. Berlin, Verlag für kunstwissenschaft, 1920.
**Schuette, Marie.** Gestickte bildteppiche und decken des mittelalters. Leipzig, Hiersemann, 1927—. v. 1—.
**Thomson, William G.** A history of tapestry from the earliest times until the present day. Rev. ed. N. Y., Putnam, 1930.
**Volbach, Wolfgang F., and Kühnel, Ernst.** Late antique Coptic and Islamic textiles of Egypt. N. Y., Weyhe, 1926.

### Costume

**Boehn, Max von.** Modes and manners. Trans. Joan Joshua. London, Harrap, 1932–36. 4 v.
**Brooke, Iris.** A history of English costume. 3d ed. London, Methuen, 1949.
**Bruhn, Wolfgang.** Das kostümwerk; eine geschichte des kostüms aller zeiten und völker vom altertum bis zur neuzeit einschliesslich der volkstrachten Europas und der trachten der aussereuropaïschen länder. Berlin, Wasmuth, 1941.
**Colas, René.** Bibliographie générale du costume et de la mode. Paris, Colas, 1933. 2 v.
**Davenport, Millia.** The book of costume. N. Y., Crown, 1948. 2 v.

**Earle, Alice M.** Two centuries of costume in America, MDCXX–MDCCCXX. N. Y., Macmillan, 1903. 2 v.

**Houston, Mary G.** Ancient Egyptian, Assyrian and Persian costumes and decorations. London, Black, 1920.

———Ancient Greek, Roman and Byzantine costume and decoration. 2d ed. London, Black, 1947.

———Medieval costume in England and France; the 13th, 14th and 15th centuries. London, Black, 1939.

**Kelly, Francis M., and Schwabe, Randolph.** Historic costume, a chronicle of fashion in western Europe, 1450–1790. London, Batsford, 1925.

**Laver, James.** Costume of the western world. London, Harrap, 1950—. v. 1—.

———Style in costume. London, Oxford Univ. press, 1949.

**McClellan, Elisabeth.** History of American costume, 1607–1870; with an introductory chapter on dress in the Spanish and French settlements in Florida and Louisiana. N. Y., Tudor, 1937.

**Monro, Isabel S., and Cook, Dorothy E.** Costume index; a subject index to plates and to illustrated text. N. Y., Wilson, 1937.

**Planché, James R.** A cyclopaedia of costume or dictionary of dress, including notices of contemporaneous fashions on the continent; a general chronological history of the costumes of the principal countries of Europe, from the commencement of the Christian era to the accession of George the third. London, Chatto and Windus, 1876–79. 2 v.

**Racinet, Auguste.** Le costume historique. Paris, Firmin-Didot, 1888. 6 v.

### Furniture

**Aronson, Joseph.** The encyclopedia of furniture. N. Y., Crown, 1938.

**Bode, Wilhelm von.** Italian renaissance furniture. Trans. M. E. Herrick. N. Y., Helburn, 1921.

**Brackett, Oliver.** English furniture illustrated; a pictorial review of English furniture from Chaucer to Queen Victoria. Rev. ed., by H. C. Smith. N. Y., Macmillan, 1950.

**Burr, Grace H.** Hispanic furniture, with examples in the collection of the Hispanic society of America. N. Y., Hispanic society, 1941.

**Byne, Arthur, and Stapley, Mildred.** Spanish interiors and furniture. N. Y., Helburn, 1921–22. 4 v.

**Cescinsky, Herbert.** English furniture from Gothic to Sheraton; a concise account of the development of English furniture and woodwork from the Gothic of the fifteenth century to the classic revival of the fifteenth century to the classic revival of the early nineteenth. Grand Rapids, Mich., Dean-Hicks, 1929.

**Cescinsky, Herbert, and Hunter, George L.** English and American furniture; a pictorial handbook of furniture made in Great Britain and in the American colonies, some in the sixteenth century but principally in the seventeenth, eighteenth and early nineteenth centuries. Grand Rapids, Mich., Dean-Hicks, 1929.

**Cornelius, Charles O.** Early American furniture. N. Y., Century, 1926.

**Dilke, Emilia F. S.** French furniture and decoration in the XVIIIth century. London, Bell, 1901.

**Dreyfus, Carle.** French furniture. N. Y., Brentano's, 1921. 2 v.

**Eberlein, Harold D., and McClure, Abbot.** The practical book of period furniture, treating of furniture of the English, American colonial and post-colonial and principal French periods. Philadelphia, Lippincott, 1914.

**Eberlein, Harold D., and Ramsdell, Roger W.** The practical book of Italian, Spanish, and Portuguese furniture. Philadelphia, Lippincott, 1927.

**Falke, Otto von.** Deutsche möbel des mittelalters und der renaissance. Stuttgart, Hoffmann, 1924.

**Félice, Roger de.** French furniture in the middle ages and under Louis XIII. Trans. F. M. Atkinson. N. Y., Stokes, 19—.

——French furniture under Louis XIV. Trans. F. M. Atkinson. N. Y., Stokes, 19—.

——French furniture under Louis XV. Trans. Florence Simmonds. London, Heinemann, 1927.

——French furniture under Louis XVI and the empire. Trans. F. M. Atkinson. London, Heinemann, 1920.

**Feulner, Adolf.** Kunstgeschichte des möbels seit dem altertum. 2 aufl. Berlin, Propyläen-verlag, 1927.

**Havard, Henry.** Dictionnaire de l'ameublement et de la décoration depuis le XIII$^e$ siècle jusqu'à nos jours. Paris, Quantin, 1894. 4 v.

**Holloway, Edward S.** American furniture and decoration, colonial and federal. Philadelphia, Lippincott, 1928.

**Hunter, George L.** Italian furniture and interiors. N. Y., Helburn, 1918. 2 v.

**Jourdain, Margaret.** English decoration and furniture of the early renaissance, 1500–1650, an account of its development and characteristic forms. London, Batsford, 1924.

——English decoration and furniture of the later XVIIIth century, 1760–1820; an account of its development and characteristic forms. London, Batsford, 1922.

**Kates, George N.** Chinese household furniture, from examples selected and measured. N. Y., Harper, 1948.

**Kettell, Russell H.** The pine furniture of early New England. Garden City, N. Y., Doubleday, 1929.

**Litchfield, Frederick.** Illustrated history of furniture from the earliest to the present time. 7th ed. London, Truslove, 1922.

**Lockwood, Luke V.** Colonial furniture in America. 3d ed. N. Y., Scribner, 1926. 2 v.

**Luthmer, Ferdinand.** Deutsche möbel der vergangenheit. Leipzig, Klinkhardt und Biermann, 1924.

**Macquoid, Percy.** A history of English furniture. London, 1926. 4 v.

**Macquoid, Percy, and Edwards, Ralph.** The dictionary of English furniture, from the middle ages to the late Georgian period. N. Y., Scribner, 1924–27. 3 v.

**Nagel, Charles.** American furniture, 1650–1850; a brief background and illustrated history. N. Y., Chanticleer press, 1949.

**Nutting, Wallace.** Furniture of the Pilgrim century (of American origin), 1620–1720, including colonial utensils and hardware. Boston, Marshall, Jones, 1921.

——Furniture treasury, mostly of American origin; all periods of American furniture with some foreign examples in America, also American hardware and household utensils. Reprint ed. N. Y., Macmillan, 1948. 2 v.

**Odom, William M.** A history of Italian furniture from the fourteenth to the early nineteenth centuries. Garden City, N. Y., Doubleday, 1918–19. 2 v.

**Olmer, Pierre.** Le mobilier français d'aujourd'hui, 1910–1925. Paris, Van Oest, 1926.

——La renaissance du mobilier français, 1890–1910. Paris, Van Oest, 1927.

**Richter, Gisela M. A.** Ancient furniture; a history of Greek, Etruscan and Roman furniture. Oxford, Clarendon press, 1926.

**Rogers, Meyric R.** American interior design; the traditions and development of domestic design from colonial times to the present. N. Y., Norton, 1947.

**Saglio, André.** French furniture. London, Batsford, 1913.

**Salverte, François de.** Les ébénistes du XVIII$^e$ siècle, leurs oeuvres et leurs marques. 3$^e$ éd. Paris, Van Oest, 1934.

**Schmitz, Hermann,** ed. The encyclopedia of furniture; an outline history of furniture design in Egypt, Assyria, Persia, Greece, Rome, Italy, France, the Netherlands, Germany, England, Scandinavia, Spain, Russia, and in the Near and Far East, up to the middle of the nineteenth century. N. Y., McBride, 1926.

**Schottmüller, Frida.** Furniture and interior decoration of the Italian renaissance. 2d rev. ed. N. Y., Westermann, 1928.

**Smith, Harold C.,** ed. Catalogue of English furniture and woodwork. London, Victoria and Albert Museum, 1929–31. 4 v. (v.1, Smith: Gothic and early Tudor; v.2, Smith: Late Tudor and early Stuart; v.3, Oliver Brackett: Late Stuart and Queen Anne; v.4, Ralph Edwards: Georgian).

**Strange, Thomas A.** English furniture, decoration, woodwork and allied arts, during the last half of the 17th century, the whole of the 18th century and the earlier part of the 19th. London, Simpkin, Marshall, Hamilton, Kent, 1903.

——An historical guide to French interiors, furniture, decoration, woodwork and allied arts during the last half of the 17th century, the whole of the 18th century, and the early part of the 19th. London, McCorquodale, 1907.

**Taullard, Alfredo.** El mueble colonial sudamericano. Buenos Aires, Ediciones Peuser, 1944.

**Viollet-le-Duc, Eugène E.** Dictionnaire raisonné du mobilier français de l'époque carlovingienne à la renaissance. Paris, Gründ, 1914. 6 v.

### Pottery and Porcelain

**Barber, Edwin A.** Marks of American potters, with facsimiles of 1000 marks, and illustrations of rare examples of American wares. Philadelphia, Patterson and White, 1904.

――The pottery and porcelain of the United States; an historical review of American ceramic art from the earliest times to the present day. 3d ed. N. Y., Putnam, 1909.

Burton, William. A general history of porcelain. London, Cassell, 1921. 2 v.

Burton, William, and Hobson, Robert L. Handbook of marks on pottery and porcelain. London, Macmillan, 1929.

Chaffers, William. Marks and monograms on pottery and porcelain of the renaissance and modern periods. 14th ed. London, Bickers, 1946.

Cox, Warren E. The book of pottery and porcelain. N. Y., Lee and Shepard, 1944. 2 v.

Dillon, Edward. Porcelain. N. Y., Putnam, 1904 (Connoisseur's library).

Eberlein, Harold D., and Ramsdell, Roger W. The practical book of chinaware. Rev. ed. Philadelphia, Lippincott, 1948.

Fontaine, Georges. La céramique française. Paris, Larousse, 1947 (Arts, styles et techniques).

Furumark, Arne. The Mycenaen pottery; analysis and classification. Stockholm, Petterson, 1941.

Hannover, Emil. Pottery and porcelain; a handbook for collectors. Trans. from the Danish; ed. by Bernard Rackham. 5th ed. rev. N. Y., Scribner, 1951. 3 v.

Hofmann, Friedrich H. Das porzellan der europäischen manufakturen im XVIII. jahrhundert; eine kunst- und kulturgeschichte. Berlin, Propyläen-verlag, 1932.

Honey, William B. The art of the potter; a book for the collector and connoisseur. N. Y., Whittlesey house, 1950.

――English pottery and porcelain. London, Black, 1933.

――Old English porcelain; a handbook for collectors. New ed. N. Y., McGraw-Hill, 1949.

Lane, Arthur. Early Islamic pottery; Mesopotamia, Egypt, and Persia. London, Faber, 1947.

――French faïence. London, Faber, 1948.

――Style in pottery. London, Oxford Univ. press, 1948.

Laufer, Berthold. The beginnings of porcelain in China. Chicago, Field Museum, 1917.

Leach, Bernard. A potter's book. London, Faber, 1940.

**Litchfield, Frederick.** Pottery and porcelain; a guide to collectors. 4th ed. N. Y., Macmillan, 1925.

**March, Benjamin.** Standards of pottery description. Ann Arbor, Univ. of Michigan press, 1934.

**Minghetti, Aurelio.** Ceramisti. Milan, B. C. Tosi, 1930.

**Ramsay, John.** American potters and pottery. Boston, Hale, Cushman and Flint, 1939.

**Solon, Louis M. E.** Ceramic literature; an analytical index to the works published in all languages on the history and the technology of the ceramic art. London, Griffin, 1910.

———A history and description of Italian majolica. N. Y., Cassell, 1907.

**Spargo, John.** Early American pottery and china. N. Y., Century, 1926.

**Thorn, C. Jordan.** Handbook of old pottery and porcelain marks. N. Y., Tudor, 1947.

**Watkins, Lura.** Early New England potters and their wares. Cambridge, Harvard Univ. press, 1950.

## Glass

**Arnold, Hugh.** Stained glass of the middle ages in England and France, painted by Lawrence B. Saint. London, Black, 1925.

**Aubert, Marcel.** Le vitrail en France. Paris, Larousse, 1946 (Arts, styles et techniques).

**Buckley, Wilfred.** European glass; a brief outline of the history of glass making. Boston, Houghton Mifflin, 1926.

**Connick, Charles J.** Adventures in light and color; an introduction to the stained glass craft. N. Y., Random house, 1937.

**Day, Lewis F.** Windows; a book about stained and painted glass. 3d ed. London, Batsford, 1909.

**Dillon, Edward.** Glass. N. Y., Putnam, 1907 (Connoisseur's library).

**Drake, Maurice.** A history of English glass-painting, with some remarks upon the Swiss glass miniatures of the sixteenth and seventeenth centuries. London, Laurie, 1912.

**Garnier, Édouard.** Histoire de la verrerie et de l'émaillerie. Tours, A. Mame, 1886.

**Honey, William B.** Glass; a handbook for the study of glass vessels of all periods and countries and a guide to the museum collection. London, Victoria and Albert Museum, 1946.

**Janneau, Guillaume.** Modern glass. London, Studio, 1931.

**Knittle, Rhea M.** Early American glass. N. Y., Century, 1927.
**McKearin, George S., and McKearin, Helen.** American glass. N. Y., Crown, 1941.
**Moore, Hannah H.** Old glass, European and American. N. Y., Tudor, 1935.
**Pazaurek, Gustav E.** Kunstgläser der gegenwart. Leipzig, Klinkhardt und Biermann, 1925.
——Moderne gläser. Leipzig, Seemann, 1901.
**Read, Herbert E.** English stained glass. N. Y., Putnam, 1926.
**Rogers, Frances, and Beard, Alice.** 5000 years of glass. New rev. ed. Philadelphia, Lippincott, 1948.
**Schmidt, Robert.** Das glas. $2^e$ aufl. Berlin, De Gruyter, 1922.
**Thorpe, William A.** English glass. 2d ed. London, Black, 1950.
——History of English and Irish glass. London, Medici Society, 1929. 2 v.
**Watkins, Lura.** American glass and glassmaking. N. Y., Chanticleer, 1950.
**Woodforde, Christopher.** The Norwich school of glass-painting in the fifteenth century. London, Oxford Univ. press, 1950.
——Stained glass in Somerset, 1250–1830. London, Oxford Univ. press, 1946.

## Enamels, Ivories, Mosaics

**Anthony, Edgar W.** A history of mosaics. Boston, Sargent, 1935.
**Babelon, Jean.** Mosaïques chrétiennes. Paris, Alpina, 1942.
**Berchem, Marguerite van, and Clouzot, Étienne.** Mosaïques chrétiennes du $IV^e$ au $X^e$ siècle. Genève, Journal de Genève, 1924.
**Chamot, Mary.** English mediaeval enamels. London, Benn, 1930.
**Cunynghame, Henry H.** European enamels. N. Y., Putnam, 1906.
**Cust, Anna M. E.** The ivory workers of the middle ages. London, Bell, 1906.
**Demus, Otto.** Byzantine mosaic decoration. London, Kegan Paul, 1948.
——The mosaics of Norman Sicily. London, Routledge and Paul, 1950.
**Goldschmidt, Adolph.** Die elfenbeinskulpturen. Berlin, Cassirer, 1914–26. 4 v.
**Goldschmidt, Adolph, and Weitzmann, Kurt.** Die byzantinischen elfenbeinskulpturen des X–XIII jahrhunderts. Berlin, Cassirer, 1930–34. 2 v.

**Grodecki, Louis.** Ivoires français. Paris, Larousse, 1947 (Arts, styles et techniques).

**Koechlin, Raymond.** Les ivoires gothiques français. Paris, Picard, 1924. 3 v.

**Longhurst, Margaret H.** Catalogue of carvings in ivory. London, Victoria and Albert Museum, 1927–29. 2 v.

——English ivories. London, Putnam, 1926.

**Marquet de Vasselot, Jean J.** Bibliographie de l'orfèvrerie et de l'émaillerie françaises. Paris, Picard, 1925.

**Maskell, Alfred.** Ivories. N. Y., Putnam, 1905 (Connoisseur's library).

**Morey, Charles R.** The mosaics of Antioch. London, Longmans, 1938.

**Pelka, Otto.** Elfenbein. 2 aufl. Berlin, Schmidt, 1923.

**Salvini, Roberto.** Mosaici medievali in Sicilia. Florence, Sansoni, 1949.

**Volbach, Wolfgang F.** Early Christian mosaics, from the fourth to the seventh centuries, Rome, Naples, Milan, Ravenna. N. Y., Oxford Univ. press, 1946 (Iris books).

## Metalwork

**Avery, Clara L.** Early American silver. N. Y., Century, 1930.

**Babelon, Jean.** La médaille en France. Paris, Larousse, 1948 (Arts, styles et techniques).

——Orfevrerie française. Paris, Larousse, 1947 (Arts, styles et techniques).

**Bell, Malcolm.** Old pewter. London, Batsford, 1913.

**Bigelow, Francis H.** Historic silver of the colonies and its makers. N. Y., Macmillan, 1925.

**Blanc, Louis.** Le fer forgé en France aux XVI et XVII siècles; oeuvres gravées des anciens maîtres, serruriers, architectes, dessinateurs et graveurs. Paris, Van Oest, 1928.

——Le fer forgé en France; la régence; aurore, apogée, déclin. Paris, Van Oest, 1930.

**Braun, Joseph.** Meisterwerke der deutschen goldschmiedekunst der vorgotischen zeit. Munich, Riehn und Reusch, 1922. 2 pts.

**Byne, Arthur, and Stapley, Mildred.** Spanish ironwork. N. Y., Hispanic society, 1915.

**Carré, Louis.** Les poinçons de l'orfèvrerie française du quatorzième siècle jusqu'au début du dix-neuvième siècle. Paris, Carré, 1928.

**Chaffers, William.** Hall marks on gold and silver plate. 10th ed. London, Reeves and Turner, 1922.

**Churchill, Sidney J. A.** The goldsmiths of Italy; some account of their guilds, statues, and work. London, Hopkinson, 1926.

**Clouzot, Henri.** Les arts du métal; métaux précieux, le bronze et le cuivre, le fer, les armes, la parure. Paris, Laurens, 1934.

**Cotterell, Howard H.** Old pewter, its makers and marks in England, Scotland and Ireland; an account of the old pewterer and his craft. London, Batsford, 1929.

**Cripps, Wilfred J.** Old English plate, ecclesiastical, decorative and domestic: its makers and marks. London, Murray, 1901.

——Old French plate, its makers and marks. 2d ed. London, Murray, 1893.

**Dawson, Nelson.** Goldsmiths' and silversmiths' work. N. Y., Putnam, 1907.

**Ensko, Stephen G. C.** American silversmiths and their marks, III. N. Y., Ensko, 1948.

——English silver, 1675–1825. N. Y., Ensko, 1937.

**Fabriczy, Cornelius von.** Italian medals. Trans. Mrs. Gustavus W. Hamilton. London, Duckworth, 1904.

**Ferrari, Giulio.** Il ferro nell'arte italiano. Milan, Hoepli, 1910.

**Forrer, Leonard.** Biographical dictionary of medallists; coin, gem, and seal-engravers, mint-masters, etc., ancient and modern, with references to their works B.C. 500–A.D. 1900. London, Spink, 1902–30. 8 v.

**Frank, Edgar B.** Old French ironwork; the craftsman and his art. Cambridge, Harvard Univ. press, 1950.

**French, Hollis.** A list of early American silversmiths and their marks. N. Y., Walpole Society, 1917.

**Gardner, John S.** English ironwork of the XVIIth and XVIIIth centuries; an historical and analytical account of the development of exterior smithcraft. London, Batsford, 1911.

——Ironwork. 4th end. London, H. M. Stationery office, 1927–30. 2 v.

**Habich, Georg.** Die medaillen der italienischen renaissance. Stuttgart, Deutsche verlags-anstalt, 1924.

**Hill, George F.** Medals of the renaissance. Oxford, Clarendon press, 1920.

**Höver, Otto.** An encyclopaedia of ironwork; examples of hand wrought ironwork from the middle ages to the end of the 18th century. N. Y., Weyhe, 1927.

**Jackson, Charles J.** English goldsmiths and their marks; a history of the goldsmiths and plate workers of England, Scotland, and Ireland. 2d ed. London, Macmillan, 1921.

**Johnson, Ada M.** Hispanic silverwork. N. Y., Hispanic society, 1944.

**Jones, Edward A.** Old silver of Europe and America from early times to the nineteenth century. Philadelphia, Lippincott, 1928.

**Kerfoot, John B.** American pewter. N. Y., Crown, 1942.

**Laughlin, Ledlie I.** Pewter in America, its makers and their marks. Boston, Houghton Mifflin, 1940. 2 v.

**Long, Basil S.** British miniaturists. London, Bles, 1929.

**Phillips, John M.** American silver. N. Y., Chanticleer, 1949.

**Planiscig, Leo.** Piccoli bronzi italiani del rinascimento. Milano, Treves, 1930.

**Rosenberg, Marc.** Der goldschmiede merkzeichen. 3 aufl. Frankfurt a/M, Frankfurter verlags-anstalt, 1922–28. 4 v.

**Schottmüller, Frida.** Bronze statuetten und geräte. 2 aufl. Berlin, Schmidt, 1921.

**Thorn, C. Jordan.** Handbook of American silver and pewter marks. N. Y., Tudor, 1949.

**Wehle, Harry B.** American miniatures, 1730–1850. N. Y., Metropolitan museum of art, 1927.

**Wenham, Edward.** Domestic silver of Great Britain and Ireland. N. Y., Oxford Univ. press, 1935.

——The practical book of American silver. Philadelphia, Lippincott, 1949.

**Williamson, George C.** The history of portrait miniatures. London, Bell, 1904. 2 v.

**Wyler, Seymour B.** The book of old silver; English, American, foreign, with all available hallmarks including Sheffield plate marks. N. Y., Crown, 1937.

# INDIVIDUAL ARTISTS

**ADAM, Robert, 1728-1792.**
  Lees-Milne, James. The age of Adam. N. Y., Batsford, 1947.
  Swarbrick, John. Robert Adam and his brothers; their lives, work and influence on English architecture, decoration and furniture. London, Batsford, 1915.

**ALBERTI, Leone Battista, 1404-1472**
  Alberti, Leone Battista. Leone Battista Alberti's kleinere kunsttheoretische schriften. Hrsg. von H. Janitschek. Vienna, Braumüller, 1877 (Quellenschriften für kunstgeschichte, 11).
  Mancini, Girolamo. Vita di Leon Battista Alberti. 2 ed. Florence, G. Carnescchi, 1911.

**ALLEGRI, Antonio, see CORREGGIO**

**ALLSTON, Washington, 1779-1843**
  Richardson, Edgar P. Washington Allston, a study of the romantic artist in America. Chicago, Univ. of Chicago press, 1948.

**ALTDORFER, Albrecht, 1488-1538**
  Becker, Hanna L. Die handzeichnungen Albrecht Altdorfers. Munich, Neuer Filser-verlag, 1938 (Münchener beitrage zur kunstgeschichte, 1).
  Benesch, Otto. Der maler Albrecht Altdorfer. Vienna, Schroll, 1939.
  Friedländer, Max J. Albrecht Altdorfer. Berlin, Cassirer, 1923.
  Waldmann, Emil. Albrecht Altdorfer. Boston, Medici society, 1923 (Masters of engraving and etching).
  Wolf, Georg J. Altdorfer. Bielefeld, Velhagen und Klasing, 1925 (Künstler-monographien, 115).

**AMADEO, Giovanni Antonio, 1447-1522**
  Malaguzzi-Valeri, Francesco. Gio. Antonio Amadeo, scultore e architetto lombardo (1447-1522). Bergamo, Istituto italiano d'arti grafiche, 1904.

**ANDREA DEL SARTO, see SARTO, Andrea Del**

**ANGELICO, Fra (Giovanni da Fiesole), 1387-1455**
  Douglas, Robert L. Fra Angelico. 2d ed. London, Bell, 1902.
  Schneider, Édouard. Fra Angelico da Fiesole (1387-1455). Paris, Michel, 1924.

**ANGELICO, Fra** (continued)

Schottmüller, Frida. Fra Angelico da Fiesole. 2ᵉ aufl. Stuttgart, Deutsche verlagsanstalt, 1924 (Klassiker der kunst, 18).

**ANTONELLO DA MESSINA, 1444?–1493?**

Bottari, Stefano. Antonello da Messina. Messina, Principato, 1939 (Monumenti ed artisti di Sicilia, 1).

Lauts, Jan. Antonello da Messina. Vienna, Schroll, 1940 (Sammlung Schroll).

**ARCHIPENKO, Alexander, 1887–**

Raynal, Maurice. A. Archipenko. Rome, Valori plastici, 1923.

**ARNOLFO DI CAMBIO, 13th century**

Mariani, Valerio. Arnolfo di Cambio. Rome, Tumminelli, 1943 (Quaderni d'arte, 6).

**ARP, Hans, 1889–**

Arp, Hans. On my way; poetry and essays, 1912–1947. N. Y., Wittenborn, Schultz, 1948 (Documents of modern art).

**BALDOVINETTI, Alesso, 1425–1499**

Kennedy, Ruth W. Alesso Baldovinetti, a critical and historical study. New Haven, Yale Univ. press, 1938.

**BALDUNG, HANS, called Grien, 1480?–1545**

Curjel, Hans. Hans Baldung Grien. Munich, Recht, 1923.

Escherich, Mela. Hans Baldung-Grien, bibliographie, 1509–1915. Strassburg, Heitz, 1916 (Studien zur deutschen kunstgeschichte, 189).

Koch, Carl. Die Zeichnungen Hans Baldung Griens. Berlin, Deutscher verein für kunstwissenschaft, 1941 (Denkmaler deutscher kunst).

Martin, Kurt. Skizzenbuch des Hans Baldung Grien; "Karlsruher Skizzenbuch." Basel, Holbein-verlag, 1950. 2 v. (Veröffentlichung der Holbein-gesellschaft, 2).

**BARBARI, Jacopo de', 1440–1515**

Servolini, Luigi. Jacopo de' Barbari. Padua, Le Tre Venezie, 1944.

**BARLACH, Ernst, 1870–1938**

Barlach, Ernst. Ernst Barlach; ein selbsterzähltes Leben. Munich, Piper, 1948.

Fechter, Paul. Zeichnungen [Ernst Barlach]. Munich, Piper, 1948.

**BAROCCI, Federigo, 1528–1612**
Krommes, Rudolf H. Studien zu Federigo Barocci. Leipzig, Seemann, 1912 (Beiträge zur kunstgeschichte, n.f. 38).
Pietro, Filippo di. Disegni sconosciuti e disegni finora non identificati di Federigo Barocci negli Uffizi. Florence, Istituto micrografico italiano, 1913.

**BARTOLOMMEO, Fra, 1472–1517**
Gabelentz, Hans von der. Fra Bartolommeo und die Florentiner renaissance. Leipzig, Hiersemann, 1922. 2 v.
Rouchès, Gabriel. Fra Bartolomeo, 1472–1517; quatorze dessins. Paris, Musées nationaux, 1942.

**BARYE, Antoine Louis, 1796–1875**
Alexandre, Arsène. A. L. Barye. Paris, Librairie de l'art, 1889 (Les artistes célèbres).

**BASSANO, Jacopo (Giacomo da Ponte), 1510–1592**
Arslan, Wart. I Bassano. Bologna, Apollo, 1931.
Bettini, Sergio. L'arte di Jacopo Bassano. Bologna, Apollo, 1933 (Ars viva, 1).

**BAYER, Herbert, 1900–**
Dorner, Alexander. The way beyond "art"; the work of Herbert Bayer. N. Y., Wittenborn, Schultz, 1947.

**BEAUX, Cecilia, 1863–1942**
Beaux, Cecilia. Background with figures; autobiography. Boston, Houghton Mifflin, 1930.

**BELLINI, Gentile, 1429?–1507**
Gronau, Georg. Die künstlerfamilie Bellini. Bielefeld, Velhagen und Klasing, 1909 (Künstler-monographien, 96).

**BELLINI, Giovanni, 1430?–1516**
Dussler, Luitpold. Giovanni Bellini. Vienna, Schroll, 1949 (Sammlung Schroll).
Gamba, Carlo. Giovanni Bellini. Milan, Hoepli, 1937 (Valori plastici).
Gronau, Georg. Giovanni Bellini. Stuttgart, Deutsche verlags-anstalt, 1930 (Klassiker der kunst, 36).
Hendy, Philip, and Goldscheider, Ludwig. Giovanni Bellini. N. Y., Oxford Univ. press, Phaidon ed., 1945.
Moschini, Vittorio. Giambellino. Bergamo, Istituto italiano d'arti grafiche, 1943 (Grandi artisti italiani).

**BELLINI, Jacopo, 1400?-1464?**
   Moschini, Vittorio. Disegni di Jacopo Bellini. Bergamo, Istituto italiano d'arti grafiche, 1943 (Disegnatori ed incisori italiani, 2).
   Ricci, Corrado. Jacopo Bellini e i suoi libri di disegni. Florence, 1908. 2 v.

**BELLOWS, George Wesley, 1882-1925**
   Bellows, George W. Paintings. N. Y., Knopf, 1929.
   ——George W. Bellows, his lithographs. Rev. ed. N. Y., Knopf, 1928.
   Eggers, George W. George Bellows. N. Y., Whitney museum, 1931. (American artists series).

**BENEDETTO DA MAIANO, 1442-1497**
   Cendali, Lorenzo. Giuliano e Benedetto da Majano, Fiesole. Florence, Società editrice Toscana, 1926.
   Dussler, Luitpold. Benedetto da Majano, ein Florentiner bildhauer des späten quattrocento. Munich, Schmidt, 1924.

**BENTON, Thomas Hart, 1889-**
   Benton, Thomas H. An artist in America. N. Y., McBride, 1937.

**BERNARD, Joseph, 1866-1931**
   Cantinelli, Richard. Joseph Bernard. Paris, Van Oest, 1928.

**BERNINI, Giovanni Lorenzo, 1598-1680**
   Baldinucci, Filippo. Vita di Gian Lorenzo Bernini. Milan, Edizioni del Milione, 1948 (Vite, lettere, testimonianze di artisti italiani).
   Boehn, Max von. Lorenzo Bernini; seine zeit, sein leben, sein werk. 2$^e$ neub. aufl. Bielefeld, Velhagen und Klasing, 1927 (Künstlermonographien, 105).
   Brauer, Heinrich, and Wittkower, Rudolf. Die zeichnungen des Gianlorenzo Bernini. Berlin, Keller, 1931. 2 v. (Römische forschungen, 9-10).
   Grassi, Luigi. Bernini pittore. Rome, Danesi, 1945.
   ——Disegni del Bernini. Bergamo, Istituto italiano d'arti grafiche, 1944 (Disegnatori ed incisori italiani, 5).
   Muñoz, Antonio. G. L. Bernini, architetto e decoratore. Rome, Società editrice d'arte illustrata, 1925 (Biblioteca d'arte illustrata: sei e settecento italiano, fasc. 26-28).

**BIDDLE, George, 1885-**
   Biddle, George. An American artist's story. Boston, Little, Brown, 1939.

**BLAKE, William, 1757-1827**
  Binyon, Laurence. The drawings and engravings of William Blake. London, Studio, 1922.
  Damon, Samuel F. William Blake, his philosophy and symbols. Boston, Houghton Mifflin, 1924.
  Figgis, Darrell. The paintings of William Blake. London, Benn, 1925.
  Keynes, Geoffrey L. A bibliography of William Blake. N. Y., Grolier club, 1921.
  ——Engravings [of William Blake]. London, Faber, 1950.
  ——Pencil drawings by William Blake. London, Nonesuch press, 1927.
  Russell, Archibald G. B. The engravings of William Blake. London, Richards, 1912.

**BOLOGNA, Giovanni, 1524-1608**
  Desjardins, Abel. La vie et l'oeuvre de Jean Bologne. Paris, Quantin, 1883.

**BONINGTON, Richard Parkes, 1801-1828**
  Curtis, Atherton. Catalogue de l'oeuvre lithographié et gravé de R. P. Bonington. Paris, Prouté, 1939.
  Dubuisson, A. Richard Parkes Bonington: his life and work. London, Lane, 1924.
  Shirley, Andrew. Bonington. London, Kegan Paul, 1940 (English master painters).

**BORROMINI, Francesco, 1599-1667**
  Hempel, Eberhard. Francesco Borromini. Vienna, Schroll, 1924.
  Muñoz, Antonio. Francesco Borromini. Rome, Società editrice d'arte illustrata, 1921 (Biblioteca d'arte illustrata: sei e settecento italiano, fasc. 1).

**BOSCH, Hieronymus van Aken, 1450?-1516**
  Baldass, Ludwig von. Hieronymus Bosch. Vienna, Schroll, 1943.
  Combe, Jacques. Jérôme Bosch. Paris, Tisné, 1946 (Collection Prométhée).
  De Tolnay, Charles. Hieronymus Bosch. Bâle, Holbein, 1937.
  Leymarie, Jean. Jérôme Bosch. Paris, Somogy, 1949 (Ars mundi).

**BOTTICELLI, Sandro, 1447?-1510**
  Bode, Wilhelm von. Botticelli: des meisters werke. Stuttgart, Deutsche verlags-anstalt, 1926 (Klassiker der kunst, 30).

**BOTTICELLI, Sandro** (continued)

    Gamba, Carlo. Botticelli. Traduction de Jean Chuzeville. Paris, Gallimard, 1937 (Collection: Musée de la Pléiade).

    Horne, Herbert P. Alessandro Filipepi, commonly called Sandro Botticelli, painter of Florence. London, Bell, 1908.

    Venturi, Lionello. Botticelli. N. Y., Oxford Univ. press, Phaidon ed., 1937.

    Yashiro, Yukio. Sandro Botticelli and the Florentine renaissance. Rev. ed. London, Medici society, 1929.

**BOUCHER, François, 1703–1770**

    Kahn, Gustave. Boucher; biographie critique. Paris, Laurens, 1904 (Les grands artistes).

    Lavallée, Pierre. François Boucher, 1703–1770. Paris, Musée nationaux, 1942.

    Michel, André. F. Boucher. Paris, Piazza, 1906 (Les artistes célèbres).

    Nolhac, Pierre de. François Boucher, premier peintre du roi, 1703–1770. Paris, Goupil, 1907.

**BOURDELLE, Émile Antoine, 1861–1929**

    Lorenz, Paul. Bourdelle, sculptures et dessins. Paris, Rombaldi, 1947.

    Varenne, Gaston. Bourdelle par lui-même; sa pensée et son art. Paris, Fasquelle, 1937.

**BOUTS, Dirck, 1420?–1475**

    Schöne, Wolfgang. Dieric Bouts und seine Schule. Berlin, Verlag für kunstwissenschaft, 1938.

**BRAMANTE, Donato, 1444?–1514**

    Baroni, Costantino. Bramante. Bergamo, Istituto italiano d'arti grafiche, 1944 (I grandi artisti italiani).

    Frey, Dagobert. Bramantes St. Peter-entwurf und seine apokryphen. Vienna, Schroll, 1915 (Bramante-studien, 1).

**BRAQUE, Georges, 1881–**

    Einstein, Carl. Georges Braque. N. Y., Weyhe, 1934.

    Hope, Henry R. Georges Braque. N. Y., Museum of modern art, 1949.

**BREUER, Marcel, 1902–**

    Blake, Peter. Marcel Breuer, architect and designer. N. Y., Museum of modern art, 1949.

**BRONZINO, Agnolo (Angelo Allori), 1502–1572**

    McComb, Arthur K. Agnolo Bronzino; his life and works. Cambridge, Harvard Univ. press, 1928.

**BROUWER, Adriaen, 1606?–1638**
 Bode, Wilhelm von. Adriaen Brouwer, sein leben und seine werke. Berlin, Euphorion-verlag, 1924.
 Schmidt-Degener, Frederik. Adriaen Brouwer et son évolution artistique. Brussels, Van Oest, 1908.

**BRUEGHEL, Jan, 1568–1625**
 Denucé, Jean. Brieven en documenten betreffend Jan Breugel I en II. Antwerpen, De Sikkel, 1934.

**BRUEGHEL, Peeter, 1520?–1570?**
 Bruhns, Leo. Das Bruegel buch. Vienna, Schroll, 1941 (Sammlung Schroll).
 De Tolnay, Charles. Pierre Bruegel l'ancien. Brussels, Nouvelle société d'éditions, 1935. 2 v. (Bibliothèque du XVIe siècle).
 Friedländer, Max J. Pieter Bruegel. Berlin, Propyläen-verlag, 1921.
 Glück, Gustav. Pieter Brueghel, the elder. Trans. Eveline Byam Shaw. London, Commodore press, 1936.
 Jedlicka, Gothard. Pieter Bruegel, der maler in seiner zeit. Erlenbach, Rentsch, 1938.

**BRUNELLESCHI, FILIPPO, 1377–1446**
 Folnesics, Hans. Brunelleschi; ein beitrag zur entwicklungsgeschichte der frührenaissance architektur. Vienna, Schroll, 1915.

**BULFINCH, Charles, 1763–1844**
 Bulfinch, Charles. The life and letters of Charles Bulfinch, architect, with other family papers. Boston, Houghton Mifflin, 1896.
 Place, Charles A. Charles Bulfinch, architect and citizen. Boston, Houghton Mifflin, 1925.

**BUONARROTI see MICHELANGO**

**BURCHFIELD, Charles, 1893–**
 Ritchie, Andrew C. Charles Burchfield; a retrospective exhibition of water colors and oils, 1916–1943. Buffalo, Holling press, 1944.

**BURGKMAIR, Hans, 1473–1531**
 Burkhard, Arthur. Hans Burgkmair d.ä. Leipzig, Insel-verlag, 1934.

**BURNE-JONES, Edward, 1833–1898**
 Bell, Malcolm. Sir Edward Burne-Jones; a record and review. 4th ed. London, Bell, 1903.
 Burne-Jones, Georgiana M. Memorials of Edward Burne-Jones. N. Y., Macmillan, 1904. 2 v.

BURNE-JONES, Edward (continued)
   Wood, T. Martin. Drawings of Sir Edward Burne-Jones. N. Y., Scribner, 1907 (Drawings of the great masters).
BURNHAM, Daniel Hudson, 1846-1912
   Moore, Charles H. Daniel H. Burnham, architect, planner of cities. Boston, Houghton Mifflin, 1921. 2 v.
CALLOT, Jacques, 1592?-1635
   Bouchot-Saupique, Jacqueline. Jacques Callot, 1592-1635; quatorze dessins. Paris, Musées nationaux, 1942.
   Lieure, J. Jacques Callot. Paris, Gazette des beaux-arts, 1924-26. 3 v.
CANALE, Antonio (Canaletto), 1697-1768
   Hadeln, Detlev von. The drawings of Antonio Canale, called Canaletto. Trans. Campbell Dodgson. London, Duckworth, 1929.
   Parker, Karl T. The drawings of Antonio Canaletto in the collection of His Majesty the King at Windsor Castle. Oxford Univ. press, Phaidon ed., 1948 (Italian drawings at Windsor Castle).
CANOVA, Antonio, 1757-1822
   Bassi, Elena. Canova. Bergamo, Istituto italiano d'arti grafiche, 1943 (I grandi artisti italiani).
   Foratti, Aldo. Antonio Canova, 1757-1822. Milan, Caddeo, 1922.
CARAVAGGIO, Michelangelo (Michelangelo Merisi), 1569?-1609
   Benkard, Ernst. Caravaggio-studien. Berlin, Keller, 1928.
   Schudt, Ludwig. Caravaggio. Vienna, Schroll, 1942 (Sammlung Schroll).
   Venturi, Lionello. Il Caravaggio. 2 ed. Rome, Società editrice d'arte illustrata, 1925 (Biblioteca d'arte illustrata: sei e settecento italiano, fasc. 23-24).
CARPACCIO, Vittore, 1455?-1525?
   Fiocco, Giuseppe. Carpaccio. Traduction de Jean Chuzeville. Paris, Crès, 1931.
   Hausenstein, Wilhelm. Das werk des Vittore Carpaccio. Stuttgart, Deutsche verlags-anstalt, 1925.
   Molmenti, Pompeo G. Vittore Carpaccio; la vita e le opere. Milan, Hoepli, 1906.
CARPEAUX, Jean Baptiste, 1827-1875
   Clément-Carpeaux, Louise. La vérité sur l'oeuvre et la vie de J.-B. Carpeaux (1827-1875). Paris, Dousset et Bigerelle, 1934-35. 2 v.

Laran, Jean, and Le Bas, Georges. Carpeaux. Paris, Librairie centrale des beaux-arts, 1912 (L'art de notre temps).

Lecomte, Georges C. La vie héroïque et glorieuse de Carpeaux. Paris, Plon, 1928.

## CARRACCI family: Agostino, 1557–1602; Annibale, 1560–1609; Ludovico, 1555–1619

Bodmer, Heinrich. Lodovico Carracci. Burg, Hopfer, 1939 (Beitrage zur kunstgeschichte, 6).

Foratti, Aldo. I Carracci nella teoria e nella pratica. Castello, Lapi, 1913.

Rouchès, Gabriel. Le peinture Bolonaise à la fin du XVI$^e$ siècle (1575–1619): Les Carrache. Paris, Alcan, 1913.

## CARRIÈRE, Eugène, 1849–1906

Dubray, Jean P. Eugène Carrière; essai critique. Paris, Seheur, 1931 (L'art et la vie).

Faure, Élie. Eugène Carrière, peintre et lithographe. Paris, Floury, 1908 (Les maîtres de l'art moderne).

Séailles, Gabriel. Eugène Carrière; essai de biographie psychologique. 2 éd. Paris, Colin, 1917.

## CASSATT, Mary, 1845–1926

Breeskin, Adelyn D. The graphic work of Mary Cassatt; a catalogue raisonné. N. Y., Bittner, 1948.

Watson, Forbes. Mary Cassatt. N. Y., Whitney museum, 1932 (American artists series).

## CASTAGNO, Andrea del, 1423–1457

Richter, George M. Andrea del Castagno. Chicago, Univ. of Chicago press, 1943.

Salmi, Maria. Paolo Uccello, Andrea del Castagno, Domenico Veneziano. Milan, Hoepli, 1938 (Valori plastici).

## CASTELFRANCO, Giorgione da, see GIORGIONE

## CELLINI, Benvenuto, 1500–1571

Cellini, Benvenuto. The life of Benvenuto Cellini, written by himself. Trans. John Addington Symonds. London, Oxford Univ. press, Phaidon ed., 1949.

Plon, Eugène. Benvenuto Cellini, orfèvre, médailleur, sculpteur; recherches sur sa vie, sur son oeuvre et sur les pièces qui lui sont attribuées. Paris, Plon, 1883. Nouvelle appendice, 1884.

**CELLINI, Benvenuto** (continued)

Supino, Igino B. L'arte di Benvenuto Cellini, con nuovi documenti sull'oreficeria fiorentina del secolo XVI. Florence, Alinari, 1901.

**CÉZANNE, Paul, 1839–1906**

Cézanne, Paul. Letters. Ed. by John Rewald. London, Cassirer, 1941.

Dorival, Bernard. Cézanne. Paris, Tisné, 1948 (Collection Prométhée).

Fry, Roger E. Cézanne, a study of his development. London, Woolf, 1927.

Loran, Erle. Cézanne's composition; analysis of his form with diagrams and photographs of his motifs. 2d ed. Berkeley, Univ. of California press, 1944.

Mack, Gerstle. Paul Cézanne. N. Y., Knopf, 1935.

Novotny, Fritz. Cézanne. London, Oxford Univ. press, Phaidon ed., 1948.

Rewald, John. Paul Cézanne, a biography. Trans. Margaret H. Liebman. N. Y., Simon and Schuster, 1948.

Venturi, Lionello. Cézanne; son art, son oeuvre. Paris, Rosenberg, 1936. 2 v.

Vollard, Ambroise. Paul Cézanne; his life and art. Trans. Harold L. Van Doren. N. Y., N. L. Brown, 1923.

**CHAGALL, Marc, 1887–**

Chagall, Marc. Ma vie. Traduit du russe par Bella Chagall. Paris, Stock, 1931 (Ateliers, 3).

Salmon, André. Chagall. Paris, Chroniques du jour, 1928 (Les maîtres nouveaux, 4).

Sweeney, James J. Marc Chagall. N. Y., Museum of modern art, 1946.

**CHARDIN, Jean Baptiste Siméon, 1699–1779**

Dayot, Armand P. M. J.-B Siméon Chardin, avec un catalogue complet de l'oeuvre du maître par Jean Guiffrey. Paris, Piazza, 1907.

Ridder, André de. J. B. S. Chardin. Paris, Floury, 1932 (Art et artistes français).

Wildenstein, Georges. Chardin. Paris, Beaux-arts, 1933 (L'art français).

**CHASSÉRIAU, Théodore, 1819–1856**

Bénédite, Léonce. Théodore Chassériau, sa vie et son oeuvre. Paris, Braun, 1932. 2 v.

**CHIRICO, Giorgio de, 1888–**
 Chirico, Giorgio de. Memorie della mia vita. Rome, Astrolabio, 1945.
 Soby, James T. The early Chirico. N. Y., Dodd, Mead, 1941.

**CIMABUE, Giovanni, 1240?–1302?**
 Nicholson, Alfred. Cimabue; a critical study. Princeton, Princeton Univ. press, 1932 (Princeton monographs in art and archaeology, 16).
 Salvini, Roberto. Cimabue. Rome, Tumminelli, 1946 (Quaderni d'arte, 9).

**CLAUDE LORRAIN (Claude Gellée), 1600–1682**
 Claude Lorrain. Liber veritatis; or, A collection of prints, after the original designs of Claude de Lorrain; in the collection of His Grace the Duke of Devonshire. London, Boydell, 1777–1819. 3 v.
 Courthion, Pierre. Claude Gellée dit Le Lorrain. Paris, Floury, 1932 (Art et artistes français).
 Friedlaender, Walter F. Claude Lorrain. Berlin, Cassirer, 1921.

**CLOUET family: François, 1505?–1572?; Jean, 1475?–1541**
 Germain, Alphonse. Les Clouet; biographie critique. Paris, Laurens, 1907 (Les grands artistes).
 Moreau-Nélaton, Étienne. Les Clouet et leurs émules. Paris, Laurens, 1924. 3 v.

**COLOMBE, Michel, 1430?–1512?**
 Vitry, Paul. Michel Colombe et la sculpture française de son temps. Paris, Librairie centrale des beaux-arts, 1901.

**CONSTABLE, John, 1776–1837**
 Constable, John. The letters of John Constable to C. R. Leslie, 1826–1837. Ed. by Peter Leslie. London, Constable, 1931.
 Holmes, Charles J. Constable and his influence on landscape painting. Westminster [Eng.], Constable, 1902.
 Key, Sydney J. John Constable, his life and work. London, Phoenix house, 1948 (British painters series).
 Leslie, Charles R. Memoirs of the life of John Constable; composed chiefly of his letters. London, Lehmann, 1949 (Chiltern library, 29).
 Shirley, Andrew. John Constable. London, Medici society, 1948.

**COPLEY, John Singleton, 1737–1815**
 Bayley, Frank W. The life and works of John Singleton Copley,

founded on the work of Augustus Thorndike Perkins. Boston, Taylor, 1915.

Copley, John S. Letters and papers of John Singleton Copley and Henry Pelham, 1739–1776. Boston, Massachusetts historical society, 1914.

Flexner, James T. John Singleton Copley. Boston, Houghton Mifflin, 1948.

Parker, Barbara N., and Wheeler, Anne B. John Singleton Copley; American portraits in oil, pastel and miniature. Boston, Museum of fine arts, 1938.

COROT, Jean Baptiste Camille, 1796–1875

Bazin, Germain. Corot. Paris, Tisné, 1942 (Collection Prométhée).

Corot, Jean B. C. Corot, raconté par lui-même et par ses amis. Geneva, Cailler, 1946. 2 v.

Delteil, Loÿs. Corot. Paris, 1910 (Le Peintre-graveur illustré, 5).

Moreau-Nélaton, Étienne. Corot, raconté par lui-même. Paris, Laurens, 1924. 2 v.

Robaut, Alfred, and Moreau-Nélaton, Étienne. L'oeuvre de Corot. Paris, Floury, 1905. 4 v. Supplement, 1905.

Schoeller, André, and Dieterle, Jean. Corot. Premier supplément à L'oeuvre de Corot par A. Robaut et Moreau-Nélaton. Paris, Arts et métiers graphiques, 1948.

Sérullaz, Maurice. Camille Corot, 1796–1875; quatorze dessins. Paris, Musées nationaux, 1939.

CORREGGIO, Antonio Allegri, 1494–1534

Bodmer, Heinrich. Correggio und die malerei der Emilia. Vienna, Deuticke, 1942.

Gronau, Georg. Correggio; des meisters gemälde. Stuttgart, Deutsche verlags-anstalt, 1907 (Klassiker der kunst, 10).

Ricci, Corrado. Correggio. N. Y., Warne, 1930.

Vito Battaglia, Silvia de. Correggio; bibliografia. Rome, Palombi, 1934.

COTMAN, John Sell, 1782–1842

Kitson, Sydney D. The life of John Sell Cotman. London, Faber, 1937.

Smith, Solomon C. K. Cotman. N. Y., Stokes, 1926 (British artists).

## COURBET, Gustave, 1819–1877

Boas, George. Courbet and the naturalistic movement. Baltimore, Johns Hopkins press, 1938.

Courbet, Gustave. Courbet, raconté par lui-même et par ses amis; sa vie et ses oeuvres. Genève, Cailler, 1948—. v. 1—.

Courthion, Pierre. Courbet. Paris, Floury, 1931 (Art et artistes français).

Duret, Théodore. Courbet. Paris, Bernheim-Jeune, 1918.

Léger, Charles. Courbet. Paris, Crès, 1929 (Maîtres d'autrefois).

## CRANACH, Lucas, 1472–1553

Friedländer, Max J., and Rosenberg, Jakob. Die gemälde von Lucas Cranach. Berlin, Deutscher verein für kunstwissenschaft, 1932.

Glaser, Curt. Lukas Cranach. Leipzig, Insel-verlag, 1923 (Deutsche meister).

Lilienfein, Heinrich. Lukas Cranach und seine zeit. Bielefeld, Velhagen und Klasing, 1942.

Posse, Hans. Lucas Cranach. Vienna, Schroll, 1942 (Sammlung Schroll).

## CRIVELLI, Carlo, 1450?–1493?

Drey, Franz. Carlo Crivelli und seine schule. Munich, Bruckmann, 1927.

Rushforth, Gordon M. Carlo Crivelli. London, Bell, 1900.

## CROME, John, 1768–1821

Baker, Charles H. C. Crome. London, Methuen, 1921.

Smith, Solomon C. K. Crome; with a note on the Norwich School. London, Allan, 1923 (British artists).

## DALI, Salvador, 1904–

Soby, James T. Paintings, drawings, prints; Salvador Dali. N. Y., Museum of modern art, 1941.

## DALOU, Aimé Jules, 1838–1902

Caillaux, Henriette. Aimé-Jules Dalou (1838–1902). Paris, Delagrave, 1935.

Dreyfous, Maurice. Dalou, sa vie et son oeuvre. Paris, Laurens, 1903.

## DAUBIGNY, Charles François, 1817–1878

Delteil, Loÿs. Charles-François Daubigny. Paris, 1921 (Peintre-graveur illustré, 13).

Moreau-Nélaton, Étienne. Daubigny, raconté par lui-même. Paris, Laurens, 1925.

**DAUMIER, Honoré, 1808-1879**

    **Courthion, Pierre.** Daumier, raconté par lui-même et par ses amis. Geneva, Cailler, 1945.

    **Delteil, Loÿs.** Honoré Daumier. Paris, 1925-30. 10 v. in 11 (Peintre-graveur illustré, 20-29 bis).

    **Escholier, Raymond.** Daumier. Paris, Floury, 1934 (Anciens et modernes).

    **Fuchs, Eduard.** Honoré Daumier; holzschnitte, 1833-1870. Munich, Langen, 1918.

    ——Honoré Daumier, lithographien. Munich, Langen, 1920-22. 3 v.

    ——Der Maler Daumier. N. Y., Weyhe, 1927. Nachtrag. Munich, Langen, 1930.

    **Hausenstein, Wilhelm.** Daumier, zeichnungen. Munich, Piper, 1918 (Marées-gesellschaft, 9).

    **Lemann, Bernard.** Honoré Daumier; 240 lithographs. N. Y., Reynal and Hitchcock, 1946.

**DAVID, Jacques Louis, 1748-1825**

    **Cantinelli, Richard.** Jacques-Louis David, 1748-1825. Paris, Van Oest, 1930.

    **Maret, Jacques.** David. Monaco, 1943 (Documents d'art).

    **Maurois, André.** J.-L. David. Paris, Dimanche, 1948 (Les demi-dieux).

    **Serullaz, Maurice.** J.-L David, 1748-1825; quatorze dessins. Paris, Musées nationaux, 1939.

**DAVID D'ANGERS, Pierre Jean, 1788-1856**

    **Jouin, Henry.** David d'Angers, sa vie, son oeuvre, ses écrits et ses contemporains. Paris, Plon, 1878. 2 v.

    **Valotaire, Marcel.** David d'Angers; étude critique. Paris, Renouard, 1932 (Les grands artistes).

**DAVIES, Arthur Bowen, 1862-1928**

    **Cortissoz, Royal.** Arthur B. Davies. N. Y., Whitney museum, 1931 (American artists).

    **Price, Frederic N.** The etchings and lithographs of Arthur B. Davies. N. Y., Kennerley, 1929.

**DAVIS, Stuart, 1894–**

    **Sweeney, James J.** Stuart Davis. N. Y., Museum of modern art, 1945.

**DEGAS, Hilaire Germain Edgar, 1834–1917**
  Degas, Hilaire G. E. Letters. Ed. by Marcel Guerin. Oxford, Cassirer, 1947.
  Delteil, Loÿs. Edgar Degas. Paris, 1919 (Peintre-graveur illustré, 9).
  Lafond, Paul. Degas. Paris, Floury, 1918–19. 2 v.
  Lemoisne, Paul A. Degas et son oeuvre. Paris, Brame et Hauke, 1947. 4 v. (Les artistes et leurs oeuvres).
  Rewald, John. Degas, works in sculpture. N. Y., Pantheon, 1944.
  Rivière, Henri. Les dessins de Degas. Ser. I–II. Paris, Demotte, 1922–23.
  Vollard, Ambroise. Degas, an intimate portrait. Trans. Randolph T. Weaver. N. Y., Greenberg, 1927.

**DELACROIX, Eugène, 1798–1863**
  Badt, Kurt. Eugène Delacroix drawings. Oxford, Cassirer, 1946.
  Cassou, Jean. Delacroix. Paris, Dimanche, 1947 (Les demi-dieux).
  Courthion, Pierre. La vie de Delacroix. 6e éd. Paris, Gallimard, 1927.
  Delacroix, Eugène. Correspondance générale d'Eugène Delacroix, publiée par André Joubin. Paris, Plon, 1936–38. 5 v.
  ——Journal de Eugène Delacroix... Nouvelle édition publiée d'après le manuscrit original, avec une introduction et des notes par André Joubin. Paris, Plon, 1932. 3 v.
  Escholier, Raymond. Delacroix, peintre, graveur, écrivain. Paris, Floury, 1926–29. 3 v. (La vie et l'art romantiques).
  Lavallée, Pierre. Eugène Delacroix; quatorze dessins. Paris, Musées nationaux, 1938.
  Moreau-Nélaton, Étienne. Delacroix, raconté par lui-même; étude biographique d'après ses lettres, son journal, etc. Paris, Laurens, 1916. 2 v.
  Robaut, Alfred. L'oeuvre complet de Eugène Delacroix, peintures, dessins, gravures, lithographies. Paris, Charavay, 1885.
  Rudrauf, Lucien. Eugène Delacroix et le problème du romantisme artistique. Paris, Laurens, 1942.

**DEMUTH, Charles Henry, 1883–1935**
  Murrell, William. Charles Demuth. N. Y., Whitney museum, 1931 (American artists series).
  Ritchie, Andrew C. Charles Demuth. N. Y., Museum of modern art, 1950.

**DERAIN, André, 1880–**
  Faure, Élie. A. Derain. Paris, Crès, 1926 (Cahiers d'aujourd'hui).
  Vaughan, Malcolm. Derain. N. Y., Hyperion, 1941 (Modern masters, 2).

**DESIDERIO DA SETTIGNANO, 1428–1464**
  Planiscig, Leo. Desiderio da Settignano. Vienna, Schroll, 1942 (Sammlung Schroll).

**DOMENICHINO (Domenico Zampieri), 1581–1641**
  Pope-Hennessy, John. The drawings of Domenichino in the collection of His Majesty the King at Windsor Castle. N. Y., Oxford Univ. press, Phaidon ed., 1948 (Italian drawings at Windsor Castle).
  Serra, Luigi. Domenico Zampieri, detto il Domenichino. Rome, Calzone, 1909.

**DONATELLO (Donato di Niccolo di Betto Bardi), 1386–1466**
  Cecchi, Emilio. Donatello. Rome, Tumminelli, 1942 (Quaderni d'arte, 2).
  Crawford, David A. E. L. (Lord Balcarres). Donatello. N. Y., Scribner, 1903.
  Goldscheider, Ludwig. Donatello. London, Oxford Univ. press, Phaidon ed., 1944.
  Planiscig, Leo. Donatello. Vienna, Schroll, 1939 (Sammlung Schroll).
  Schubring, Paul. Donatello; des meisters werke. 2ᵉ aufl. Stuttgart, Deutsche Verlags-anstalt, 1922 (Klassiker der kunst, 11).

**DOU, Gerard, 1613–1675**
  Martin, Wilhelm. Gerard Dou. Stuttgart, Deutsche verlags-anstalt, 1913 (Klassiker der kunst, 24).

**DUCCIO DI BUONINSEGNA, 1255?–1319**
  Weigelt, Curt H. Duccio di Buoninsegna; studien zur geschichte der frühsienesischen tafelmalerei. Leipzig, Hiersemann, 1911 (Kunstgeschichtliche monographien, 15).

**DÜRER, Albrecht, 1471–1528**
  Conway, William M. C. Literary remains of Albrecht Dürer. Cambridge [Eng.], University press, 1889.
  Dodgson, Campbell. Albrecht Dürer. Boston, Medici society, 1926 (Masters of engraving and etching).
  Flechsig, Eduard. Albrecht Dürer; sein leben und seine künstlerische entwickelung. Berlin, Grote, 1928–31. 2 v.

**Friedländer, Max J.** Albrecht Dürer. Leipzig, Insel-verlag, 1921.

**Kurth, Willi.** The complete woodcuts of Albrecht Dürer. Trans. Silvia M. Welsh. N. Y., Crown, 1946.

**Lippmann, Friedrich.** Drawings by Albrecht Dürer. Berlin, Grote, 1883–1929. 7 v.

**Meder, Joseph.** Dürer katalog; ein handbuch über Albrecht Dürers stiche, radierungen, holzschnitte, deren zustände, ausgaben und wasserzeichen. Vienna, Gilhofer und Ranschburg, 1932.

**Panofsky, Erwin.** Albrecht Dürer. 3d ed. Princeton, Princeton Univ. press, 1948. 2 v.

**Scherer, Valentin.** Dürer; des meisters gemälde, kupferstiche und holzschnitte. 4$^{te}$ aufl. Stuttgart, Deutsche Verlags-anstalt, 192– (Klassiker der kunst, 4).

**Singer, Hans W.** Versuch einer Dürer bibliographie. 2 aufl. Strassburg, Heitz, 1928 (Studien zur deutschen kunstgeschichte, 41).

**Tietze, Hans, and Tietze-Conrat, Erika.** Kritisches verzeichnis der werke Albrecht Dürers. Augsburg, Filser, 1928—. v. 1—.

**Waetzoldt, Wilhelm.** Dürer and his times. Trans. R. H. Boothroyd. London, Oxford Univ. press, Phaidon ed., 1950.

**Winkler, Friedrich.** Die zeichnungen Albrecht Dürers. Berlin, Deutscher verein für kunstwissenschaft, 1936–39. 4 v.

## DUFY, Raoul, 1877–

**Courthion, Pierre.** Raoul Dufy. Geneva, Cailler, 1951.

**Zervos, Christian.** Raoul Dufy. Paris, Cahiers d'art, 1928 (Grands peintres d'aujourd'hui).

## DYCK, Anthony van, 1599–1641

**Cust, Lionel H.** Anthony van Dyck; an historical study of his life and works. London, Bell, 1900.

**Delacre, Maurice.** Le dessin dans l'oeuvre de van Dyck. Brussels, Hayez, 1934.

**Dyck, Anthony van.** Italienisches skizzenbuch, herausgegeben von Gert Adriani. Vienna, Schroll, 1940.

**Glück, Gustav.** Van Dyck; des meisters gemälde. 2$^{te}$ aufl. N. Y., Kleinberger, 1931 (Klassiker der kunst, 13).

**Knackfuss, Hermann.** Van Dyck. Trans. Campbell Dodgson. Bielefeld, Velhagen und Klasing, 1899 (Monographs on artists, 4).

**EAKINS, Thomas, 1844–1916**
  Goodrich, Lloyd. Thomas Eakins, his life and work. N. Y., Whitney museum, 1933.
  McKinney, Roland J. Thomas Eakins. N. Y., Crown, 1942.

**ELSHEIMER, Adam, 1578–1620**
  Drost, Willi. Adam Elsheimer und sein kreis. Potsdam, Akademische verlagsgesellschaft Athenaion, 1933 (Grossen deutschen maler, 1).
  Weizsäcker, Heinrich. Adam Elsheimer, der maler von Frankfurt. Berlin, Deutscher verein für kunstwissenschaft, 1936—. v. 1—. (Denkmaler deutscher kunst).

**EPSTEIN, Jacob, 1880–**
  Epstein, Jacob. Let there be sculpture. N. Y., Putnam, 1940.

**ERNST, Max, 1891–**
  Ernst, Max. Beyond painting, and other writings by the artist and his friends. N. Y., Wittenborn, Schultz, 1948 (Documents of modern art).

**EYCK family: Hubert van, 1366–1426; Jan van, 1390–1440**
  Beenken, Hermann T. Hubert und Jan van Eyck. Munich, Bruckmann, 1941.
  Conway, William M. The Van Eycks and their followers. London, Murray, 1921.
  De Tolnay, Charles. Le Maître de Flémalle et les frères Van Eyck. Brussels, Connaissance, 1939.
  Renders, Émile. Hubert van Eyck, personnage de légende. Paris, Van Oest, 1933.
  Schmarsow, August. Hubert und Jan van Eyck. Leipzig, Hiersemann, 1924 (Kunstgeschichtliche monographien, 19).
  Weale, William H. J., and Brockwell, Maurice W. The Van Eycks and their art. N. Y., Lane, 1912.

**FALCONET, Étienne Maurice, 1716–1791**
  Réau, Louis. Étienne Maurice Falconet. Paris, Demotte, 1922. 2 v.

**FANTIN-LATOUR, Ignace Henri Jean Théodore, 1836–1904**
  Fantin-Latour, Victoria D. Catalogue de l'oeuvre complet (1849–1904) de Fantin-Latour. Paris, Floury, 1911.
  Jullien, Adolphe. Fantin-Latour, sa vie et ses amitiés; lettres inédites et souvenirs personnels. Paris, Laveur, 1909.

**FEKE, Robert, 1705?-1750**
 Foote, Henry W. Robert Feke, colonial portrait painter. Cambridge, Harvard Univ. press, 1930.

**FINIGUERRA, Tommaso, 1426-1464**
 Finiguerra, Tommaso. A Florentine picture-chronicle; being a series of ninety-nine drawings representing scenes and personages of ancient history, sacred and profane, by Maso Finiguerra, reproduced from the originals in the British museum. Critical and descriptive text by Sidney Colvin. London, Quaritch, 1898.

**FOPPA, Vincenzo, 1425?-1516?**
 Ffoulkes, Constance J., and Maiocchi, Rodolfo. Vincenzo Foppa of Brescia, founder of the Lombard school, his life and work. N. Y., Lane, 1909.

 Wittgens, Fernanda. Vincenzo Foppa. Milan, Pizzi, 1949.

**FOUQUET, Jean, 1415-1485?**
 Cox, Trenchard. Jehan Foucquet, native of Tours. London, Faber, 1931.

 Perls, Klaus G. Jean Fouquet. London, Hyperion, 1940.

 Wescher, Paul R. Jean Fouquet and his time. Trans. Eveline Winkworth. London, Pleiades books, 1947.

**FRAGONARD, Jean Honoré, 1732-1806**
 Algoud, Henri. Fragonard. Monaco, 1941 (Documents d'art, 1).

 Grappe, Georges. Fragonard, la vie et l'oeuvre. Monaco, 1946 (Documents d'art).

 Lavallée, Pierre. J.-H. Fragonard; quatorze dessins. Paris, Musées nationaux, 1938.

 Nolhac, Pierre de. Fragonard, 1732-1806. Paris, Goupil, 1918.

**FRANCESCHI, Pietro di Benedetto dei, 1416?-1492**
 Clark, Kenneth M. Piero della Francesca. London, Oxford Univ. press, Phaidon ed., 1951.

 Fasola, Giustina N. De prospectiva pingendi. Firenze, Sansoni, 1942 (Raccolti di fonti per la storia del' arte, 5).

 Longhi, Roberto. Piero della Francesca. 2. ed. Milan, Hoepli, 1946.

 Salmi, Mario. Piero della Francesca e il Palazzo ducale di Urbino. Florence, Le Monnier, 1945.

**FRANCESCO DI GIORGIO MARTINI, 1439–1502**
  Papini, Roberto. Francesco di Giorgio, architetto. Florence, Electa, 1946. 3 v.
  Weller, Allen S. Francesco di Giorgio, Siena, 1439–75. Chicago, Univ. of Chicago press, 1942.

**FRENCH, Daniel Chester, 1850–1931**
  Adams, Adeline V. P. Daniel Chester French, sculptor. Boston, Houghton Mifflin, 1932.
  Cresson, Margaret F. Journey into fame; the life of Daniel Chester French. Cambridge, Harvard Univ. press, 1947.
  French, Mary F. Memories of a sculptor's wife. Boston, Houghton Mifflin, 1928.

**GAINSBOROUGH, Thomas, 1727–1788**
  Armstrong, Walter. Gainsborough and his place in English art. London, Heinemann, 1898.
  Gower, Ronald C. S. Drawings of Gainsborough. N. Y., Scribner, 1910 (Drawings of the great masters).
  Whitley, William T. Thomas Gainsborough. London, Murray, 1915.
  Woodall, Mary. Gainsborough's landscape drawings. London, Faber, 1939.
  ——— Thomas Gainsborough, his life and work. London, Phoenix house, 1949 (British painters).

**GAUGUIN, PAUL, 1848–1903**
  Cogniat, Raymond. Gauguin. Paris, Tisné, 1947.
  Gauguin, Paul. Intimate journals. Trans. Van Wyck Brooks. N. Y., Crown, 1936.
  ——— Letters to his wife and friends. Ed. by M. Malingue. Cleveland, World pub. co., 1949.
  Guérin, Marcel. L'oeuvre gravé de Gauguin. Paris, Floury, 1927. 2 v.
  Malingue, Maurice. Gauguin, le peintre et son oeuvre; avant-propos de Pola Gauguin. Paris, Presses de la cité, 1948.
  Rewald, John. Gauguin. Paris, Hyperion, 1938.
  Rotonchamp, Jean de. Paul Gauguin, 1848–1903. Paris, Crès, 1925.

**GENTILE DA FABRIANO, 1360?–1427**
  Colasanti, Arduino. Gentile da Fabriano. Bergamo, Istituto italiano d'arti grafiche, 1909.

## GÉRICAULT, Jean Louis André Théodore, 1791-1824

Berger, Klaus. Géricault; drawings and watercolors. N. Y., Bittner, 1946.

Clément, Charles. Géricault; étude biographique et critique. 3 éd. Paris, Didier, 1879.

Delteil, Loÿs. Théodore Géricault. Paris, 1924 (Peintre-graveur illustré, 18).

## GÉRÔME, Jean Léon, 1824-1904

Moreau-Vauthier, Charles. Gérôme, peintre et sculpteur, l'homme et l'artiste. Paris, Hachette, 1906.

## GHIBERTI, Lorenzo, 1378-1455

Goldscheider, Ludwig. Ghiberti. London, Oxford Univ. press, Phaidon ed., 1949.

Planiscig, Leo. Lorenzo Ghiberti. Vienna, Schroll, 1940 (Sammlung Schroll).

Schlosser, Julius. Leben und meinungen des florentinischen bildners Lorenzo Ghiberti. Basel, Holbein, 1941.

## GHIRLANDAIO, Domenico, 1449-1494

Bargellini, Piero. Il Ghirlandaio del bel mondo fiorentino. Florence, Arnaud, 1945.

Lauts, Jan. Domenico Ghirlandajo. Vienna, Schroll, 1943 (Sammlung Schroll).

Steinmann, Ernst. Ghirlandajo. Bielefeld, Velhagen und Klasing, 1897 (Künstler-monographien, 25).

## GILL, Eric, 1882-1940

Gill, Eric. Autobiography. London, Cape, 1940.

——Letters. Ed. by Walter Shewring. N. Y., Devin-Adair, 1948.

## GIORGIONE DA CASTELFRANCO (Giorgio Barbarelli), 1477-1510

Conway, William M. Giorgione, a new study of his art as a landscape painter. London, Benn, 1929.

Cook, Herbert F. Giorgione. 2d ed. London, Bell, 1904 (Great masters in painting and sculpture).

Fiocco, Giuseppe. Giorgione. 2 cd. Bergamo, Istituto italiano d'arti grafiche, 1948 (Grandi artisti italiani, ser. 1).

Justi, Ludwig. Giorgione. Berlin, Reimer, 1926. 2 v.

Richter, George M. Giorgio da Castelfranco, called Giorgione. Chicago, Univ. of Chicago press, 1937.

## GIOTTI DI BONDONE, 1266-1337

Cecchi, Emilio. Giotto. Milan, Hoepli, 1937 (Valori plastici).

Hausenstein, Wilhelm. Giotto. Berlin, Propyläen-verlag, 1923.

Salvini, Roberto. Giotto bibliografia. Rome, Palombi, 1938.

Sirén, Osvald. Giotto and some of his followers. Trans. Frederic Schenck. Cambridge, Harvard Univ. press, 1917. 2 v.

Weigelt, Curt H. Giotto: des meisters gemälde. Stuttgart, Deutsche verlags-anstalt, 1925 (Klassiker der kunst, 29).

## GIOVANNI DA BOLOGNA see BOLOGNA, Giovanni da

## GIOVANNI DI PAOLO, 1403?-1483?

Brandi, Cesare. Giovanni di Paolo. Florence, Le Monnier, 1947.

Pope-Hennessy, John. Giovanni di Paolo, 1403-1483. London, Chatto, 1937.

## GIRARDON, François, 1628-1715

Francastel, Pierre. Girardon; biographie et catalogue critiques; l'oeuvre complète de l'artiste. Paris, Beaux-arts, 1928 (L'art français)

## GIRTIN, Thomas, 1775-1802

Binyon, Laurence. Thomas Girtin. London, Seeley, 1900.

Davies, Randall. Thomas Girtin's water-colours. London, Studio, 1924.

Mayne, Jonathan. Thomas Girtin. Leigh-on-Sea [Eng.], Lewis, 1949.

## GLEYRE, Marc Charles Gabriel, 1806-1874

Clément, Charles. Gleyre; étude biographique et critique. 2d ed. Paris, Perrin, 1886.

## GOES, Hugo van der, 1435?-1482

Destrée, Joseph. Hugo van der Goes. Brussels, Van Oest, 1914.

Rey, Robert. Hugo van der Goes. Brussels, Cercle d'art, 1945 (L'art en Belgique).

## GOGH, Vincent van, 1853-1890

Brooks, Charles M. Vincent van Gogh, a bibliography, comprising a catalogue of the literature published from 1890 through 1940. N. Y., Museum of modern art, 1942.

Duret, Théodore. Van Gogh, Vincent. Paris, Bernheim-Jeune, 1919.

Gogh, Vincent van. The letters of Vincent van Gogh to his brother, 1872-1886. Trans. Johanna van Gogh-Bonger. Boston, Houghton Mifflin, 1927. 2 v.

——Letters to Emile Bernard. Ed. by Douglas Lord. N. Y., Museum of modern art, 1938.

Goldscheider, Ludwig. Vincent van Gogh. London, Oxford Univ. press, Phaidon ed., 1947.

Hautecoeur, Louis. Van Gogh. Monaco, 1946 (Documents d'art).

La Faille, J. Bernard de. Les faux van Gogh. Paris, Van Oest, 1930.

——L'oeuvre de Vincent van Gogh; catalogue raisonné. Paris, Van Oest, 1928. 4 v.

Meier-Graefe, Julius. Vincent van Gogh, a biographical study. Trans. John H. Reece. N. Y., Harcourt, Brace, 1933.

——Vincent van Gogh, der zeichner. Berlin, Wacker, 1928.

Schapiro, Meyer. Vincent van Gogh. N. Y., Abrams, 1950 (Library of great painters).

Uhde, Wilhelm. Vincent van Gogh. 2d ed. London, Oxford Univ. press, Phaidon ed., 1936.

## GOUJON, Jean, 1515?–1568?

Du Colombier, Pierre. Jean Goujon. Paris, Michel, 1949 (Maîtres du moyen âge, 11).

Vitry, Paul. Jean Goujon; biographie critique. Paris, Laurens, 1908? (Les grands artistes).

## GOYA Y LUCIENTES, Francisco José de, 1746–1828

Adhémar, Jean. Goya. Paris, Tisné, 1941 (Bibliotheque française des arts).

Beruete y Moret, Aureliano de. Goya as portrait painter. Trans. Selwyn Brinton. 2d ed. London, Constable, 1922.

Delteil, Loÿs. Francisco Goya. Paris, 1922. 2 v. (Peintre-graveur illustré, 14–15).

Desparmet Fitz-Gerald, Xavière. L'oeuvre peint de Goya; catalogue raisonné. Paris, Nobele, 1928–50. 2 v. in 4.

Estrada, Genaro. Bibliografía de Goya. México, Casa de España, 1940.

Gudiol Ricart, Josep. Goya. N. Y., Hyperion, 1941.

Huxley, Aldous L. The complete etchings of Goya. N. Y., Crown, 1943.

Malraux, André. Dessins de Goya au Musée du Prado. Paris, Skira, 1947.

Mayer, August L. Francisco de Goya. Trans. Robert West. London, Dent, 1924.

**GOYA Y LUCIENTES, Francisco José de** (continued)

Rothe, Hans. Francisco Goya; handzeichnungen. Munich, Piper, 1943.

Wehle, Harry B. Fifty drawings by Francisco Goya. N. Y., Metropolitan museum of art, 1938.

**GOZZOLI, Benozzo, 1420–1498**

Bargellini, Piero. La fiaba pittorica di Benozzo Gozzoli. Florence, Arnaud, 1946.

Stokes, Hugh. Benozzo Gozzoli. London, Newnes, 1912.

**GRECO, El (Domenico Theotocopuli), 1542?–1614**

Babelon, Jean. El Greco. Paris, Tisné, 1946 (Coll. Colombier).

Bronstein, Leo. El Greco (Domenicos Theotocopoulos). N. Y., Abrams, 1950 (Library of great painters).

Camón Aznar, José. Dominico Greco. Madrid, Espasa-Calpe, 1950. 2 v.

Goldscheider, Ludwig. El Greco. N. Y., Oxford Univ. press, Phaidon ed., 1938.

Mayer, August L. El Greco. Berlin, Klinkhardt und Biermann, 1931.

Trapier, Elizabeth du Gué. El Greco. N. Y., Hispanic society, 1925.

Zervos, Christian. Les oeuvres du Greco en Espagne. Paris, Cahiers d'art, 1939.

**GREUZE, Jean Baptiste, 1725–1805**

Bouchot-Saupique, Jacqueline. J.-B. Greuze, 1725–1805; quatorze dessins. Paris, Musées nationaux, 1939.

Mauclair, Camille. Jean-Baptiste Greuze. Paris, Piazza, 1905.

**GRIS, Juan, 1887–1927**

Kahnweiler, Daniel H. Juan Gris, his life and work. N. Y., Valentin, 1947.

**GROPIUS, Walter, 1883–**

L'Architecture d'aujourd'hui. Walter Gropius et son école; Walter Gropius the spread of an idea. Paris, 1950.

Cook, Ruth R. A bibliography: Walter Gropius, 1919 to 1950. Chicago, American institute of architects, 1951.

Gropius, Walter. The new architecture and the Bauhaus. Trans. P. M. Shand. N. Y., Museum of modern art, 1937.

**GROS, Antoine Jean, 1771–1835**

Escholier, Raymond. Gros, ses amis et ses élèves. Paris, Floury, 1936.

Lemonnier, Henry. Gros; biographie critique. Paris, Laurens, 1905 (Grands artistes).

## GROSZ, George, 1893–
Grosz, George. Drawings. N. Y., Bittner, 1944.

——A little yes and a big no; autobiography. N. Y., Dial, 1946.

## GRÜNEWALD, Mathias, 1470?–1530
Burkhard, Arthur. Matthias Grünewald; personality and accomplishment. Cambridge, Harvard Univ. press, 1936.

Escherich, Mela. Grünewald-bibliographie (1489–juni 1914). Strassburg, Heitz, 1914 (Studien zur deutschen kunstgeschichte, 177).

Hagen, Oskar F. L. Matthias Grünewald. 4$^e$ aufl. Munich, Piper, 1923.

Huerlimann, Martin. Grünewald, das werk des meisters Mathis Gothardt Neithardt. Berlin, Atlantis, 1939.

Schoenberger, Guido. The drawings of Mathis Gothart Nithart, called Gruenewald. N. Y., Bittner, 1948.

## GUARDI, Francesco, 1712–1793
Fiocco, Giuseppe. Francesco Guardi. Florence, Battistelli, 1923.

Goering, Max. Francesco Guardi. Vienna, Schroll, 1944 (Sammlung Schroll).

Pallucchini, Rodolfo. I disegni del Guardi al Museo Correr di Venezia. Venice, Guaranti, 1943.

Shaw, James B. The drawings of Francesco Guardi. London, Faber, 1951.

## GUERCINO, Il (Giovanni Francesco Barbieri), 1591–1666
Russell, Archibald G. B. Drawings by Guercino. London, Arnold, 1923.

## HALS, Frans, 1584–1666
Davies, Gerald S. Frans Hals. London, Bell, 1902.

Moes, Ernst W. Frans Hals, sa vie et son oeuvre. Trans. Jean de Bosschere. Brussels, Van Oest, 1909.

Trivas, Numa S. The paintings of Frans Hals. 2d ed. London, Oxford Univ. press, Phaidon ed., 1949.

Valentiner, Wilhelm R. Frans Hals; des meisters gemalde. 2$^e$ aufl. Berlin, Deutsche verlags-anstalt, 1923 (Klassiker der kunst, 28).

## HASSAM, Childe, 1859–1935
Adams, Adeline V. P. Childe Hassam. N. Y., American academy of arts and letters, 1938.

HASSAM, Childe (continued)
> Cortissoz, Royal. Catalogue of the etchings and dry-points of Childe Hassam. N. Y., Scribner, 1925.

HEEMSKERK, Martin van, 1498-1574
> Huelsen, Christian, and Egger, Hermann. Die römischen skizzenbücher von Marten van Heemskerk, im Königlichen kupferstichkabinett zu Berlin. Berlin, Bard, 1913-16. 2 v.

HENRI, Robert, 1865-1929
> Henri, Robert. The art spirit; notes, articles, fragments of letters and talks to students, bearing on the concept and technique of picture making, the study of art generally, and on appreciation. Compiled by Margery Ryerson. Philadelphia, Lippincott, 1939.
>
> Read, Helen A. Robert Henri. N. Y., Whitney museum, 1931 (American artists series).

HOBBEMA, Meindert, 1638-1709
> Broulhiet, Georges. Meindert Hobbema (1638-1709). Paris, Firmin-Didot, 1938.
>
> Michel, Émile. Hobbema et les paysagistes de son temps en Hollande. Paris, Librairie de l'art, 1890 (Les artistes célèbres).

HOFFMAN, Malvina Cornell, 1887-
> Alexandre, Arsène. Malvina Hoffmann. Paris, Pouterman, 1930.
>
> Hoffman, Malvina C. Sculpture inside and out. N. Y., Norton, 1939.

HOGARTH, William, 1697-1764
> Ayrton, Michael. Hogarth's drawings. London, Avalon, 1948.
>
> Beckett, Ronald B. Hogarth. London, Routledge, 1949 (English master painters).
>
> Brown, Gerard B. William Hogarth. N. Y., Scribner, 1905 (Makers of British art).
>
> Dobson, Austin. William Hogarth. New and enl. ed. London, Heinemann, 1907.
>
> Hind, Arthur M. William Hogarth, his original engravings and etchings. N. Y., Stokes, 1912 (Great engravers).
>
> Moore, Robert E. Hogarth's literary relationships. Minneapolis, Univ. of Minnesota press, 1948.
>
> Oppé, Adolf P. The drawings of William Hogarth. N. Y., Oxford Univ. press, Phaidon ed., 1948.
>
> Wheatley, Henry B. Hogarth's London; pictures of the manners of the eighteenth century. N. Y., Dutton, 1909.

## HOLBEIN, Hans, 1460-1524

Glaser, Curt. Hans Holbein der ältere. Leipzig, Hiersemann, 1908 (Kunstgeschichtliche monographien, 11).

Schilling, Edmund. Zeichnungen der künstlerfamilie Holbein. Frankfurt a/M, Prestel-verlag, 1937.

Woltmann, Alfred F. G. A. Holbein und seine zeit. 2 aufl. Leipzig, Seemann, 1874-76. 2 v.

## HOLBEIN, Hans, 1497-1543

Chamberlain, Arthur B. Hans Holbein the younger. London, Allen, 1913. 2 v.

Ganz, Paul. Les dessins de Hans Holbein le jeune. Geneva, Boissonnas, 1939. 9 v.

——Die handzeichnungen Hans Holbein, d.j.; kritischer katalog. Berlin, Bard, 1937.

——Hans Holbein d.j.; des meisters gemälde. Stuttgart, Deutsche verlags-anstalt, 1912 (Klassiker der kunst, 20).

——The paintings of Hans Holbein. Trans. R. H. Boothroyd. London, Oxford Univ. press, Phaidon ed., 1950.

Glaser, Curt. Hans Holbein d.j. N. Y., Weyhe, 1924.

Holbein, Hans. The dance of death. Introduction and notes by James M. Clark. London, Oxford Univ. press, Phaidon ed., 1947.

Koegler, Hans. Hans Holbein d.j. Die bilder zum gebetbuch Hortulus animae. Basel, Schwabe, 1943. 2 v. in 1.

Leroy, Alfred. Hans Holbein et son temps. Paris, Michel, 1943.

Parker, Karl T. The drawings of Hans Holbein in the collection of His Majesty the King at Windsor castle. London, Oxford Univ. press, Phaidon ed., 1945.

Schmid, Heinrich A. Hans Holbein der Jüngere, sein aufstieg zur meisterschaft und sein senglischer stil. Basel, Holbein, 1948—. v. 1—.

Waetzoldt, Wilhelm. Hans Holbein der Jüngere; werk und welt. Berlin, Grote, 1938.

## HOMER, Winslow, 1836-1910

Downes, William H. The life and works of Winslow Homer. Boston, Houghton Mifflin, 1911.

Goodrich, Lloyd. American watercolor and Winslow Homer. Minneapolis, Walker art center, 1945.

——Winslow Homer. N. Y., Whitney museum, 1944.

**HOOCH, Pieter de, 1629?–1681**

Valentiner, William R. Des meisters gemälde; mit einem anhang über die genremaler um Pieter de Hooch und die kunst Hendrik van der Burch. Stuttgart, Deutsche verlags-anstalt, 1929 (Klassiker der kunst, 35).

**HOPPER, Edward, 1882–**

Du Bois, Guy P. Edward Hopper. N. Y., Whitney museum, 1931 (American artists).

Goodrich, Lloyd. Edward Hopper. Harmondsworth, Penguin, 1949 (Penguin modern painters).

**HOPPNER, John, 1758–1810**

McKay, William, and Roberts, William. John Hoppner. London, Colnaghi, 1909.

**HOUDON, Jean Antoine, 1741–1828**

Giacometti, Georges. Un lévrier, terre-cuite originale de Jean-Antoine Houdon (1741–1828). Paris, Nouvelle imprimerie, 1904.

Maillard, Élisa. Houdon. Paris, Rieder, 1931 (Maîtres de l'art ancien).

Réau, Louis. Houdon; biographie critique. Paris, Laurens, 1930 (Les grands artistes).

**HUGUET, Jaime, 1448?–1487**

Gudiol Ricart, José. Huguet. Barcelona, Instituto Amatller de arte hispánico, 1948.

Rowland, Benjamin. Jaume Huguet; a study of late Gothic painting in Catalonia. Cambridge, Harvard Univ. press, 1932.

**HUNT, William Holman, 1827–1910**

Gissing, Alfred C. William Holman Hunt, a biography. London, Duckworth, 1936.

Hunt, William H. Pre-Raphaelitism and the pre-Raphaelite brotherhood. 2d ed. N. Y., Dutton, 1914. 2 v.

**INGRES, Jean Auguste Dominique, 1780–1867**

Alazard, Jean. Ingres et l'ingrisme. Paris, Michel, 1950.

——J.-D. Ingres, 1780–1867; quatorze dessins. Paris, Musées nationaux, 1942.

Cassou, Jean. Ingres. Brussels, Éditions de la Connaissance, 1947.

Courthion, Pierre. Ingres, raconté par lui-même et par ses amis; pensées et écrits du peintre. Geneva, Cailler, 1947–48. 2 v.

Delteil, Loÿs. Ingres et Delacroix. Paris, 1908 (Peintre-graveur illustré, 3).

Fröhlich-Bum, Lili. Ingres, his life and art. Trans. Maude V. White. London, Heinemann, 1926.

Lapauze, Henry. Les dessins de J. A. D. Ingres du Musée de Montauban. Paris, Bulloz, 1901.

——Ingres, sa vie et son oeuvre (1780–1867) d'après des documents inédits. Paris, Petit, 1911.

Malingue, Maurice. Ingres. Monaco, 1943 (Documents d'art).

Pach, Walter. Ingres. N. Y., Harper, 1939.

## INNESS, George, 1825–1894

Inness, George, Jr. Life, art, and letters of George Inness. N. Y., Century, 1917.

McCausland, Elizabeth. George Inness, an American landscape painter, 1825–1894. N. Y., American artists group, 1946.

## JACOPO DELLA QUERCIA see QUERCIA

## JEFFERSON, Thomas, 1743–1826

Frary, Ihna T. Thomas Jefferson, architect and builder. Richmond, Garrett and Massie, 1931.

Kimball, Sidney Fiske. Thomas Jefferson, architect; original designs in the collection of Thomas Jefferson Coolidge, junior. Boston, Riverside press, 1916.

## JONES, Inigo, 1573–1652

Gotch, John A. Inigo Jones. London, Methuen, 1928.

## JONGKIND, Johan Barthold, 1819–1891

Moreau-Nélaton, Étienne. Jongkind raconté par lui-même. Paris, Laurens, 1918.

Roger-Marx, Claude. Jongkind. Paris, Crès, 1932.

## JORDAENS, Jakob, 1593–1678

Fierens-Gevaert, Hippolyte. Jordaens; biographie critique. Paris, Laurens, 1905 (Grands artistes).

Rooses, Max. Jacob Jordaens, his life and work. Trans. Elisabeth C. Broers. N. Y., Dutton, 1908.

## KANDINSKY, Wassily, 1866–1944

Grohmann, Will. Kandinsky. Paris, Cahiers d'art, 1930.

**KANDINSKY, Wassily** (continued)
    Kandinsky, Wassily. Concerning the spiritual in art, and painting in particular. A revision of the translation by Michael Sadleir. N. Y., Wittenborn, Schultz, 1947 (Documents of modern art).

**KLEE, Paul, 1879–1940**
    Grohmann, Will. The drawings of Paul Klee. N. Y., Valentin, 1944.
    Klee, Paul. On modern art. Trans. Paul Findlay. London, Faber, 1948.
    ——Pedagogical sketch book. Trans. Sibyl Peech. N. Y., Nierendorf, 1944.
    Miller, Margaret, ed. Paul Klee. 2d ed. N. Y., Museum of modern art, 1945.
    Nierendorf, Karl. Paul Klee; paintings, watercolors, 1913 to 1939. N. Y., Oxford Univ. press, 1941.
    Soby, James T. The prints of Paul Klee. N. Y., Valentin, 1945.

**KNELLER, Godfrey, 1646–1723**
    Killanin, Michael M. Sir Godfrey Kneller and his times, 1646–1723, being a review of English portraiture of the period. N. Y., Batsford, 1948.

**KOKOSCHKA, Oscar, 1886–**
    Hoffmann, Edith. Kokoschka, his life and work. London, Faber, 1947.
    Plaut, James S. Oskar Kokoschka. N. Y., Chanticleer, 1948.

**KOLBE, Georg, 1877–1947**
    Justi, Ludwig. Georg Kolbe. Berlin, Klinkhardt und Biermann, 1931 (Junge kunst, 60).
    Valentiner, Wilhelm R. Georg Kolbe, plastik und zeichnung. Munich, Wolff, 1922.

**KOLLWITZ, Käthe Schmidt, 1867–1945**
    Kollwitz, Käthe S. Tagebuchblätter und Briefe. Berlin, Mann, 1948.
    Zigrosser, Carl. Kaethe Kollwitz. N. Y., Bittner, 1946.

**KONINCK, Philips de, 1619–1688**
    Gerson, Horst. Philips Koninck; ein beitrag zur erforschung der holländischen malerei des XVII. jahrhunderts. Berlin, Mann, 1936.

**KUHN, Walt, 1880–1949**
    Bird, Paul. Fifty paintings by Walt Kuhn. N. Y., Studio, 1940.
    Kuhn, Walt. The story of the Armory Show. N. Y., 1938.

**KULMBACH, Hans Suess von, 1480?–1522**
    Winkler, Friedrich. Die zeichnungen Hans Süss von Kulmbachs und Hans Leonhard Schäufeleins. Berlin, Deutscher verein für kunstwissenschaft, 1942 (Denkmaler deutscher kunst).

**LA FARGE, John, 1835–1910**
    Cortissoz, Royal. John La Farge, a memoir and a study. Boston, Houghton Mifflin, 1911.
    La Farge, John. Considerations on painting. N. Y., Macmillan, 1901.
    Waern, Cecilia. John La Farge, artist and writer. N. Y., Macmillan, 1896 (Portfolio artistic monographs, 26).

**LANCRET, Nicolas, 1690–1743**
    Wildenstein, Georges. Lancret; biographie et catalogue critiques. Paris, Servant, 1924 (L'art français).

**LA TOUR, Georges Dumésnil de, 1593–1652**
    Furness, S. M. M. Georges de La Tour, of Lorraine, 1593–1652. London, Routledge, 1949.
    Jamot, Paul. Georges de La Tour. Paris, Floury, 1942.
    Pariset, François G. Georges de La Tour. Paris, Laurens, 1948.

**LATOUR, Henri Fantin, see FANTIN-LATOUR, Henri**

**LA TOUR, Maurice Quentin de, 1704–1788**
    Besnard, Albert, and Wildenstein, Georges. La Tour; la vie et l'oeuvre de l'artiste. Paris, Beaux-arts, 1928 (L'art français).
    Lapauze, Henry. La Tour et son oeuvre au Musée de Saint Quentin. Paris, Manzi, 1905. 2 v.
    ——Les pastels de Maurice-Quentin de La Tour du Musée Lécuyer à Saint-Quentin. Paris, La Renaissance, 1919.

**LAURANA, Francesco, 1425?–1502**
    Burger, Fritz. Francesco Laurana, eine studie zur italienischen quattrocentoskulptur. Strassburg, Heitz, 1907 (Zur kunstgeschichte des auslandes, 50).
    Rolfs, Wilhelm. Franz Laurana. Berlin, Bong, 1907. 2 v.

**LAWRENCE, Thomas, 1769–1830**
    Armstrong, Walter. Lawrence. N. Y., Scribner, 1913.
    Gower, Ronald C. S. Sir Thomas Lawrence. London, Goupil, 1900.

**LE BRUN, Mme Marie Louise Élisabeth Vigée, 1755–1842**
    Hautecoeur, Louis. Madame Vigée-Lebrun; étude critique. Paris, Laurens, 1917 (Grands artistes).

**LE BRUN, Mme Marie L. E. V.** (continued)

    **Lebrun, Marie L. E. V.** The memoirs of Mme. Élisabeth Louise Vigée-Le Brun, 1755–1789. Trans. Gerard Shelley. N. Y., Doran, 1927.

    **Nolhac, Pierre de.** Madame Vigée-Le Brun, peintre de la reine Marie Antoinette, 1755–1842. Paris, Goupil, 1908.

**LE CORBUSIER** (Charles Édouard Jeanneret-Gris), 1887–

    **Jeanneret-Gris, Charles E.** Oeuvre complète. Zürich, Girsberger, 1930—. v. 1—.

    ——Toward a new architecture, by Le Corbusier [pseud.]. Trans. Frederick Etchells. London, Architectural press, 1948.

    **Papadaki, Stamo,** ed. Le Corbusier, architect, painter, writer. N. Y., Macmillan, 1948.

**LÉGER, Fernand, 1881–**

    **Cooper, Douglas.** Fernand Léger et le nouvel espace. London, Lund, Humphries, 1949.

    **Tériade E.** Fernand Léger. Paris, Cahiers d'art, 1928.

**LEHMBRUCK, Wilhelm, 1881–1919**

    **Hoff, August.** Wilhelm Lehmbruck; seine sendung und sein werk. Berlin, Rembrandt-verlag, 1936 (Zeichner des volkes, 16).

    **Westheim, Paul.** Wilhelm Lehmbruck. 2$^{te}$ aufl. Potsdam, Kiepenheuer, 1922.

**LELY, Peter, 1618–1680**

    **Baker, Charles H. C.** Lely and the Stuart portrait painters; a study of English portraiture before and after Van Dyck. London, Warner, 1912. 2 v.

    **Beckett, Ronald B.** Lely. London, Routledge, 1951 (English master painters).

**LE NAIN family: Antoine, 1588?–1648; Louis, 1593?–1648; Mathieu, 1607–1677**

    **Fierens, Paul.** Les Le Nain. Paris, Floury, 1933 (Art et artistes français).

    **Jamot, Paul.** Les Le Nain; biographie critique. Paris, Laurens, 1929 (Grands artistes).

**LE NÔTRE, André, 1613–1700**

    **Guiffrey, Jules M. J.** André Le Nostre. Paris, Laurens, 1912 (Grands artistes).

## LEONARDO DA VINCI, 1452-1519

Bodmer, Heinrich. Disegni di Leonardo. 2ª ed. Florence, Sansoni, 1943.

——Leonardo, des meisters gemälde und zeichnungen. Stuttgart, Deutsche verlags-anstalt, 1931 (Klassiker der kunst, 37).

Clark, Kenneth M. A catalogue of the drawings of Leonardo da Vinci in the collection of His Majesty the King at Windsor Castle. Cambridge [Eng.], University press, 1935. 2 v.

——Leonardo da Vinci; an account of his development as an artist. Cambridge [Eng.], University press, 1939.

Douglas, Robert L. Leonardo da Vinci; his life and his pictures. Univ. press, Phaidon ed., 1944.

Goldscheider, Ludwig. Leonardo da Vinci. 2d ed. N. Y., Oxford Univ. press, Phaidon ed., 1944.

Mabbott, Mrs. Maureen C. A check list of the editions of Leonardo da Vinci's works in college and public libraries in the United States. N. Y., New York Public library, 1935.

McCurdy, Edward. The notebooks of Leonardo da Vinci. N. Y., Reynal and Hitchcock, 1938. 2 v.

Panofsky, Erwin. The Codex Huygens and Leonardo da Vinci's art theory. The Pierpont Morgan library, Codex M.A. 1139. London, Warburg institute, 1940 (Studies of the Warburg institute, 13).

Popham, Arthur E. The drawings of Leonardo da Vinci. N. Y., Reynal and Hitchcock, 1945.

Richter, Irma A. Paragone; a comparison of the arts. N. Y., Oxford Univ. press, 1949.

Richter, Jean P. Literary works [of Leonardo]. Compiled and edited from the original manuscripts. 2d ed. London, Oxford Univ. press, 1939. 2 v.

Suida, Wilhelm. Leonardo und sein kreis. Munich, Bruckmann, 1929.

Verga, Ettore. Bibliografia vinciana, 1493-1930. Bologna, Zanichelli, 1931. 2 v.

## LESCAZE, William, 1896–

Lescaze, William H. On being an architect. N. Y., Putnam, 1942.

## LIPPI, Filippino, 1457?-1504

Neilson, Katharine B. Filippino Lippi, a critical study. Cambridge, Harvard Univ. press, 1938 (Harvard-Radcliffe fine arts series).

**LIPPI, Filippino** (continued)
   Scharf, Alfred. Filippino Lippi. Vienna, Schroll, 1950 (Sammlung Schroll).

**LIPPI, Filippo, 1406?–1469**
   Oertel, Robert. Fra Filippo Lippi. Vienna, Schroll, 1942 (Sammlung Schroll).
   Pittaluga, Mary. Filippo Lippi. Florence, Del Turco, 1949 (Monografie e studi d'arte antica e moderna).

**LORENZETTI, Pietro, 1305?–1348**
   Cecchi, Emilio. Pietro Lorenzetti. Milan, Treves, 1930.
   Dewald, Ernest T. Pietro Lorenzetti. Cambridge, Harvard Univ. press, 1930.
   Sinibaldi, Giulia. I Lorenzetti. Siena, Istituto comunale d'arte e di storia, 1933 (Coll. di monografie d'arte senese).

**LOTTO, Lorenzo, 1480–1556**
   Berenson, Bernhard. Lorenzo Lotto; an essay in constructive art criticism. Rev. ed. London, Bell, 1905.
   Biagi, Luigi. Lorenzo Lotto. 2$^a$ ed. Rome, Tumminelli, 1943 (Quaderni d'arte, 4).

**LUCAS VAN LEYDEN, 1494–1533**
   Baldass, Ludwig von. Die gemälde des Lucas van Leyden. Vienna, Hölzel, 1923.
   Beets, Nicholaas. Lucas de Leyde. Brussels, Van Oest, 1913 (Grands artistes des Pays-Bas).
   Friedländer, Max J. Lucas van Leyden. Leipzig, Klinkhardt und Biermann, 1925 (Meister der graphik, 13).

**LUINI, Bernardino, 1475?–1533?**
   Williamson, George C. Bernardino Luini. London, Bell, 1907 (Great masters).

**MACINTIRE, Samuel, 1757–1811**
   Kimball, Sidney Fiske. Mr. Samuel McIntire, carver, the architect of Salem. Portland [Me.], Southworth-Anthoensen press, 1940.

**McKIM, Charles Follen, 1847–1909**
   Moore, Charles H. The life and times of Charles Follen McKim. Boston, Houghton Mifflin, 1929.

**MADERNO, Carlo, 1556–1629**
   Caflisch, Nina. Carlo Maderno; ein beitrag zur geschichte der römischen barockarchitektur. Munich, Bruckmann, 1934.

Muñoz, Antonio. Carlo Maderno. Rome, Società editrice d'arte illustrata, 1922 (Biblioteca d'arte illustrata: sei e settecento italiano, 12).

**MAES, Nicolaes, 1632-1693**

Valentiner, Wilhelm R. Nicolaes Maes. Stuttgart, Deutsche verlagsanstalt, 1924.

**MAGNASCO, Alessandro, 1667?-1749?**

Geiger, Benno. I disegni del Magnasco. Padua, Le Tre Venezie, 1945.

——Magnasco. Bergamo, Istituto italiano d'arti grafiche, 1949.

Pospisil, Maria. Magnasco. Florence, Alinari, 1944.

**MAILLOL, Aristide Joseph Bonaventure, 1861-1944**

Denis, Maurice. A. Maillol. Paris, Crès, 1925 (Coll. des cahiers d'aujourd'hui).

——Maillol: dessins et pastels. Paris, Carré, 1942.

Rewald, John. Maillol. N. Y., Hyperion, 1939.

——The woodcuts of Aristide Maillol. N. Y., Pantheon, 1943.

Ritchie, Andrew C. Aristide Maillol; with an introduction and survey of the artist's work in American collections. Buffalo, Albright art gallery, 1945.

**MANET, Édouard, 1832-1883**

Duret, Théodore. Manet and the French impressionists: Pissarro—Claude Monet—Sisley—Renoir—Berthe Morisot—Cézanne—Guillaumin. Philadelphia, Lippincott, 1910.

Florisoone, Michel. Manet. Monaco, 1947 (Documents d'art).

Guerin, Marcel, and Wildenstein, Georges. L'oeuvre gravé de Manet. Paris, Floury, 1944.

Jamot, Paul. Manet. Paris, Beaux-arts, 1932. 2 v. (L'art français).

Moreau-Nélaton, Étienne. Manet, raconté par lui-même. Paris, Laurens, 1926. 2 v.

Rewald, John. Édouard Manet pastels. Oxford, Cassirer, 1947.

Tabarant, Adolphe. Manet et ses oeuvres. Paris, Gallimard, 1947.

**MANSART, François, 1598-1666**

Blunt, Anthony. François Mansart and the origins of French classical architecture. London, Warburg institute, 1941 (Studies of the Warburg institute, 14).

**MANSHIP, Paul, 1885–**
  **Vitry, Paul.** Paul Manship, sculpteur américain. Paris, Gazette des beaux-arts, 1917 (Artistes étrangers contemporains).

**MANTEGNA, Andrea, 1431–1506**
  **Cruttwell, Maud.** Andrea Mantegna. London, Bell, 1908 (Great masters in painting and sculpture).
  **Fiocco, Giuseppe.** Mantegna. Paris, Gallimard, 1938 (Le Musée de la Pléiade).
  **Hind, Arthur M.** Andrea Mantegna and the Italian pre-Raphaelite engravers. N. Y., Stokes, 1911 (Great engravers).
  **Knapp, Fritz.** Andrea Mantegna, des meisters gemälde und kupferstiche. 2 ver. aufl. Stuttgart, Deutsche Verlags-anstalt, 191– (Klassiker der kunst, 16).

**MARIN, John, 1870–**
  **Helm, MacKinley.** John Marin. Boston, Pellegrini and Cudahy, 1948.
  **Marin, John.** Letters. Ed. by H. J. Seligmann. N. Y., An American Place, 1931.
  ——Selected writings. N. Y., Pellegrini and Cudahy, 1949.

**MARTINI, Simone, 1285?–1344**
  **Marle, Raimond van.** Simone Martini et les peintres de son école. Strasbourg, Heitz, 1920 (Études sur l'art de tous les pays et de toutes les époques, 1).
  **Rinaldis, Aldo de.** Simone Martini. Rome, Palombi, 1936.

**MASACCIO (Tommaso Guidi), 1401–1428?**
  **Mesnil, Jacques.** Masaccio et les débuts de la renaissance. The Hague, Nijhoff, 1927.
  **Pittaluga, Mary.** Masaccio. Florence, Le Monnier, 1935.
  **Salmi, Mario.** Masaccio. Rome, Valori plastici, 1932.
  **Steinbart, Kurt.** Masaccio. Vienna, Schroll, 1948 (Sammlung Schroll).

**MASOLINO DA PANICALE (Tommaso Fini), 1383–1440?**
  **Toesca, Pietro.** Masolino da Panicale. Bergamo, Istituto italiano d'arti grafiche, 1908.

**MATISSE, Henri, 1869–**
  **Faure, Élie.** Henri Matisse. Éd. nouv. Paris, Crès, 1923.
  **Fry, Roger Eliot.** Henri-Matisse. Paris, Éditions des chroniques du jour, 1935.

Testori, Gianni. Henri Matisse; 25 disegni. 2d ed. Milan, Görlich, 1943.
Zervos, Christian. Henri-Matisse. N. Y., Weyhe, 1931.

**MAZZOLA, Francesco, see PARMIGIANINO**

**MELOZZO DA FORLI, 1438-1494**
Buscaroli, Rezio. Melozzo da Forlì, nei documenti delle testimonianze dei contemporanei e nella bibliografia. Rome, Reale accademia d'Italia, 1938.

**MEMLING, Hans, 1430?-1494**
Baldass, Ludwig von. Hans Memling. Vienna, Schroll, 1942 (Sammlung Schroll).
Bazin, Germain. Memling. Paris. Tisné, 1939.
Voll, Karl. Memling. Stuttgart, Deutsche verlags-anstalt, 1909 (Klassiker der kunst, 14).

**MENDELSOHN, Erich, 1887–**
Mendelsohn, Erich. Three lectures on architecture: architecture in a world crisis; architecture today; architecture in a rebuilt world. Berkeley, Univ. of California press, 1944.
Whittick, Arnold. Eric Mendelsohn. London, Faber, 1940.

**MEŠTROVIĆ, Ivan, 1883–**
Ćurchin, Milan. Ivan Meštrović; a monograph. London, Williams and Norgate, 1919.
Meštrović, Ivan. Meštrović. Zagreb, Nova Evropa, 1933.

**MEUNIER, Constantin, 1831-1905**
Lemonnier, Camille. Constantin Meunier, sculpteur et peintre. Paris, Floury, 1904.
Thiery, A. Catalogue complet des oeuvres dessinées, peintes, et sculptées de Constantin Meunier. Louvain, Nova et Vetera, 1909.

**MICHELANGELO BUONARROTI, 1475-1564**
Boyer d'Agen, Jean A. B. Michel Ange. Les sculptures. The sculptures of Michel Angelo. Paris, Tel, 1935.
Carli, Enzo. Michelangelo. Bergamo, Istituto italiano l'arti grafiche, 1946 (Grandi artisti italiani).
Delacre, Maurice. Le dessin de Michel-Ange. Brussels, Palais des académies, 1938.
Delogu, Giuseppe. Michelangelo, plastik, gemälde und handzeichnungen. Zürich, Fretz und Wasmuth, 1939.

**MICHELANGELO BUONARROTI** (continued)

De Tolnay, Charles. The youth of Michel Angelo. 2d ed., rev. Princeton, Princeton Univ. press, 1947 (Michelangelo, 1).

——The Sistine ceiling. Princeton, Princeton Univ. press, 1949 (Michelangelo, 2).

——The Medici Chapel. Princeton, Princeton Univ. press, 1948 (Michelangelo, 3).

Frey, Carl. Die handzeichnungen Michelagniolos Buonarroti. Berlin, Bard, 1909–11. 3 v. Nachtrag. Hrsg. von Fritz Knapp. Berlin, Bard, 1925.

Goldscheider, Ludwig. The paintings of Michelangelo. N. Y., Oxford Univ. press, Phaidon ed., 1940.

——The sculptures of Michelangelo. 2d ed., rev. London, Oxford Univ. press, Phaidon ed., 1950.

Knapp, Fritz. Michelangelo. Stuttgart, Deutsche verlags-anstalt, 1906 (Klassiker der kunst, 7).

Kriegbaum, Friedrich. Michelangelo Buonarroti, die bildwerke. Berlin, Rembrandt-verlag, 1940.

Schiavo, Armando. Michelangelo architetto. Michelangelo as an architect. Rome, Libreria dello Stato, 1949.

Steinmann, Ernst, and Wittkower, Rudolf. Michelangelo bibliographie 1510–1926. Leipzig, Klinkhardt und Biermann, 1927 (Römische forschungen der Biblioteca Hertziana, 1).

**MIES VAN DER ROHE, Ludwig, 1886–**

Johnson, Philip C. Mies van der Rohe. N. Y., Museum of modern art, 1947.

**MILLAIS, John Everett, 1829–1896**

Baldry, Alfred L. Sir John Everett Millais, his art and influence. London, Bell, 1899.

Millais, John G. The life and letters of Sir John Everett Millais. London, Methuen, 1902. 2 v.

**MILLER, Kenneth Hayes, 1876–**

Burroughs, Alan. Kenneth Hayes Miller. N. Y., Whitney museum, 1931 (American artists series).

Goodrich, Lloyd. Kenneth Hayes Miller. N. Y., The Arts, 1930.

**MILLES, Carl, 1875–**

Rogers, Meyric R. Carl Milles; an interpretation of his work. New Haven, Yale Univ. press, 1940.

Verneuil, Maurice P. Carl Milles, sculpteur suédois; suivi de deux études. Paris, Van Oest, 1929. 2 v.

## MILLET, Jean François, 1814-1875

Bénédite, Léonce. The drawings of Jean François Millet. Philadelphia, Lippincott, 1906.

Moreau-Nélaton, Étienne. Millet; raconté par lui-même. Paris, Laurens, 1921. 3 v.

Sensier, Alfred. Jean-François Millet, peasant and painter. Trans. Helena de Kay. Boston, Osgood, 1881.

## MINO DA FIESOLE, 1430?-1484

Angeli, Diego. Mino da Fiesole. Florence, Alinari, 1905.

## MIRÓ, Joán, 1893-

Greenberg, Clement. Joán Miró. N. Y., Quadrangle press, 1948.

## MODIGLIANI, Amadeo, 1884-1920

Soby, James T. Modigliani; paintings, drawings, sculpture. N. Y., Museum of modern art, 1951.

## MONDRIAAN, Pieter Cornelis, 1872-1944

Mondriaan, Pieter C. Plastic art and pure plastic art, 1937, and other essays, 1941-1943. N. Y., Wittenborn, Schultz, 1945 (Documents of modern art).

## MONET, Claude, 1840-1926

Fels, Marthe de. La vie de Claude Monet. Paris, Gallimard, 1929.

Geffroy, Gustave. Claude Monet, sa vie, son oeuvre. Paris, Crès, 1924. 2 v. (Artistes d'hier et d'aujourd'hui).

Malingue, Maurice. Claude Monet. Monaco, 1943 (Documents d'art).

## MOORE, Henry Spencer, 1898-

Read, Herbert E. Henry Moore; sculpture and drawings. N. Y., Valentin, 1944.

Sweeney, James J. Henry Moore. N. Y., Museum of modern art, 1947.

## MOREAU family: Jean Michel, 1741-1814; Louis Gabriel, 1740-1805

Moureau, Adrien. Les Moreau. Paris, Librairie de l'art, 1893 (Artistes célèbres).

Schéfer, Gaston. Moreau le jeune, 1741-1814. Paris, Goupil, 1915.

Wildenstein, Georges. Un peintre de paysage au XVIII$^e$ siècle: Louis Moreau. Paris, Beaux-arts, 1923.

**MORETTO, Il (Alessandro Bonvicino), 1498?–1554**
   Gombosi, György. Moretto da Brescia. Basel, Holbein, 1943 (Ars docta, 4).

**MORISOT, Berthe (Mme. Eugène Manet), 1841–1895**
   Morisot, Berthe. Correspondance de Berthe Morisot avec sa famille et ses amis: Manet, Puvis de Chavannes, Degas, Monet, Renoir et Mallarmé. Ed. by Denis Rouart. Paris, Quatre chemins-éditart, 1950.
   Fourreau, Armand. Berthe Morisot. Paris, Rieder, 1925 (Maîtres de l'art moderne).

**MORRIS, William, 1834–1896**
   Cary, Elisabeth L. William Morris, poet, craftsman, socialist. N. Y., Putnam, 1902.
   Mackail, John W. The life of William Morris. London, Oxford Univ. press, 1950 (World's classics, 521).
   Morris, William. The letters of William Morris to his family and friends. Ed. by Philip Henderson. N. Y., Longmans, 1950.

**MORSE, Samuel Finley Breese, 1791–1872**
   Mabee, Carleton. The American Leonardo, a life of Samuel F. B. Morse. N. Y., Knopf, 1943.

**MOUNT, William Sidney, 1807–1868**
   Cowdrey, Bartlett, and Williams, Hermann W. William Sidney Mount, 1807–1868, an American painter. N. Y., Columbia Univ. press, 1944.

**MUNCH, Edvard, 1863–1944**
   Deknatel, Frederick B. Edvard Munch. Boston, Institute of Contemporary Art, 1950.
   Glaser, Curt. Edvard Munch. Berlin, Cassirer, 1917.
   Schiefler, Gustav. Edvard Munch; das graphische werk, 1906–1926. Berlin, Euphorion verlag, 1928.

**MURILLO, Bartolomé Esteban, 1617–1682**
   Calvert, Albert F. Murillo, a biography and appreciation. N. Y., Lane, 1907 (Spanish series).
   Mayer, August L. Murillo. 2d ed. Stuttgart, Deutsche verlags-anstalt, 1923 (Klassiker der kunst, 22).
   Muñoz, Antonio. Murillo. Novara, Istituto geografico De Agostini, 1942 (Grandi pittori).

**NASH, John, 1752-1835**
    Summerson, John N. John Nash, architect to King George IV. 2d ed. London, Allen, 1949.

**NASH, Paul, 1889-1946**
    Nash, Paul. Outline, an autobiography, and other writings. London, Faber, 1949.
    Read, Herbert E. Paul Nash. 2d ed. Harmondsworth, Middlesex, Penguin, 1944 (Penguin modern painters).

**NATTIER, Jean Marc, 1685-1766**
    Nolhac, Pierre de. Nattier, peintre de la cour de Louis XV. Paris, Floury, 1925.

**NICOLA D'APULIA see PISANO, Nicola**

**O'KEEFE, Georgia (Mrs. Alfred Stieglitz), 1887-**
    Rich, Daniel C. Georgia O'Keefe. Chicago, Art institute, 1943.

**ORCAGNA, Andrea (Andrea di Cione), 1308?-1368?**
    Steinweg, Klara. Andrea Orcagna; quellengeschichtliche und stilkritische untersuchung. Strassburg, Heitz, 1929 (Zur kunstgeschichte des auslandes, 131).

**OROZCO, José Clemente, 1883-1949**
    Fernández, Justino. José Clemente Orozco; forma e idea. México, Porrua, 1942.
    Orozco, José C. Autobiografia. México, Ediciones occidente, 1945.

**ORPEN, William, 1878-1931**
    Konody, Paul G., and Dark, Sidney. Sir William Orpen, artist and man. London, Seeley, 1932.

**OSTADE family: Adriaen van, 1610-1685; Isaac van, 1621-1649**
    Godefroy, Louis. L'oeuvre gravé de Adriaen van Ostade. Paris, L'auteur, 1930 (Monographies de peintres-graveurs illustrées, 3).
    Rosenberg, Adolf. Adriaen und Isack van Ostade. Bielefeld, Velhagen und Klasing, 1900 (Künstler-monographien, 44).
    Wiele, Marguerite van de. Les frères van Ostade. Paris, Librairie de l'art, 1893 (Artistes célèbres).

**OUDRY, Jean Baptiste, 1686-1755**
    Lavallée, Pierre. J.-B. Oudry, 1686-1755; quatorze dessins. Paris, Musées nationaux, 1938.
    Locquin, Jean. Catalogue raisonné de l'oeuvre de J. B. Oudry, peintre du roi, 1686-1755. Paris, Schemit, 1912.

**PACHER, Michael, 1435?-1498**
  Allesch, Gustav J. von. Michael Pacher. Leipzig, Insel-verlag, 1931 (Deutsche meister).
  Hempel, Eberhard. Das werk Michael Pachers. 4. aufl. Vienna, Schroll, 1940 (Sammlung Schroll).

**PALLADIO, Andrea, 1518-1580**
  Burger, Fritz. Die villen des Andrea Palladio; ein beitrag zur entwicklungsgeschichte der renaissance-architektur. Leipzig, Klinkhardt und Biermann, 1909.
  Pane, Roberto. Andrea Palladio. Turin, Einaudi, 1948 (Biblioteca d'arte, 4).

**PALMA, Giacomo (Palma Vecchio), 1480?-1528**
  Gombosi, György. Palma Vecchio, des meisters gemälde und zeichnungen. Stuttgart, Deutsche verlags-anstalt, 1937 (Klassiker der kunst, 38).
  Spahn, Annemarie. Palma Vecchio. Leipzig, Hiersemann, 1932 (Kunstgeschichtliche monographien, 20).

**PARMIGIANINO, Il (Francesco Mazzuoli), 1503-1540**
  Freedberg, Sydney J. Parmigianino: his works in painting. Cambridge, Harvard Univ. press, 1950.
  Fröhlich-Bum, Lili. Parmigianino und der manierismus. Vienna, Schroll, 1921.
  Quintavalle, Armando O. Il Parmigianino. Milan, Istituto editoriale italiano, 1948.

**PATER, Jean Baptiste Joseph, 1695-1736**
  Ingersoll-Smouse, Florence. Pater, biographie et catalogue critiques. Paris, Beaux-arts, 1928 (L'art français).

**PEALE, Charles Willson, 1741-1827**
  Sellers, Charles C. Charles Willson Peale. Philadelphia, American Philosophical Society, 1947. 2 v.

**PERRAULT, Claude, 1613-1688**
  Hallays, André. Les Perrault. Paris, Perrin, 1926 (Essais sur le XVII$^e$ siècle).

**PERUGINO (Pietro Vannucci), 1446-1524**
  Bombe, Walter. Perugino, des meisters gemälde. Stuttgart, Deutsche verlags-anstalt, 1914 (Klassiker der kunst, 25).
  Canuti, Fiorenzo. Il Perugino. Siena, La Diana, 1931. 2 v.

Williamson, George C. Pietro Vannucci, called Perugino. London, Bell, 1903 (Great masters in painting and sculpture).

## PERUZZI, Baldassare, 1481–1536
Kent, William W. The life and works of Baldassare Peruzzi of Siena. N. Y., Architectural book co., 1925.

## PESELLINO (Francesco di Stefano Giuochi), 1422–1457
Weisbach, Werner. Francesco Pesellino und die romantik der renaissance. Berlin, Cassirer, 1901.

## PIAZZETTA, Giovanni Battista, 1682–1754
Pallucchini, Rodolfo. L'arte di Giovanni Battista Piazzetta. Bologna, Maylender, 1934.

## PICASSO, Pablo (Pablo Ruiz y Picasso), 1881–
Barr, Alfred H. Picasso: fifty years of his art. N. Y., Museum of modern art, 1946.

Geiser, Bernhard. Picasso, peintre-graveur; catalogue illustré de l'oeuvre gravé et lithographié, 1899–1931. Berne, Chez l'auteur, 1933.

——Pablo Picasso; lithographs, 1945–1948. N. Y., Valentin, 1948.

Kahnweiler, Daniel H. Les sculptures de Picasso. Paris, Éditions du Chêne, 1948.

Stein, Gertrude. Picasso. London, Batsford, 1938.

Zervos, Christian. Pablo Picasso. Paris, Cahiers d'art, 1932—. v. 1—.

## PIERO DELLA FRANCESCA see FRANCESCHI, Pietro di Benedetto dei

## PIERO DI COSIMO (Piero di Lorenzo), 1462–1521
Douglas, Robert L. Piero di Cosimo. Chicago, Univ. of Chicago press, 1946.

Knapp, Fritz. Piero di Cosimo; ein übergangsmeister vom Florentiner quattrocento zum cinquecento. Halle, 1899.

## PIGALLE, Jean Baptiste, 1714–1785
Réau, Louis. J.-B. Pigalle. Paris, Tisné, 1950 (Grands sculpteurs français).

Rocheblave, Samuel. Jean-Baptiste Pigalle. Paris, Lévy, 1919 (Grands sculpteurs français du XVIII$^e$ siècle).

## PILON, Germain, 1536?–1590
Babelon, Jean. Germain Pilon; biographie et catalogue critiques, l'oeuvre complète de l'artiste. Paris, Beaux-arts, 1927 (L'art français).

**PILON, Germain** (continued)

Terrasse, Charles. Germain Pilon. Paris, Laurens, 1930 (Grands artistes).

**PINTURICCHIO (Bernardino Betti), 1454-1513**

Ricci, Corrado. Pintoricchio (Bernardino di Betto of Perugia), his life, work and time. Trans. Florence Simmonds. Philadelphia, Lippincott, 1902.

Steinmann, Ernst. Pinturicchio. Bielefeld, Velhagen und Klasing, 1898 (Künstler-monographien, 37).

**PIOMBO, Sebastiano Luciani, 1485-1547**

Dussler, Luitpold. Sebastiano del Piombo. Basel, Holbein-verlag, 1942.

Pallucchini, Rodolfo. Sebastian Viniziano (fra Sebastiano del Piombo). Milan, Mondadori, 1944.

**PIRANESI, Giovanni Battista, 1720-1778**

Giesecke, Albert. Studien über Giov. Batt. Piranesi (1720-1778). Leipzig, Hedrick, 1911 (Meister der graphik, 6).

Hermanin, Federico. Giambattista Piranesi. Rome, Sansaini, 1922.

Hind, Arthur M. Giovanni Battista Piranesi; a critical study, with a list of his published works and detailed catalogues of the prisons and the views of Rome. London, Cotswold, 1922.

**PISANELLO (Vittore Pisano), 1395-1455**

Degenhart, Bernhard. Pisanello. Vienna, Schroll, 1940 (Sammlung Schroll).

Hill, George F. Dessins de Pisanello. Paris, Van Oest, 1929.

——Pisanello. N. Y., Scribner, 1905.

Venturi, Adolfo. Pisanello. Rome, Palombi, 1939.

**PISANO, Andrea, 1270?-1348**

Toesca, Ilaria. Andrea e Nino Pisani. Florence, Sansoni, 1950 (Collezione di "Proporzioni").

**PISANO, Giovanni, 1240?-1320?**

Keller, Harald. Giovanni Pisano. Vienna, Schroll, 1942 (Sammlung Schroll).

Venturi, Adolfo. Giovanni Pisano; sein leben und sein werk. Florence, Pantheon, 1925. 2 v.

**PISANO, Niccolò, 1206?-1280?**

Fasola, Giustina N. Nicola Pisano; orientamenti sulla formazione del gusto italiano. Rome, Palombi, 1941.

Swarzenski, Georg. Nicolo Pisano. Frankfurt a/M, Iris, 1926 (Meister der plastik).

## PISSARRO, Camille Jacob, 1830–1903
Pissarro, Camille J. Camille Pissarro; letters to his son Lucien. Ed by John Rewald; trans. Lionel Abel. 2d ed. N. Y., Pantheon, 1943.

Pissarro, Ludovic R. Camille Pissarro; son art—son oeuvre. Paris, Rosenberg, 1939. 2 v.

Tabarant, Adolphe. Pissarro. Paris, Rieder, 1924 (Maîtres de l'art moderne).

## POLLAIUOLO, Antonio, 1429–1498
Colacicchi, Giovanni. Antonio del Pollaiuolo. Florence, Chessa, 1945 (Astarte, 1).

Cruttwell, Maud. Antonio Pollaiuolo. London, Duckworth, 1911.

Ortolani, Sergio. Il Pollaiuolo. Milan, Hoepli, 1948 (Valori plastici).

Sabatini, Attilio. Antonio e Piero del Pollaiolo. Florence, Sansoni, 1944.

## PONTORMO, Jacopo da (Jacopo Carrucci), 1494–1557
Becherucci, Luisa. Disegni del Pontormo. Bergamo, Istituto italiano d'arti grafiche, 1943 (Disegnatori ed incisori italiani, 1).

Clapp, Frederick M. Les dessins de Pontormo; catalogue raisonné. Paris, Champion, 1914.

——Jacopo Carucci da Pontormo, his life and work. New Haven, Yale Univ. press, 1916.

Toesca, Elena. Il Pontormo. Rome, Tumminelli, 1943 (Quaderni d'arte, 5).

## POUSSIN, Nicolas, 1593–1665
Félibien, André. Entretiens sur la vie et les ouvrages de Nicolas Poussin. Geneva, Cailler, 1947 (Écrits et documents de peintres, 5).

Friedlaender, Walter F. The drawings of Nicolas Poussin. London, Warburg institute, 1939—. v. 1—.

——Nicolas Poussin; die entwicklung seiner kunst. Munich, Piper, 1914.

Jamot, Paul. Connaissance de Poussin. Paris, Floury, 1948.

Poussin, Nicolas. Lettres. Intro. by Pierre du Colombier. Paris, Cité des livres, 1929.

Rouchès, Gabriel. Nicolas Poussin; quatorze dessins. Paris, Musées nationaux, 1938.

**PRENDERGAST, Maurice Brazil, 1859-1924**
   **Breuning, Margaret.** Maurice Prendergast. N. Y., Whitney museum, 1931 (American artists series).

**PRIMATICCIO, Francesco, 1504-1570**
   **Dimier, Louis.** Le Primatice. Paris, Michel, 1928.

**PRUD'HON, Pierre Paul, 1758-1823**
   **Goncourt, Edmond L. A. H. de.** Catalogue raisonné de l'oeuvre peint, dessiné et gravé de P. P. Prud'hon. Paris, Rapilly, 1876.
   **Guiffrey, Jean.** L'oeuvre de P. P. Prud'hon. Paris, Colin, 1924.

**PUGET, Pierre, 1622-1694**
   **Alibert, François P.** Pierre Puget. Paris, Rieder, 1930 (Maîtres de l'art ancien).
   **Auquier, Philippe.** Pierre Puget. Paris, Laurens, 1903 (Grands artistes).

**PUVIS DE CHAVANNES, Pierre, 1824-1898**
   **Laran, Jean, and Michel, André.** Puvis de Chavannes, with a biographical and critical study by André Michel. Philadelphia, Lippincott, 1912 (French artists of our day).
   **Werth, Léon.** Puvis de Chavannes. Paris, Crès, 1926 (Peintres et sculpteurs).

**QUERCIA, Jacopo Della, 1372?-1438**
   **Bacci, Pèleo.** Jacopo della Quercia; nuovi documenti e commenti. Siena, Lib. ed. Senese, 1929.
   **Biagi, Luigi.** Jacopo della Quercia. Florence, Arnaud, 1946 (Monografie e studi d'arte antica e moderna).
   **Gielly, Louis J.** Jacopo della Quercia. Paris, Michel, 1930 (Maîtres du moyen âge et de la renaissance, 6).

**RAEBURN, Henry, 1756-1823**
   **Armstrong, Walter.** Sir Henry Raeburn. London, Heinemann, 1901.

**RAPHAEL (Raffaelo Sanzio d'Urbino), 1483-1520**
   **Fischel, Oskar.** Raphael. Trans. Bernard Rackham. London, Kegan Paul, 1948. 2 v.
   ——[Raphael Sanzio] zeichnungen. Berlin, Grote, 1913—. Abt. 1—.
   **Middeldorf, Ulrich A.** Raphael's drawings. N. Y., Bittner, 1945.
   **Rosenberg, Adolf.** Raffael, des meisters gemälde. 5$^e$ aufl. Stuttgart, Deutsche verlags-anstalt, 1923 (Klassiker der kunst, 1).

Rouchès, Gabriel. Raphaël; quatorze dessins. Paris, Musées nationaux, 1938.

Serra, Luigi. Raffaello. Turin, Unione tipografico-editrice torinese, 1945 (Grandi italiani).

Suida, Wilhelm. Raphael. 2d ed. N. Y., Oxford Univ. press, Phaidon ed., 1948.

## REDON, Odilon, 1840-1916

Destrée, Jules. L'oeuvre lithographique de Odilon Redon. Brussels, Deman, 1891.

Mellerio, André. Odilon Redon, peintre, dessinateur et graveur. Paris, Floury, 1923.

Redon, Odilon. A soi-même, journal (1867-1915); notes sur la vie, l'art et les artistes. Paris, Fleury, 1922.

——Lettres d'Odilon Redon, 1878-1916. Paris, Van Oest, 1923.

## REGNAULT, Henri, 1843-1871

Cazalis, Henry. Henri Regnault; sa vie et son oeuvre. Paris, Lemerre, 1872.

Marx, Roger. Henri Regnault, 1843-1871. Paris, Rouam, 1886 (Artistes célèbres).

Regnault, Henri. Correspondance. Recueille et annotée par Arthur Duparc. 2ᵉ éd. Paris, Charpentier, 1873.

## REMBRANDT HERMANSZOON VAN RIJN, 1606-1669

Benesch, Otto. Rembrandt; selected drawings. London, Oxford Univ. press, Phaidon ed., 1947. 2 v.

Blum, André. Rembrandt, 1606-1669; quatorze dessins. Paris, Musées nationaux, 1939.

Borenius, Tancred. Rembrandt; selected paintings. London, Oxford Univ. press, Phaidon ed., 1942.

Bredius, Abraham. The paintings of Rembrandt. Vienna, Phaidon-verlag, 1936.

Hamann, Richard. Rembrandt. Potsdam, Stichnote, 1948.

Hind, Arthur M. Rembrandt. Cambridge, Harvard Univ. press, 1932.

——Rembrandt's etchings; an essay and a catalogue. London, Methuen, 1912. 2 v.

Hofstede de Groot, Cornelis. Die handzeichnungen Rembrandts. Haarlem, Bohn, 1906.

**REMBRANDT** (continued)

**Michel, Émile.** Rembrandt, his life, his work, and his time. Trans. Florence Simmonds. New ed. London, Heinemann, 1903. 2 v.

**Rosenberg, Adolf.** Rembrandt; des meisters gemälde. 3ᵉ aufl. Stuttgart, Deutsche verlags-anstalt, 1908 (Klassiker der kunst, 2).

**Rosenberg, Jakob.** Rembrandt. Cambridge, Harvard Univ. press, 1948. 2 v.

**Singer, Hans W.** Rembrandt; des meisters radierungen. 2ᵉ aufl. Stuttgart, Deutsche verlags-anstalt, 1910 (Klassiker der kunst, 8).

**Valentiner, Wilhelm R.** Rembrandt; wiedergefundene gemälde (1910–1922). 2ᵉ aufl. Stuttgart, Deutsche verlags-anstalt, 1923 (Klassiker der kunst, 27).

——[Rembrandt], handzeichnungen. Stuttgart, Deutsche verlags-anstalt, 1925–34. 2 v. (Klassiker der kunst, 31, 32).

**RENI, Guido, 1575–1642**

**Boehn, Max von.** Guido Reni. Bielefeld, Velhagen und Klasing, 1910 (Künstler-monographien, 100).

**Malaguzzi-Valeri, Francesco.** Guido Reni. Florence, Le Monnier, 1929.

**RENOIR, Pierre Auguste, 1841–1919**

**Coquiot, Gustave.** Renoir. Paris, Michel, 1925.

**Drucker, Michel.** Renoir. Paris, Tisné, 1944.

**Duret, Théodore.** Renoir. Trans. Madeleine Boyd. N. Y., Crown, 1937.

**Meier-Graefe, Julius.** Renoir. Leipzig, Klinkhardt und Biermann, 1929.

**Pach, Walter.** Pierre Auguste Renoir. N. Y., Abrams, 1950 (Library of great painters).

**Rewald, John.** Renoir; drawings. N. Y., Bittner, 1946.

**Rivière, Georges.** Renoir et ses amis. Paris, Floury, 1921.

**Vollard, Ambroise.** Renoir, an intimate record. Trans. H. L. Van Doren and R. T. Weaver. N. Y., Knopf, 1934.

**REYNOLDS, Joshua, 1723–1792**

**Armstrong, Walter.** Sir Joshua Reynolds. London, Heinemann, 1900.

**Graves, Algernon, and Cronin, William V.** A history of the works of Sir Joshua Reynolds. London, Graves, 1899–1901. 4 v.

**Reynolds, Joshua.** Discourses delivered to the students of the Royal academy. Intro. and notes by Roger Fry. London, Seeley, 1905.

——Letters. Collected and edited by Frederick Whiley Hilles. Cambridge [Eng.], University press, 1929.

Steegmann, John. Sir Joshua Reynolds. London, Duckworth, 1933 (Great lives, 5).

Waterhouse, Ellis K. Reynolds. London, Kegan Paul, 1939 (English master painters).

RIBERA, Jusepe de (Lo Spagnoletto), 1588?–1652

Lafond, Paul. Ribera et Zurbaran. Paris, Laurens, 1909 (Les grands artistes).

Mayer, August L. Jusepe de Ribera (lo Spagnoletto). 2$^e$ aufl. Leipzig, Hiersemann, 1923 (Kunstgeschichtliche monographien, 10).

Pillement, Georges. Ribera. Paris, Rieder, 1929 (Maîtres de l'art ancien, 12).

RICHARDSON, Henry Hobson, 1838–1886

Hitchcock, Henry-Russell. The architecture of H. H. Richardson and his times. N. Y., Museum of modern art, 1936.

RIEMENSCHNEIDER, Tilman, 1460?–1531

Bier, Justus. Tilmann Riemenschneider. 6$^{te}$ aufl. Vienna, Schroll, 1948 (Sammlung Schroll).

Gerstenberg, Kurt. Tilman Riemenschneider. 2$^{te}$ aufl. Vienna, Schroll, 1943 (Sammlung Schroll).

Schrade, Hubert. Tilman Riemenschneider. Heidelberg, Hain, 1927. 2 v.

RIVERA, Diego, 1886–

Wolfe, Bertram D. Diego Rivera; his life and times. London, Hale, 1939.

ROBBIA family: Andrea della, 1435?–1525?; Giovanni della, 1469–1529?; Luca della, 1400?–1482

Cruttwell, Maud. Luca and Andrea della Robbia and their successors. N. Y., Dutton, 1902.

Marquand, Allan. Andrea della Robbia and his atelier. Princeton, Princeton Univ. press, 1922. 2 v. (Princeton monographs in art and archaeology, 11).

——The brothers of Giovanni della Robbia; Fra Mattia, Luca, Girolamo, Fra Ambrogio. Princeton, Princeton Univ. press, 1928 (Princeton monographs in art and archaeology, 13).

——Giovanni della Robbia. Princeton, Princeton Univ. press, 1920 (Princeton monographs in art and archaeology, 8).

**ROBBIA family** (continued)

——Luca della Robbia. Princton, Princeton Univ. press, 1914 (Princeton monographs in art and archaeology, 3).

——Robbia heraldry. Princeton, Princeton Univ. press, 1919 (Princeton monographs in art and archaeology, 7).

**Planiscig, Leo.** Luca della Robbia. Vienna, Schroll, 1940 (Sammlung Schroll).

**Reymond, Marcel.** Les Della Robbia. Florence, Alinari, 1897.

**ROBERT, Hubert, 1733–1898**

**Leclère, Tristan.** Hubert Robert et les paysagistes français de XVIII$^e$ siècle. Paris, Laurens, 1913 (Les grands artistes).

**Nolhac, Pierre de.** Hubert Robert, 1733–1808. Paris, Goupil, 1910.

**RODIN, Auguste, 1840–1917**

**Cladel, Judith.** Rodin; the man and his art. Trans. S. K. Star. N. Y., Century, 1917.

**Grappe, Georges.** Le Musée Rodin. Paris, Taupin, 1947.

**Rodin, Auguste.** Art. Trans. Mrs. Romilly Fedden. N. Y., Dodd, 1928.

**Story, Sommerville.** Rodin. London, Oxford Univ. press, Phaidon ed., 1951.

**Waldmann, Emil.** Auguste Rodin. Vienna, Schroll, 1945 (Sammlung Schroll).

**ROGERS, John, 1829–1904**

**Smith, Chetwood.** Rogers groups, throught and wrought. Boston, Goodspeed, 1934.

**ROMNEY, George, 1734–1802**

**Chamberlain, Arthur B.** George Romney. N. Y., Scribner, 1910.

**Gower, Ronald C. S.** George Romney. London, Duckworth, 1904.

**Maxwell, Herbert E.** George Romney. N. Y., Scribner, 1902 (Makers of British art).

**Ward, Thomas H., and Roberts, William.** Romney; a biographical and critical essay, with a catalogue raisonné of his work. N. Y., Scribner, 1904. 2 v.

**ROSA, Salvatore, 1615–1673**

**Cattaneo, Irene.** Salvatore Rosa. Milan, Alpes, 1929.

**ROSSELLINO family: Antonio, 1427–1478; Bernardo, 1409–1464**

**Planiscig, Leo.** Bernardo und Antonio Rossellino. Vienna, Schroll, 1942 (Sammlung Schroll).

**ROSSETTI, Dante Gabriel, 1828–1882**

Cary, Elisabeth L. The Rossettis: Dante Gabriel and Christina. N. Y., Putnam, 1900.

Marillier, Henry C. Dante Gabriel Rossetti. 3d ed. London, Bell, 1904 (British artists).

Rossetti, Dante G. Letters of Dante Gabriel Rossetti to William Allingham, 1854–1870. Ed. by George B. N. Hill. London, Unwin, 1897.

Rossetti, William M. Praeraphaelite diaries and letters. 3 pts. (I, Some early correspondence of Dante Gabriel Rossetti, 1835–54; II, Madox Brown's diary, 1844–56; III, The P.R.B. journal kept by W. M. Rossetti, 1849–53). London, Hurt, 1900.

Waugh, Evelyn. Rossetti, his life and works. London, Duckworth, 1928.

**ROSSO, Giovanni Battista, 1494–1541**

Barocchi, Paola. Il Rosso Fiorentino. Rome, Gismondi, 1950.

Kusenberg, Kurt. Le Rosso. Paris, Michel, 1931 (Maîtres du moyen âge et de la renaissance, 7).

**ROUAULT, Georges, 1871–**

Jewell, Edward A. Georges Rouault. Paris, Hypérion, 1947.

Soby, James T. Georges Rouault: paintings and prints. 3d ed. N. Y., Museum of modern art, 1947.

Venturi, Lionello. Georges Rouault. 2$^e$ éd. Paris, Skira, 1948.

Wheeler, Monroe. The prints of Georges Rouault. N. Y., Museum of modern art, 1938.

**ROUBILIAC, Louis François, 1695?–1762**

Esdaile, Katharine A. M. The life and works of Louis François Roubiliac. London, Oxford Univ. press, 1928.

**ROUSSEAU, Henri Julien Félix (Le Douanier), 1844–1910**

Courthion, Pierre. Henri Rousseau, le douanier. Geneva, Skira, 1944.

Grey, Roch. Henri Rousseau. Paris, Tel, 1943.

Rich, Daniel C. Henri Rousseau. 2d ed., rev. N. Y., Museum of modern art, 1946.

**ROUSSEAU, Pierre Étienne Théodore, 1812–1867**

Dorbec, Prosper. Théodore Rousseau. Paris, Laurens, 1910 (Les grands artistes).

**RUBENS, Peter Paul, 1577–1640**
  **Arents, Prosper.** Rubens-bibliografie, geschriften van en aan Rubens. Brussels, De Lage Landen, 1943.
  **Burckhardt, Jakob C.** Recollections of Rubens. N. Y., Oxford Univ. press, Phaidon ed., 1950.
  **Evers, Hans G.** Peter Paul Rubens. Munich, Bruckmann, 1942.
  ——Rubens und sein Werk; neue Forschungen. Brussels, De Lage Landen, 1944.
  **Glück, Gustav.** Rubens, Van Dyck und ihr kreis. Wien, Schroll, 1933 (Gesammelte aufsatze, 1).
  **Goris, Jan-A., and Held, Julius S.** Rubens in America. N. Y., Pantheon, 1947.
  **Oldenbourg, Rudolf.** P. P. Rubens; des meisters gemälde. 4$^e$ neub. aufl. Stuttgart, Deutsche verlags-anstalt, 19— (Klassiker der kunst, 5).
  **Puyvelde, Leo van.** Les esquisses de Rubens. Basel, Holbein, 1940.
  **Rooses, Max.** Rubens. Trans. Harold Child. London, Duckworth, 1904. 2 v.
  **Rubens, Peter P.** Briefe. Ubersetzt von Otto Zoff. Vienna, Schroll, 1918.
  **Stevenson, Robert A. M.** Rubens, paintings and drawings. N. Y., Oxford Univ. press, Phaidon ed., 1939.

**RUDE, François, 1784–1855**
  **Calmette, Joseph L. A.** François Rude. Paris, Floury, 1920.
  **Fourcaud, Louis de.** François Rude, sculpteur; ses oeuvres et son temps, 1784–1855. Paris, Librairie de l'art, 1904.

**RUSH, William, 1756–1833**
  **Marceau, Henri.** William Rush, 1756–1833, the first native American sculptor. Philadelphia, Pennsylvania museum of art, 1937.

**RUYSDAEL, Jacob Isaacszoon van, 1629?–1682**
  **Riat, Georges.** Ruysdael. Paris, Laurens, 1907 (Les grands artistes).
  **Rosenberg, Jakob.** Jacob van Ruisdael. Berlin, Cassirer, 1928.
  **Stechow, Wolfgang.** Salomon van Ruysdael; eine einführung in seine kunst. Berlin, Mann, 1938.

**RYDER, Albert Pinkham, 1847–1917**
  **Price, Frederic N.** Ryder (1847–1917); a study of appreciation. N. Y., Rudge, 1932.
  **Sherman, Frederic F.** Albert Pinkham Ryder. N. Y., priv. pr., 1920.

**SAARINEN, Eliel, 1873-1950**
  Christ-Janer, Albert. Eliel Saarinen. Chicago, Univ. of Chicago press, 1948.
  Saarinen, Eliel. Search for form; a fundamental approach to art. N. Y., Reinhold, 1948.

**SAINT-AUBIN, Gabriel Jacques de, 1724-1780**
  Dacier, Émile. Gabriel de Saint-Aubin, peintre, dessinateur et graveur (1724-1780). Paris, Van Oest, 1929-31. 2 v.

**SAINT-GAUDENS, Augustus, 1848-1907**
  Cortissoz, Royal. Augustus Saint-Gaudens. Boston, Houghton Mifflin, 1907.
  Hind, Charles L. Augustus Saint-Gaudens. N. Y., Lane, 1908.
  Saint-Gaudens, Augustus. Reminiscences. Ed. by Homer Saint-Gaudens. N. Y., Century, 1913. 2 v.

**SANGALLO family: Antonio da, d.1516; Antonio da, d.1534; Giuliano da, d.1546**
  Clausse, Gustave. Les San Gallo, architectes, peintres, sculpteurs, médailleurs, XV$^e$ et XVI$^e$ siècles. Paris, Leroux, 1900-02. 3 v.
  Marchini, Giuseppe. Giuliano da Sangallo. Florence, Sansoni, 1942.

**SANO DI PIETRO, 1406-1481**
  Gaillard, Émile. Un peintre siennois aux XV$^e$ siècle, Sano di Pietro, 1406-1481. Chambéry, Dardel, 1923.
  Trübner, Jörg. Die stilistische entwickelung der tafelbilder des Sano di Pietro, 1405-1481. Strassburg, Heitz, 1925.

**SANSOVINO, Andrea, 1460-1529**
  Huntley, George Haydn. Andrea Sansovino, sculptor and architect of the Italian renaissance. Cambridge, Harvard Univ. press, 1935.

**SANSOVINO, Jacopo (Jacopo Tatti), 1486-1570**
  Sapori, Francesco. Jacopo Tatti detto il Sansovino. Rome, Libr. dello stato, 1928.

**SARGENT, John Singer, 1856-1925**
  Charteris, Evan E. John Sargent. N. Y., Scribner, 1927.
  Downes, William H. John S. Sargent, his life and work. Boston, Little, Brown, 1925.

**SARTO, Andrea del, 1486-1531**
  Fraenckel, Ingeborg. Andrea del Sarto; gemälde und zeichnungen. Strassburg, Heitz, 1935.

**SARTO, Andrea del** (continued)

   **Guinness, H.** Andrea del Sarto. London, Bell, 1901 (Great masters in painting and sculpture).

   **Knapp, Fritz.** Andrea del Sarto. Bielefeld, Velhagen und Klasing, 1907 (Künstler-monographien, 90).

   **Rouchès, Gabriel.** Andrea del Sarto, 1486–1531; quatorze dessins. Paris, Musée nationaux, 1939.

**SASSETTA (Stefano di Giovanni), 1392–1450**

   **Berenson, Bernhard.** A Sienese painter of the Franciscan legend. London, Dent, 1910.

   **Pope-Hennessy, John.** Sassetta. London, Chatto, 1939.

**SCHLÜTER, Andreas, 1664–1714**

   **Benkard, Ernst.** Andreas Schlüter. Frankfurt a/M, Iris-verlag, 1925 (Meister der plastik, 2).

   **Ladendorf, Heinz.** Andreas Schlüter. Berlin, Rembrandt-verlag, 1937.

**SCHONGAUER, Martin, 1430?–1491**

   **Baum, Julius.** Martin Schongauer. Vienna, Schroll, 1948 (Sammlung Schroll).

   **Rosenberg, Jakob.** Martin Schongauer; handzeichnungen. Munich, Piper, 1923.

**SCOREL, Jan van, 1495–1562**

   **Hoogewerff, Godfried J.** Jan van Scorel, peintre de la renaissance hollandaise. The Hague, Nijhoff, 1923.

**SEGHERS, Hercules Pietersz, 1590–1640**

   **Springer, Jaro.** Die radierungen des Hercules Seghers. Berlin, Cassirer, 1910–12. 3 v. (Graphische gesellschaft, 13–14, 16 veroffentlichung).

**SEURAT, Georges Pierre, 1859–1891**

   **Kahn, Gustave.** Les dessins de Georges Seurat, 1859–1891. Paris, Bernheim-Jeune, 1928. 2 v.

   **Laprade, Jacques de.** Georges Seurat. Monaco, Taupin, 1945 (Documents d'art).

   **Rewald, John.** Georges Seurat. 2d rev. ed. N. Y., Wittenborn, Schultz, 1946.

   **Rich, Daniel C.** Seurat and the revolution of "La Grande Jatte." Chicago, Univ. of Chicago press, 1935.

   **Seligman, Germain.** The drawings of Georges Seurat. N. Y., Valentin, 1947.

**SHEELER, Charles, 1883–**
  Rourke, Constance M. Charles Sheeler, artist in the American tradition. N. Y., Harcourt, Brace, 1938.
  Williams, William C. Charles Sheeler; paintings, drawings, photographs. N. Y., Museum of modern art, 1939.

**SICKERT, Walter Richard, 1860–1942**
  Emmons, Robert. The life and opinions of Walter Richard Sickert. London, Faber, 1941.
  Sickert, Walter R. A free house! or, The artist as craftsman. London, Macmillan, 1947.

**SIGNAC, Paul, 1863–1935**
  Besson, George. Signac, dessins. Paris, Braun, 1950 (Plastique, 7).
  Signac, Paul. D'Eugène Delacroix au néo-impressionnisme. 4$^e$ éd. Paris, Floury, 1939 (Écrits d'artistes).

**SIGNORELLI, Luca, 1441?–1523**
  Cruttwell, Maud. Luca Signorelli. London, Bell, 1907 (Great masters in painting and sculpture).
  Dussler, Luitpold. Signorelli, des meisters gemälde. Stuttgart, Deutsche verlags-anstalt, 1927 (Klassiker der kunst, 34).
  Venturi, Adolfo. Luca Signorelli. Florence, Alinari, 1922 (Grandi maestri dell' arte italiana).

**SIMONE MARTINI see MARTINI, Simone**

**SLOAN, John, 1871–1951**
  Du Bois, Guy P. John Sloan. N. Y., Whitney museum, 1931 (American artists series).
  Sloan, John. Gist of art; principles and practice expounded in the classroom and studio. N. Y., American artists group, 1939.

**SLUTER, Claus, 1340?–1406?**
  Kleinclausz, Arthur J. Claus Sluter, et la sculpture bourguignonne au XV$^e$ siècle. Paris, Librairie de l'art, 1905 (Maîtres de l'art).
  Liebreich, Aenne. Claus Sluter. Brussels, Dietrich, 1936.

**SMIBERT, John, 1688–1751**
  Foote, Henry W. John Smibert, painter. Cambridge, Harvard Univ. press, 1950.

**SOANE, John, 1753–1837**
  Bolton, Arthur T. The portrait of Sir John Soane (1753–1837) set forth in letters from his friends (1775–1837). London, Butler, 1927 (Sir John Soane's museum publication).

**SODOMA, Il (Giovanni Antonio Bazzi), 1477?-1549**

Cust, Robert H. H. Giovanni Antonio Bazzi, hitherto usually styled "Sodoma," the man and the painter, 1477-1549; a study. N. Y., Dutton, 1906.

Hauvette, Henri. Le Sodoma, biographie critique. Paris, Laurens, 1911 (Les grands artistes).

Segard, Achille. Giov.-Antonio Bazzi detto Sodoma et la fin de l'école de Sienne au XVI. siècle. Paris, Floury, 1910.

**SPINELLO ARETINO (Spinello di Luca Spinelli), 1346?-1410**

Gombosi, György. Spinello Aretino; eine stilgeschichtliche studie über die florentinische malerei des ausgehenden XIV. jahrhunderts. Budapest, Im selbstverlag des ferfassers, 1926.

**STEEN, Jan Havicksz, 1626-1679**

Schmidt-Degener, Frederik. Jan Steen. London, Lane, 1927.

**STEVENS, Alfred, 1823-1906**

Vanzype, Gustave. Les frères Stevens. Brussels, Nouvelle société d'éditions, 1936.

**STEVENS, Alfred George, 1817-1875**

Armstrong, Walter. Alfred Steven's; a biographical study. Paris, Librairie de l'art, 1881.

Stevens, Alfred G. Drawings of Alfred Stevens. N. Y., Scribner, 1908 (Drawings of the great masters).

Towndrow, Kenneth R. The works of Alfred Stevens, sculptor, painter, designer in the Tate Gallery. London, Tate Gallery, 1950.

**STOSS, Veit, d.1533**

Daun, Berthold. Veit Stoss und seine schule in Deutschland, Polen, Ungarn und Siebenbürgen. 2$^e$ aufl. Leipzig, Hiersemann, 1916 (Kunstgeschichtliche monographien, 17).

Lutze, Eberhard. Veit Stoss. Berlin, Deutscher kunstverlag, 1938 (Deutsche lande, deutsche kunst).

**STRICKLAND, William, 1788-1854**

Gilchrist, Agnes E. A. William Strickland, architect and engineer, 1788-1854. Philadelphia, Univ. of Pennsylvania press, 1950.

**STUART, Gilbert, 1755-1828**

Morgan, John H. Gilbert Stuart and his pupils. N. Y., New York historical society, 1939.

Park, Lawrence, Morgan, John H., and Cortissoz, Royal. Gilbert Stuart; an illustrated descriptive list of his works. N. Y., Rudge, 1926. 4 v.

Whitley, William T. Gilbert Stuart. Cambridge, Harvard Univ. press, 1932.

## SULLIVAN, Louis Henry, 1856–1924

Morrison, Hugh. Louis Sullivan, prophet of modern architecture. N. Y., Museum of modern art, 1935.

Sullivan, Louis H. The autobiography of an idea. Foreword by Claude Bragdon. N. Y., Smith, 1949.

——Kindergarten chats (revised 1918) and other writings. Ed. by Isabella Athey. N. Y., Wittenborn, Schultz, 1947 (Documents of modern art).

## SULLY, Thomas, 1783–1872

Biddle, Edward, and Fielding, Mantle. The life and works of Thomas Sully (1783–1872). Philadelphia, 1921.

Hart, Charles H. A register of portraits painted by Thomas Sully, 1801–1871. Philadelphia, 1909.

## TAFT, Lorado, 1860–1936

Taft, Ada B. Lorado Taft, sculptor and citizen. Greensboro, N. C., 1946.

## TENIERS, David, 1610–1690

Peyre, Roger R. David Teniers, biographie critique. Paris, Laurens, 1910 (Les grands artistes).

Rosenberg, Adolf. Teniers der jüngere. 2 aufl. Bielefeld, Velhagen und Klasing, 1901 (Künstler-monographien, 8).

## TERBORCH, Gerard, 1617–1681

Michel, Émile. Gérard Terburg (Ter Borch) et sa famille. Paris, Rouam, 1887 (Les artistes célèbres).

Plietzsch, Eduard. Gerard ter Borch. Vienna, Schroll, 1944 (Sammlung Schroll).

Rosenberg, Adolf. Terborch und Jan Steen. Bielefeld, Velhagen und Klasing, 1897 (Künstler-monographien, 19).

## THORVALDSEN, Bertel, 1770–1844

Rosenberg, Adolf. Thorwaldsen. Bielefeld, Velhagen und Klasing, 1896 (Künstler-monographien, 16).

**TIEPOLO, Giovanni Battista, 1696–1770**
    Hadeln, Detlev von. The drawings of Giovanni Battista Tiepolo. Paris, Pegasus press, 1928. 2 v.
    Hegemann, Hans W. Giovanni Battista Tiepolo. Berlin, Rembrandt-verlag, 1940 (Kunst italiens, 2).
    Molmenti, Pompeo G. G. B. Tiepolo, la sua vita e le sue opere. Milan, Hoepli, 1909.
    Morassi, Antonio. Tiepolo. Bergamo, Istituto italiano d'arti grafiche, 1943 (Grandi artisti italiani).

**TINO DA CAMAINO, 1280?–1337**
    Carli, Enzo. Tino di Camaino, scultore. Florence, Le Monnier, 1934.
    Valentiner, Wilhelm R. Tino di Camaino, a Sienese sculptor of the fourteenth century. Paris, Pegasus press, 1935.

**TINTORETTO, Il (Jacopo Robusti), 1518–1594**
    Bercken, Erich von der. Die gemälde des Jacopo Tintoretto. Munich, Piper, 1942.
    Coletti, Luigi. Il Tintoretto. 2. ed. Bergamo, Istituto italiano d'arti grafiche, 1944.
    Hadeln, Detlev von. Zeichnungen des Giacomo Tintoretto. Berlin, Cassirer, 1922.
    Osmaston, Francis P. B. The art and genius of Tintoret. London, Bell, 1915. 2 v.
    Pittaluga, Mary. Il Tintoretto. Bologna, Zanichelli, 1925.
    Tietze, Hans. Tintoretto; the paintings and drawings. London, Oxford Univ. press, Phaidon ed., 1948.

**TITIAN (Tiziano Vecelli), 1477–1576**
    Babelon, Jean. Titien. Paris, Plon, 1950 (Mâitres de l'histoire).
    Fischel, Oskar. Tizian. 5$^e$ aufl. Stuttgart, Deutsche verlags-anstalt, 192– (Klassiker der kunst, 3).
    Hadeln, Detlev von. Titian's drawings. London, Macmillan, 1927.
    Tietze, Hans. [Titian], paintings and drawings. 2d ed., rev. London, Oxford Univ. press, Phaidon ed., 1950.

**TOULOUSE-LAUTREC, Henri Marie Raymond de, 1864–1901**
    Coquiot, Gustave. H. de Toulouse-Lautrec. Paris, Blaizot, 1913.
    Delteil, Loÿs. H. de Toulouse-Lautrec. Paris, 1920. 2 v. (Peintre-graveur illustré, 10–11).
    Jedlicka, Gothard. Henri de Toulouse-Lautrec. Erlenbach-Zürich, Rentsch, 1943.

Joyant, Maurice. Henri de Toulouse-Lautrec, 1864–1901. Paris, Floury, 1926–27. 2 v.

Mack, Gerstle. Toulouse-Lautrec. N. Y., Knopf, 1938.

TRUMBULL, John, 1756–1843

Sizer, Theodore. The works of Colonel John Trumbull, artist of the American Revolution. New Haven, Yale Univ. press, 1950.

TURNER, Joseph Mallord William, 1775–1851

Armstrong, Walter. Turner. N. Y., Scribner, 1902. 2 v.

Finberg, Alexander J. The history of Turner's Liber studiorum, with a new catalogue raisonné. London, Benn, 1924.

—— The life of J. M. W. Turner. Oxford, Clarendon press, 1939.

—— Turner's sketches and drawings. N. Y., Scribner, 1910.

Mauclair, Camille. Turner. Trans. Eveline Byam Shaw. London, Heinemann, 1939.

Rawlinson, William G. The engraved work of J. M. W. Turner. London, Macmillan, 1908–13. 2 v.

UCCELLO, Paolo (Paolo di Dono), 1397–1475

Boeck, Wilhelm. Paolo Uccello, der Florentiner meister und sein werk. Berlin, Grote, 1939.

Pittaluga, Mary. Paolo Uccello. Rome, Tumminelli, 1946 (Quaderni d'arte, 10).

Pope-Hennessy, John. The complete work of Paolo Uccello. N. Y., Oxford Univ. press, Phaidon ed., 1950.

UPJOHN, Richard, 1802–1878

Upjohn, Everard M. Richard Upjohn, architect and churchman. N. Y., Columbia Univ. press, 1939.

UTRILLO, Maurice, 1883–

Gros, Gabriel J. Maurice Utrillo. Paris, Crès, 1927.

Tabarant, Adolphe. Utrillo. Paris, Bernheim-Jeune, 1926.

VANBRUGH, John, 1664–1726

Whistler, Laurence. Sir John Vanbrugh, architect and dramatist, 1664–1726. N. Y., Macmillan, 1939.

VELÁZQUEZ, Diego Rodríguez de Silva y, 1599–1660

Allende-Salazar, Juan. Velazquez; des meisters gemälde. 4$^e$ aufl. Stuttgart, Deutsche verlags-anstalt, 1925 (Klassiker der kunst, 6).

Angulo Íniguez, Diego. Velázquez; cómo compuso sus principales cuadros. Seville, Universidad de Sevilla, 1947.

**VELÁZQUEZ** (continued)

    **Gensel, Walther.** Velazquez. 2. aufl. Stuttgart, Deutsche verlagsanstalt, 1908 (Klassiker der kunst, 6).

    **Lafuente Ferrari, Enrique.** Velazquez. London, Oxford Univ. press, Phaidon ed., 1943.

    **Mayer, August L.** Velazquez. Paris, Tisné, 1940.

    **Muñoz, Antonio.** Velázquez. Leipzig, Goldmann, 1941.

    **Trapier, Elizabeth du Gué.** Velazquez. N. Y., Hispanic society, 1948.

**VERMEER, Johannes (Jan Vermeer van Delft), 1632–1675**

    **Bodkin, Thomas.** The paintings of Jan Vermeer. N. Y., Oxford Univ. press, Phaidon ed., 1940.

    **Hale, Philip L.** Vermeer. Ed by W. Coburn and R. T. Hale. Boston, Hale, 1937.

    **Swillens, P. T. A.** Johannes Vermeer, painter of Delft, 1632–1675. Utrecht, Spectrum, 1950.

    **Vries, Ary B. de.** Jan Vermeer van Delft. Trans. Robert Allen. N. Y., Batsford, 1948.

**VERNET family: Joseph, 1712–1789; Carle, 1758–1836; Horace, 1789–1863**

    **Blanc, Charles.** Une famille d'artistes, les trois Vernet: Joseph, Carle, Horace. Paris, Renouard, 1898.

    **Dayot, Armand P. M.** Carle Vernet; étude sur l'artiste, suivie d'un catalogue de l'oeuvre gravé et lithographie et du catalogue de l'exposition rétrospective de 1925. Paris, Le Goupy, 1925.

    **Ingersoll-Smouse, Florence.** Joseph Vernet, peintre de marine, 1714–1789. Paris, Bignou, 1926. 2 v.

**VERONESE, Paolo (Paolo Cagliari), 1528–1588**

    **Fiocco, Giuseppe.** Paolo Veronese, 1528–1588. Bologna, Apollo, 1928.

    **Lukomskii, Georgii K.** Les fresques de Paul Véronese et de ses disciples. Paris, Seheur, 1928 (L'art et la vie).

    **Pallucchini, Rodolfo.** Veronese. 2 ed. Bergamo, Istituto italiano d'arti grafiche, 1943.

    **Venturi, Adolfo.** Paolo Veronese (per il IV centenario dalla nascita). Milan, Hoepli, 1928.

**VERROCCHIO, Andrea del, 1435–1488**

    **Cruttwell, Maud.** Verrocchio. London, Duckworth, 1911.

    **Planiscig, Leo.** Andrea del Verrocchio. Vienna, Schroll, 1941 (Sammlung Schroll).

Reymond, Marcel. Verrocchio. Paris, Librairie de l'art, 1906 (Maîtres de l'art).

## VIGNOLA (Giacomo Barozzi), 1507-1573

Lukomskii, Georgii K. Vignole (Jacopo Barozzi da Vignola). Paris, Vincent, 1927 (Grands architectes).

Willich, Hans. Giacomo Barozzi da Vignola. Strassburg, Heitz, 1906 (Zur kunstgeschichte des auslandes, 44).

## VISCHER family: Peter, 1460-1529; Peter, 1487-1528

Daun, Berthold. P. Vischer und A. Krafft. Bielefeld, Velhagen und Klasing, 1905 (Künstler-monographien, 75).

Meller, Simon. Peter Vischer der ältere und seine werkstatt. Leipzig, Insel-verlag, 1925 (Deutsche meister).

Réau, Louis. Peter Vischer et la sculpture franconienne du XIVe au XVIe siècle. Paris, Plon-Nourrit, 1909 (Maîtres de l'art).

Seeger, Georg. Peter Vischer der jüngere. Leipzig, Seemann, 1897 (Beiträge zur kunstgeschichte, n.f. 23).

## VLAMINCK, Maurice de, 1876-

Kahnweiler, Daniel H. Maurice de Vlaminck. Leipzig, Klinkhardt und Biermann, 1920 (Junge kunst, 11).

Perls, Klaus G. Vlaminck. N. Y., Harper, 1941.

## WATTEAU, Jean Antoine, 1684-1721

Adhémar, Hélène. Watteau, sa vie, son oeuvre. Paris, Tisné, 1950.

Brinckmann, Albert E. J. A. Watteau. Vienna, Schroll, 1943 (Sammlung Schroll).

Dacier, Émile. Jean de Jullienne et les graveurs de Watteau au XVIIIe siècle. Paris, Société pour l'étude de la gravure française, 1921-29. 3 v.

Gillet, Louis. Watteau, un grand maître du XVIIIe siècle. 4e éd. Paris, Plon, 1943.

Lavallée, Pierre. Antoine Watteau, 1684-1721; quatorze dessins. Paris, Musées nationaux, 1939.

Parker, Karl T. The drawings of Antoine Watteau. London, Batsford, 1931.

Zimmermann, Ernest H. Watteau. Stuttgart, Deutsche verlags-anstalt, 1912 (Klassiker der kunst, 21).

**WATTS, George Frederick, 1817–1904**
  Chesterton, Gilbert K. G. F. Watts. N. Y., Dutton, 1909.
  Schleinitz, Otto J. W. George Frederick Watts. Bielefeld, Velhagen und Klasing, 1904 (Künstler-monographien, 73).
  Watts, Mary S. George Frederic Watts. London, Macmillan, 1912. 3 v.

**WEBER, Max, 1881–**
  Cahill, Holger. Max Weber. N. Y., Downtown gallery, 1930.
  Goodrich, Lloyd. Max Weber. N. Y., Whitney museum, 1949.

**WEYDEN, Roger van der, 1400?–1464?**
  Destrée, Jules. Roger de La Pasture van der Weyden. Paris, Van Oest, 1930. 2 v.
  Lafond, Paul. Roger van der Weyden. Brussels, Van Oest, 1912 (Grands artistes des Pays-Bas).
  Renders, Émile. La solution du problème Van der Weyden—Flémalle—Campin. Bruges, Beyaert, 1931. 2 v.
  Winkler, Friedrich. Der meister von Flémalle und Rogier van der Weyden. Strassburg, Heitz, 1913 (Zur kunstgeschichte des auslandes, 103).

**WHISTLER, James Abbot McNeill, 1834–1903**
  Cary, Elisabeth L. The works of James McNeill Whistler. N. Y., Moffat, 1913.
  Duret, Théodore. Whistler. Trans. Frank Rutter. Philadelphia, Lippincott, 1917.
  Kennedy, Edward G. The etched work of Whistler. N. Y., Grolier club, 1910. 4 v.
  Laver, James. Whistler. London, Faber, 1930.
  Pennell, Elizabeth R. The life of James McNeill Whistler. 6th ed. Philadelphia, Lippincott, 1919.
  ——The Whistler journal. Philadelphia, Lippincott, 1921.
  Salaman, Malcolm C. James McNeill Whistler. London, Studio, 1927–32. 2 v. (Modern masters of etching, 13, 32).
  Wedmore, Frederick. Whistler's etchings; a study and a catalogue. 2d ed., rev. and enl. London, Colnaghi, 1899.
  Whistler, James A. M. The gentle art of making enemies, as pleasingly exemplified in many instances. London, Heinemann, 1916.

**WILSON, Richard, 1714-1782**
  Bury, Adrian. Richard Wilson, the grand classic. Leigh-on-Sea [Eng.], Lewis, 1947.
  Ford, Brinsley. The drawings of Richard Wilson. London, Faber, 1950.
**WITZ, Konrad, 1433?-1447**
  Gantner, Joseph. Konrad Witz. 2$^{te}$ aufl. Vienna, Schroll, 1943 (Sammlung Schroll).
  Ganz, Paul L. Meister Konrad Witz von Rottweil. Bern, Urs Graf-verlag, 1947.
  Meng-Koehler, Mathilde. Die bilder des Konrad Witz und ihre quellen: Legenda aurea, Speculum humanae salvationis, Bibel. Basel, Holbein-verlag, 1947 (Ars docta, 9).
**WREN, Christopher, 1632-1723**
  Dirks, Rudolf. Sir Christopher Wren, A.D. 1632-1723; bicentenary memorial volume published under the auspices of the Royal institute of British architects. London, Hodder and Stoughton, 1923.
  Whitaker-Wilson, Cecil. Sir Christopher Wren, his life and times. London, Methuen, 1932.
  Wren, Christopher. Life and works of Sir Christopher Wren; from the Parentalia or memoirs by his son, Christopher. Campden, Gloucestershire, Essex house press, 1903.
**WRIGHT, Frank Lloyd, 1867-**
  Hitchcock, Henry-Russell. In the nature of materials, 1887-1941; the buildings of Frank Lloyd Wright. N. Y., Duell, Sloan, and Pearce, 1942.
  Wright, Frank Lloyd. An autobiography. N. Y., Duell, Sloan, and Pearce, 1943.
  ———Frank Lloyd Wright on architecture; selected writings, 1894-1940. Ed. by Frederick Gutheim. N. Y., Duell, Sloan, and Pearce, 1941.
**ZORACH, William, 1887-**
  Wingert, Paul S. The sculpture of William Zorach. N. Y., Pitman, 1938.
  Zorach, William. Zorach explains sculpture, what it means and how it is made. N. Y., American artists group, 1947.

**ZORN, Anders Leonard, 1860–1920**
 Asplund, Karl. Anders Zorn, his life and work. London, Studio, 1921.
 ——Zorn's engraved work; a descriptive catalogue. Trans. Edward Adams-Ray. Stockholm, Bukowski's konsthandel, 1920.
 Delteil, Loÿs. Anders Zorn. Paris, 1909 (Peintre-graveur illustré, 4).

**ZURBARÁN, Francisco, 1598–1662**
 Calzada, Andrés M. Estampas de Zurbarán. Barcelona, Canosa, 1929.
 Gaya Nuño, Juan A. Zurbarán. Barcelona, Aedos, 1948 (Grandes maestros de la pintura, 6).

# INDEX OF ARTISTS AND AUTHORS

Abbot, Edith R., 39
Abell, Walter, 4
Ackerman, Phyllis, 64
ADAM, Robert, 77
Adams, Adeline V. P., 96, 101
Adams, Henry, 27
Adhémar, Hélène, 137
Adhémar, Jean, 99
Aeschlimann, Erardo, 1
Agard, Walter R., 34
Alazard, Jean, 104
ALBERTI, Leone Battista, 77
Aldred, Cyril, 6
Alexandre, Arsène, 79, 102
Algoud, Henri, 64, 95
Alibert, François P., 122
ALLEGRI, Antonio, see CORREGGIO
Allen, Beverly S., 21
Allende-Salazar, Juan, 135
Allesch, Gustav J. von, 118
ALLSTON, Washington, 77
Alpatov, Mikhail V., 23
ALTDORFER, Albrecht, 77
AMADEO, Giovanni Antonio, 77
American Art Annual, 1
American Art Directory, 1
Ancona, Paolo d', 1, 22, 45, 61
Anderson, Lawrence L., 13
Anderson, William J., 7, 30
Andrae, Walter, 12
ANDREA DEL SARTO, see SARTO, Andrea Del
Angeli, Diego, 115
ANGELICO, Fra (Giovanni da Fiesole), 77-78
Angulo Íniguez, Diego, 135
Antal, Frederick, 46
Anthony, Edgar W., 73
ANTONELLO DA MESSINA, 78
Apollinaire, Guillaume, 42
ARCHIPENKO, Alexander, 78
L'Architecture d'Aujourd'hui, 100

Arents, Prosper, 128
Arms, John T., 52
Armstrong, Walter, 96, 107, 122, 124, 132, 135
Arnold, Hugh, 72
Arnold, Thomas W., 10
ARNOLFO DI CAMBIO, 78
Aronson, Joseph, 67
ARP, Hans, 78
Arslan, Wart, 79
Art Index, 1
Arts, Musées et Curiosité en France, 1
Ashby, Thomas, 14
Ashton, Leigh, 10
Asplund, Karl, 140
Aubert, Marcel, 27, 35, 72
Auquier, Philippe, 122
Avery, Clara L., 74
Ayrton, Michael, 102

Babelon, Jean, 73, 74, 100, 119, 134
Bacci, Pèleo, 122
Bachhofer, Ludwig, 10
Badt, Kurt, 91
Baikie, James, 7
Baker, Charles H. C., 45, 48, 89, 108
Balcarres, Lord, see Crawford, David A. E. L.
Baldass, Ludwig von, 81, 110, 113
Baldinucci, Filippo, 80
BALDOVINETTI, Alesso, 78
Baldry, Alfred L., 114
BALDUNG, Hans, 78
BARBARI, Jacopo de', 78
Barber, Edwin A., 70-71
Barbier de Montault, Xavier, 3
Bargellini, Piero, 97, 100
Barker, Virgil, 50
BARLACH, Ernst, 78
Barocchi, Paola, 127
BAROCCI, Federigo, 79
Baroni, Costantino, 37, 82

141

Barr, Alfred H., 25, 39, 47, 119
BARTOLOMMEO, Fra, 79
Bartsch, Adam von, 52
BARYE, Antoine Louis, 79
Baschet, Jacques, 64
BASSANO, Jacopo (Giacomo da Ponte), 79
Bassi, Elena, 84
Baudi di Vesme, Alessandro, 52
Bauer, Catherine, 26
Baum, Julius, 14, 28, 30, 130
Baur, John I. H., 25
Baxter, Sylvester, 32
BAYER, Herbert, 79
Bayley, Frank W., 87
Bazin, Germain, 88, 113
Beard, Alice, 73
BEAUX, Cecilia, 79
Beazley, John D., 7
Becherucci, Luisa, 121
Becker, Felix, 2, 52
Becker, Hanna L., 77
Beckett, Ronald B., 102, 108
Beenken, Hermann T., 20, 35, 94
Beets, Nicholaas, 110
Behne, Adolf B., 52
Behrendt, Walter C., 26
Bell, Clive, 4, 39, 42
Bell, Edward, 26
Bell, Malcolm, 74, 83
BELLINI, Gentile, 79
BELLINI, Giovanni, 79
BELLINI, Jacopo, 80
BELLOWS, George Wesley, 80
Benavides Rodríguez, Alfredo, 33
BENEDETTO DA MAIANO, 80
Bénédite, Léonce, 86, 115
Benesch, Otto, 17, 52, 77, 123
Bénézit, Emmanuel, 1
Benkard, Ernst, 84, 130
Benoist, Luc, 35
BENTON, Thomas Hart, 80
Benz, Richard E., 20
Berchem, Marguerite van, 73

Bercken, Erich von der, 134
Berenson, Bernhard, 4, 46, 52, 110, 130
Berger, Klaus, 52, 97
Berliner, Rudolf, 63
BERNARD, Joseph, 80
BERNINI, Giovanni Lorenzo, 80
Bersier, Jean E., 52
Beruete y Moret, Aureliano de, 49, 99
Besnard, Albert, 107
Besson, George, 131
Bettini, Sergio, 79
Bevan, Bernard, 31
Biagi, Luigi, 110, 122
Biddle, Edward, 133
BIDDLE, George, 80
Biehl, Walter, 37
Bier, Justus, 125
Bigelow, Francis H., 74
Binyon, Laurence, 10, 45, 81, 98
Bird, Paul, 106
Blake, Peter, 82
Blake, Vernon, 52
BLAKE, William, 81
Blanc, Charles, 136
Blanc, Louis, 74
Bliss, Douglas P., 52
Blomfield, Reginald T., 28, 29
Blum, André, 52, 61, 123
Blunt, Anthony, 22, 52, 111
Boas, Franz, 6
Boas, George, 89
Bock, Elfried, 52–53, 54
Bode, Wilhelm von, 22, 37, 48, 67, 81, 83
Bodkin, Thomas, 136
Bodmer, Heinrich, 85, 88, 109
Boeck, Wilhelm, 135
Boehn, Max von, 39, 66, 80, 124
Boinet, Amédée, 61
BOLOGNA, Giovanni, 81
Bolton, Arthur T., 131
Bombe, Walter, 118
Bond, Francis, 29

BONINGTON, Richard Parkes, 81
Borenius, Tancred, 45, 46, 123
Born, Wolfgang, 50
Borovka, Grigorii I., 10
BORROMINI, Francesco, 81
BOSCH, Hieronymus van Aken, 81
Bossert, Helmuth T., 7, 63
Bottari, Stefano, 78
BOTTICELLI, Sandro, 81–82
BOUCHER, François, 82
Bouchot-Saupique, Jacqueline, 84, 100
BOURDELLE, Émile Antoine, 82
BOUTS, Dirck, 82
Bovy, Adrien, 50
Boyer d'Agen, Jean A. B., 113
Brackett, Oliver, 67, 70
Bradley, Morton C., 39
BRAMANTE, Donato, 82
Brandi, Cesare, 46, 98
BRAQUE, Georges, 82
Brauer, Heinrich, 80
Braun, Joseph, 74
Bredius, Abraham, 123
Breeskin, Adelyn D., 85
Bréhier, Louis, 3, 14, 19
Breton, André, 18
BREUER, Marcel, 82
Breuning, Margaret, 122
Brière, Gaston, 35
Briggs, Martin S., 26
Brinckmann, Albert E., 17, 30, 34, 137
Briquet, Charles M., 1
Brizio, Anna M., 18
Brockwell, Maurice W., 94
Bronstein, Leo, 100
BRONZINO, Agnolo (Angelo Allori), 82
Brooke, Iris, 66
Brooks, Charles M., 98
Broulhiet, Georges, 102
BROUWER, Adrian, 83
Brown, Bolton, 53
Brown, Gerard B., 21, 102

Brown, Percy, 10
Brownell, Baker, 26
Brownell, William C., 19
BRUEGHEL, Jan, 83
BRUEGHEL, Peeter, 83
Bruhn, Wolfgang, 66
Bruhns, Leo, 83
BRUNELLESCHI, Filippo, 83
Brunov, Nikolai I., 23
Bryan, Michael, 1
Buchanan, Donald W., 50
Buckley, Wilfred, 72
BULFINCH, Charles, 83
Bunim, Miriam S., 14
Bunt, Cyril G. E., 23
BUONARROTI, see MICHELANGELO
BURCHFIELD, Charles, 83
Burckhardt, Jakob C., 22, 128
Burger, Fritz, 44, 107, 118
BURGKMAIR, Hans, 83
Burkhard, Arthur, 83, 101
BURNE-JONES, Edward, 83–84
Burne,-Jones, Georgiana M., 85
BURNHAM, Daniel Hudson, 84
Burr, Grace H., 67
Burroughs, Alan, 50, 114
Burton, William, 71
Bury, Adrian, 139
Buscaroli, Rezio, 113
Buschiazzo, Mario J., 33
Buschor, Ernst, 7
Bushell, Stephen W., 10
Butler, Howard C., 14
Buxton, David R., 31
Byne, Arthur, 67, 74
Byron, Robert, 15

Cabrol, Fernand, 3
Caflisch, Nina, 110
Cahill, Holger, 25, 138
Caillaux, Henriette, 89
Calabi, Augusto, 53
CALLOT, Jacques, 84

Calmette, Joseph L. A., 128
Calvert, Albert F., 116
Calzada, Andrés M., 140
Camón Aznar, José, 33, 100
CANALE, Antonio (Canaletto), 84
CANOVA, Antonio, 84
Cantinelli, Richard, 80, 90
Canuti, Fiorenzo, 118
Capart, Jean, 6
CARAVAGGIO, Michelangelo (Michelangelo Merisi), 84
Carli, Enzo, 113, 134
CARPACCIO, Vittore, 84
CARPEAUX, Jean Baptiste, 84–85
Carpenter, Rhys, 7
CARRACCI, Agostino, 85
CARRACCI, Annibale, 85
CARRACCI, Ludovico, 85
Carré, Louis, 74
CARRIÈRE, Eugène, 85
Carrington, Fitz Roy, 53
Cary, Elisabeth L., 116, 127, 138
CASSATT, Mary, 85
Casson, Stanley, 7, 34
Cassou, Jean, 91, 104
CASTAGNO, Andrea, 85
CASTELFRANCO, Giorgione da, see GIORGIONE
Cattaneo, Irene, 126
Cavalcaselle, Giovanni B., 46
Cazalis, Henry, 123
Cecchi, Emilio, 46, 92, 98, 110
CELLINI, Benvenuto, 85–86
Cendali, Lorenzo, 80
Cennini, Cennino, 39
Cescinsky, Herbert, 68
CÉZANNE, Paul, 86
Chaffers, William, 71, 75
CHAGALL, Marc, 86
Chamberlain, Arthur B., 103, 126
Chambers, Frank P., 4
Chamot, Mary, 73
CHARDIN, Jean Baptiste Siméon, 86
Charteris, Evan E., 129

Chase, George H., 34
CHASSÉRIAU, Théodore, 86
Cheney, Martha C., 50
Cheney, Sheldon, 4, 18, 26, 39
Chesterton, Gilbert K., 138
Childe, Vere G., 6
CHIRICO, Giorgio de, 87
Chisholm, Hugh J., 7
Christ-Janer, Albert, 129
Christie, Archibald H., 63
Christie, Grace, 64
Christoffel, Ulrich, 20
Churchill, Sidney J. A., 75
CIMABUE, Giovanni, 87
Cladel, Judith, 126
Clapham, Alfred W., 26, 29
Clapp, Frederick M., 121
Clark, George N., 17
Clark, Kenneth M., 26, 39, 95, 109
CLAUDE LORRAIN (Claude Gellée), 87
Clausse, Gustave, 129
Clemen, Paul, 20, 22
Clément, Charles, 97, 98
Clément-Carpeaux, Louise, 84
CLOUET, François, 87
CLOUET, Jean, 87
Clouzot, Étienne, 73
Clouzot, Henri, 64, 75
Codrington, Kenneth de B., 11
Cogniat, Raymond, 53, 96
Cohn, William, 11
Colacicchi, Giovanni, 121
Colas, René, 28, 66
Colasanti, Arduino, 96
Coletti, Luigi, 134
Colgate, William G., 25
Colin, Paul, 53
Collins Baker, C. H., see Baker, Charles H. C.
Collison-Morley, Lacy, 22
COLOMBE, Michel, 87
Combe, Jacques, 81
Connick, Charles J., 72

CONSTABLE, John, 87
Constable, William G., 45
Contenau, Georges, 6
Conway, William M., 23, 92, 94, 97
Cook, Dorothy E., 67
Cook, Herbert F., 97
Cook, Ruth V., 100
Coomaraswamy, Ananda K., 11
Cooper, Douglas, 108
COPLEY, John Singleton, 87–88
Coquiot, Gustave, 124, 134
Cornelius, Charles O., 68
Cornette, Arthur J. H., 48
COROT, Jean Baptiste Camille, 88
CORREGGIO, Antonio Allegri, 88
Cortissoz, Royal, 90, 102, 107, 129, 133
Costa Torres, Raul, 33
Costantini, Vincenzo, 22
COTMAN, John Sell, 88
Cotterell, Howard H., 75
COURBET, Gustave, 89
Courboin, François, 53
Courthion, Pierre, 87, 89, 90, 91, 93, 104, 127
Cowdrey, Bartlett, 116
Cox, John C., 29
Cox, Trenchard, 17, 95
Cox, Warren E., 71
CRANACH, Lucas, 89
Craven, Thomas, 18, 39, 53
Crawford, David A. E. L., 37, 92
Cresson, Margaret F., 96
Cripps, Wilfred J., 75
CRIVELLI, Carlo, 89
Croce, Benedetto, 4
CROME, John, 89
Cronin, William V., 124
Crossley, Frederick H., 36
Crowe, Joseph A., 46
Cruttwell, Maud, 112, 121, 125, 131, 136
Cumming, David, 53
Cummings, Charles A., 30
Cundall, Joseph, 53

Cunynghame, Henry H., 73
Curchin, Milan, 113
Curjel, Hans, 78
Cursiter, Stanley, 45
Curtis, Atherton, 81
Cust, Anna M. E., 73
Cust, Lionel H., 93
Cust, Robert H. H., 132

Dacier, Émile, 53, 129, 137
DALI, Salvador, 89
DALOU, Aimé Jules, 89
Dalton, Ormonde M., 15
Damon, Samuel F., 81
Daremberg, Charles V., 8
Dark, Sidney, 117
DAUBIGNY, Charles François, 89
DAUMIER, Honoré, 90
Daun, Berthold, 132, 137
Daux, Georges, 8
Davenport, Cyril J. H., 39, 53
Davenport, Millia, 66
DAVID, Jacques Louis, 90
DAVID D'ANGERS, Pierre Jean, 90
DAVIES, Arthur Bowen, 90
Davies, Gerald S., 101
Davies, Randall, 98
DAVIS, Stuart, 90
Dawson, Nelson, 75
Day, Lewis F., 72
Dayot, Armand P. M., 86, 136
DEGAS, Edgar, 91
Degenhart, Bernhard, 53, 120
Dehio, Georg G., 20, 28
Deknatel, Frederick B., 116
Delacre, Maurice, 53, 93, 113
DELACROIX, Eugène, 91, 105
Delen, Adrien J. J., 53
Delogu, Giuseppe, 30, 37, 46, 53, 113
Delteil, Loÿs, 53–54, 88, 89, 90, 91, 97, 99, 105, 134, 140
Demotte, G. J., 64
Demus, Otto, 15, 73
DEMUTH, Charles Henry, 91

145

Denis, Maurice, 111
Denucé, Jean, 83
Deonna, Waldemar, 8, 36
DERAIN, André, 92
Deschamps, Paul, 35
Deshoulières, François, 28
DESIDERIO DA SETTIGNANO, 92
Desjardins, Abel, 81
Desparmet Fitz-Gerald, Xavière, 99
Destrée, Joseph, 98
Destrée, Jules, 123, 138
De Tolnay, Charles, 54, 81, 83, 94, 114
Dewald, Ernest T., 110
Dewey, John, 4
Dickins, Guy, 8
Dickinson, Goldsworthy, 8
Dickinson, Helena A. S., 44
Didron, Adolphe N., 3
Diehl, Charles, 15
Dieterle, Jean, 88
Dieulafoy, Marcel A., 24
Diez, Ernst, 11, 15
Dilke, Emilia F. S., 54, 68
Dilley, Arthur U., 64
Dillon, Edward, 71, 72
Dimier, Louis, 42, 54, 122
Dinsmoor, William B., 7
Dirks, Rudolf, 139
Dobson, Austin, 102
Dodgson, Campbell, 54, 92
Doehring, Heinrich, 14
Doering, Oskar, 20
Dörner, Max, 39
Dörries, Bernhard, 54
DOMENICHINO (Domenico Zampieri), 92
Domínguez Bordona, Jesús, 61
DONATELLO (Donato di Niccolo di Betto Bardi), 92
Donati, Lamberto, 54
Dorbec, Prosper, 127
Dorival, Bernard, 42–43, 86
Dorner, Alexander, 79
DOU, Gerard, 92

Douglas, Frederic H., 13
Douglas, Robert L., 77, 109, 119
Downes, William H., 103, 129
Drake, Maurice, 3, 72
Drepperd, Carl W., 25
Drey, Franz, 89
Dreyfous, Maurice, 89
Dreyfus, Carle, 68
Drioton, Étienne, 6
Drost, Willi, 44, 94
Drucker, Michel, 124
Du Bois, Guy P., 104, 131
Dubray, Jean P., 85
Dubuisson, A., 81
Ducati, Pericle, 8
DUCCIO DI BUONINSEGNA, 92
Du Colombier, Pierre, 19, 99
DÜRER, Albrecht, 92–93
DUFY, Raoul, 93
Dunlap, William, 25
Duret, Théodore, 89, 98, 111, 124, 138
Durrieu, Paul, 61
Dussler, Luitpold, 54, 79, 80, 120, 131
DYCK, Anthony van, 93

EAKINS, Thomas, 94
Earle, Alice M., 67
Eastlake, Charles L., 39
Eberlein, Harold D., 32, 68, 71
Ebersolt, Jean, 15, 61
Ede, Harold S., 54
Edgell, George H., 26, 32, 46
Édouard-Joseph, René, 1
Edwards, Ralph, 69, 70
Eggers, George W., 80
Einstein, Carl, 18, 82
ELSHEIMER, Adam, 94
Elst, Joseph J. M. I. van der, 48
Emmons, Robert, 131
Encyclopédie Photographique de l'Art, 4
Enlart, Camille, 19
Ensko, Stephen G. C., 75
EPSTEIN, Jacob, 94

ERNST, Max, 94
Erréra, Isabelle, 1
Escherich, Mela, 78, 101
Escholier, Raymond, 43, 90, 91, 100
Esdaile, Katharine A. M., 36, 127
Estrada, Genaro, 99
Evans, Joan, 19, 21, 28, 63
Evans, Ralph M., 39
Evers, Hans G., 128
EYCK, Hubert van, 94
EYCK, Jan van, 94

Fabriczy, Cornelius von, 75
FALCONET, Étienne Maurice, 94
Falke, Otto von, 64, 68
FANTIN-LATOUR, Ignace Henri Jean Théodore, 94
Fantin-Latour, Victoria D., 94
Farbman, Michael S., 49
Fasola, Giustina N., 95, 120
Faure, Élie, 4, 85, 92, 112
Fechter, Paul, 78
FEKE, Robert, 95
Félibien, André, 121
Félice, Roger de, 68
Fels, Marthe de, 115
Fenaille, Maurice, 64
Fenollosa, Ernest F., 11
Ferguson, John C., 11
Fergusson, James, 11
Fergusson, John D., 45
Fernández, Justino, 117
Ferrari, Giulio, 75
Feulner, Adolf, 36, 68
Ffoulkes, Constance J., 95
Fielding, Mantle, 1, 54, 133
Fierens, Paul, 22, 48, 108
Fierens-Gevaert, Hippolyte, 48, 105
Figgis, Darrell, 81
Filov, Bogdan D., 23
Finberg, Alexander J., 135
FINIGUERRA, Tommaso, 95
Fiocco, Giuseppe, 46, 84, 97, 101, 112, 136

Fischel, Oskar, 54, 122, 134
Fischer, Otto, 11, 44
Flechsig, Eduard, 92
Flemming, Ernst R., 64
Fletcher, Banister F., 26
Flexner, James T., 50, 88
Florisoone, Michel, 43, 111
Focillon, Henri, 4, 15, 34, 43
Fokker, Timon H., 17
Folnesics, Hans, 83
Fontaine, Georges, 71
Foote, Henry W., 95, 131
FOPPA, Vincenzo, 95
Foratti, Aldo, 84, 85
Ford, Brinsley, 139
Forrer, Leonard, 75
Foster, Joshua J., 39
FOUQUET, Jean, 95
Fourcard, Louis de, 128
Fourreau, Armand, 116
Fowler, Harold N., 8
Fraenckel, Ingeborg, 129
FRAGONARD, Jean Honoré, 95
Francastel, Pierre, 98
FRANCESCHI, Pietro di Benedetto dei, 95
FRANCESCO DI GIORGIO MARTINI, 96
Frank, Edgar B., 75
Frary, Ihna T., 105
Freedberg, Sydney J., 118
FRENCH, Daniel Chester, 96
French, Hollis, 75
French, Mary F., 96
Frey, Carl, 114
Frey, Dagobert, 17, 30, 82
Friedländer, Max J., 39, 48, 54, 77, 83, 89, 93, 110
Friedlaender, Walter F., 87, 121
Fröhlich-Bum, Lili, 105, 118
Fromentin, Eugène, 48
Fry, Roger E., 4, 11, 21, 86, 112
Fuchs, Eduard, 90
Furness, S. M. M., 107

Furst, Herbert, 54
Furtwängler, Adolf, 8
Furumark, Arne, 71

Gabelentz, Hans von der, 79
Gadd, Cyril J., 6
Gaillard, Émile, 129
Gaillard, Georges, 37
GAINSBOROUGH, Thomas, 96
Galassi, Giuseppe, 37
Gamba, Carlo, 79, 82
Gantner, Joseph, 139
Ganz, Paul, 54, 103, 139
Gardner, Alfred H., 29
Gardner, Arthur, 28, 35, 36
Gardner, Ernest A., 8
Gardner, Helen, 4
Gardner, John S., 75
Gardner, Percy, 8
Garner, Thomas, 29
Garnier, Édouard, 72
Garrison, Edward B., 46
Garrison, J. J., 5
Garzarolli-Thurnlackh, Karl, 54
Gascoyne, David, 18
GAUGUIN, Paul, 96
Gaunt, William, 18
Gauss, Charles E., 43
Gaya Nuño, Juan A., 24, 140
Geffroy, Gustave, 115
Geiger, Benno, 54, 111
Geisberg, Max, 54
Geiser, Bernhard, 119
Gengaro, Mario L., 17
Gensel, Walther, 136
GENTILE DA FABRIANO, 96
George, Waldemar, 55
GÉRICAULT, Jean Louis André Théodore, 97
Germain, Alphonse, 87
GÉRÔME, Jean Léon, 97
Gerson, Horst, 106
Gerstenberg, Kurt, 125

Gerstinger, Hans, 61
Gettens, Rutherford J., 40
GHIBERTI, Lorenzo, 97
GHIRLANDAIO, Domenico, 97
Giacometti, Georges, 104
Giedion, Sigfried, 26
Giedion-Welcker, C., 34
Gielly, Louis J., 122
Giesecke, Albert, 120
Gilchrist, Agnes E. A., 132
Giles, Herbert A., 11
GILL, Eric, 97
Gillet, Louis, 137
GIORGIONE DA CASTELFRANCO (Giorgio Barbarelli), 97
GIOTTO DI BONDONE, 98
GIOVANNI DA BOLOGNA, see BOLOGNA, Giovanni da
GIOVANNI DI PAOLO, 98
GIRARDON, François, 98
GIRTIN, Thomas, 98
Gischia, Léon, 20
Gissing, Alfred C., 104
Glaser, Curt, 44, 55, 89, 103, 116
Glazier, Richard, 63, 64
Gleizes, Albert, 18
GLEYRE, Marc Charles Gabriel, 98
Glück, Gustav, 18, 83, 93, 128
Glück, Heinrich, 11
Godefroy, Louis, 117
Godfrey, Walter H., 29
Göbel, Heinrich, 64
Goering, Max, 44, 46, 101
GOES, Hugo van der, 98
GOGH, Vincent van, 98-99
Goldscheider, Ludwig, 4, 8, 79, 92, 97, 99, 100, 109, 114
Goldschmidt, Adolph, 61, 73
Goldsmith, Elizabeth E., 3
Goldwater, Robert J., 4, 40
Gombosi, György, 116, 118, 132
Gombrich, E. H., 4
Gómez-Moreno, Manuel, 31

Gómez Sicre, José, 55
Goncourt, Edmond L. A. H. de, 43, 122
Goodrich, Lloyd, 94, 103, 104, 114, 138
Goodwin, Philip L., 33
Goris, Jan-A., 128
Gotch, John A., 29, 105
GOUJON, JEAN, 99
Gower, Ronald C. S., 96, 107, 126
GOYA Y LUCIENTES, Francisco José de, 99–100
GOZZOLI, Benozzo, 100
Grabar, André, 15
Gradmann, Erwin, 50, 55
Grappe, Georges, 95, 126
Grassi, Luigi, 80
Graves, Algernon, 124
Gray, Basil, 10, 55
GRECO, El (Domenico Theotocopuli), 100
Greenberg, Clement, 115
Greene, Theodore M., 4
GREUZE, Jean Baptiste, 100
Grey, Roch, 127
GRIS, Juan, 100
Grodecki, Louis, 74
Grohman, Will, 105, 106
Gromort, Georges, 30
Gronau, Georg, 79, 88
GROPIUS, Walter, 100
GROS, Antoine Jean, 100–101
Gros, Gabriel J., 135
GROSZ, George, 101
Grousset, René, 11
GRÜNEWALD, Mathias, 101
GUARDI, Francesco, 101
Gudiol Ricart, José, 24, 99, 104
GUERCINO, Il (Giovanni Francesco Barbieri), 101
Guérin, Marcel, 96, 111
Guiffrey, Jean, 122
Guiffrey, Jules M. J., 64, 108

Guinness, H., 130

Haack, Friedrich, 19
Habich, Georg, 75
Hackin, Joseph, 11
Hadeln, Detlev von, 55, 84, 134
Hagen, Oskar F. L., 5, 20, 24, 50, 55, 101
Hale, Philip L., 136
Hall, H. Van, 1
Hall, Harry R. H., 8
Hallays, André, 118
Halm, Philipp M., 36
HALS, Frans, 101
Hamann, Richard, 44, 123
Hamerton, Philip G., 55
Hamlin, Alfred D. F., 63
Hamlin, Talbot F., 26, 32
Handcock, Percy S. P., 6
Hannover, Emil, 23, 71
Harcourt-Smith, Simon, 6
Harnoncourt, René d', 13
Harris, Enriqueta, 49
Hart, Charles H., 133
Harvey, John D. M., 29
Harvey, John H., 15
Haseloff, Arthur E. G., 37
HASSAM, Childe, 101–102
Hausenstein, Wilhelm, 84, 90, 98
Hauser, Arnold, 5
Hautecoeur, Louis, 28, 99, 107
Hauttmann, Max, 15
Hauvette, Henri, 132
Havard, Henry, 68
Havell, Ernest B., 11
Hawley, Walter A., 65
Hayden, Arthur, 55
Hayes, Bartlett H., 41
Hayter, Stanley W., 55
Head, Barclay V., 8
Heath, Dudley, 40
HEEMSKERK, Martin van, 102
Hegemann, Hans W., 134

Hekler, Antal, 8
Held, Julius S., 128
Helm, MacKinley, 13, 112
Hempel, Eberhard, 28, 81, 118
Hendy, Philip, 79
Henkel, Max D., 55
HENRI, Robert, 102
Henry, Françoise, 15
Herbert, John A., 61
Hermanin, Federico, 120
Herzfeld, Ernst E., 11
Hill, George F., 75, 120
Hind, Arthur M., 55, 102, 112, 120, 123
Hind, Charles L., 129
Hinks, Roger P., 15
Hitchcock, Henry-Russell, 26, 32, 125, 139
HOBBEMA, Meindert, 102
Hobson, Robert L., 12, 71
Höver, Otto, 76
Hoff, August, 108
HOFFMAN, Malvina Cornell, 102
Hoffmann, Edith, 106
Hofmann, Friedrich H., 71
Hofstede de Groot, Cornelis, 48, 123
HOGARTH, William, 102
HOLBEIN, Hans, 103
Holloway, Edward S., 68
Hollstein, F. W. H., 55
Holman, Louis A., 55
Holme, Bryan, 56
Holme, Charles, 23, 56
Holme, Geoffrey, 23, 56
Holmes, Charles J., 40, 87
Holt, Elizabeth B. G., 1
Holt, Rosa B., 65
HOMER, Winslow, 103
Honey, William B., 12, 71, 72
HOOCH, Pieter de, 104
Hoogewerff, Godfried J., 130
Hope, Henry R., 82
HOPPER, Edward, 104
Hoppin, Joseph C., 8

HOPPNER, JOHN, 104
Horne, Herbert P., 82
HOUDON, Jean Antoine, 104
Hourticq, Louis, 20
Houston, Mary G., 67
Hubbard, Eric H., 40, 56
Hubert, Jean, 15
Hudnut, Joseph, 26
Huelsen, Christian, 102
Huerlimann, Martin, 101
Hugelshofer, Walter, 56
HUGUET, Jaime, 104
HUISH, Marcus B., 8
Huizinga, Johan, 15
HUNT, William Holman, 104
Hunter, George L., 65, 68, 69
Huntley, George Haydn, 129
Huxley, Aldous L., 99
Huyghe, René, 19, 43, 56

Industrial Arts Index, 1
Ingersoll-Smouse, Florence, 118, 136
INGRES, Jean Auguste Dominique, 104–105
INNESS, George, 105
Internationale Bibliographie der Kunstwissenschaft, 2
Isham, Samuel, 50
Ivins, William M., 56

Jackson, Charles J., 76
Jackson, Thomas G., 15
Jacobsthal, Paul, 15
Jacobus de Varagine, 3
JACOPO DELLA QUERCIA, see QUERCIA
James, Macgill, 51
James, William, 25
Jameson, Anna B., 3
Jamot, Paul, 43, 107, 108, 111, 121
Janis, Sidney, 50
Janneau, Guillaume, 72
Jantzen, Hans, 36
JEANNERET-GRIS, Charles E., see LE CORBUSIER

Jedlicka, Gothard, 50, 83, 134
JEFFERSON, Thomas, 105
Jewell, Edward A., 43, 127
Johnson, Ada M., 76
Johnson, Charles, 40, 45
Johnson, Philip C., 114
Johnston, Edward, 61
Jones, Edward A., 76
JONES, Inigo, 105
Jones, Owen, 63
JONGKIND, Johan Barthold, 105
JORDAENS, Jakob, 105
Jouin, Henry, 90
Jourdain, Margaret, 69
Joyant, Maurice, 135
Joyce, Thomas A., 13
Jullian, René, 37
Jullien, Adolphe, 94
Justi, Ludwig, 97, 106

Kahn, Gustave, 82, 130
Kahnweiler, Daniel H., 40, 100, 119, 137
Kallen, Horace M., 5
KANDINSKY, Wassily, 105–106
Karlinger, Hans, 15
Kates, George N., 69
Kelemen, Pál, 13
Keller, Harald, 120
Kelly, Francis M., 67
Kendrick, Albert F., 65
Kendrick, Thomas D., 21
Kennedy, Edward G., 138
Kennedy, Ruth W., 78
Kent, Norman, 56
Kent, William W., 119
Kepes, Gyorgy, 5
Kerfoot, John B., 76
Kettell, Russell H., 69
Key, Sydney J., 87
Keynes, Geoffrey L., 81
Kidder, Alfred V., 13
Kilham, Walter H., 33
Killanin, Michael M., 106

Kimball, Sidney Fiske, 18, 26, 32, 51, 105, 110
Kitson, Sydney D., 88
Kitzinger, Ernst, 16
KLEE, Paul, 106
Kleinclausz, Arthur J., 131
Knackfuss, Hermann, 21, 93
Knapp, Fritz, 112, 114, 119, 130
KNELLER, Godfrey, 106
Knittle, Rhea M., 73
Koch, Carl, 78
Koechlin, Raymond, 74
Koegler, Hans, 103
Köhler, Wilhelm R. W., 61
KOKOSCHKA, Oscar, 106
KOLBE, Georg, 106
KOLLWITZ, Käthe Schmidt, 106
Kondakov, Nikodim P., 16, 49
KONINCK, Philips de, 106
Konody, Paul G., 117
Koop, Albert J., 12
Kouwenhoven, John A., 25
Kowalczyk, Georg, 34
Kramrisch, Stella, 12
Kriegbaum, Friedrich, 114
Kristeller, Paul, 56
Krommes, Rudolf H., 79
Kubler, George, 33
Kühnel, Ernst, 66
Künstle, Karl, 3
Kuhn, Alfred, 34
KUHN, Walt, 106
KULMBACH, Hans Suess von, 107
Kuo, Hsi, 12
Kurth, Betty, 65
Kurth, Willi, 93
Kurz, Otto, 2
Kusenberg, Kurt, 127

Ladendorf, Heinz, 130
La Faille, J. Bernard de, 99
LA FARGE, John, 107
La Follette, Suzanne, 25
Lafond, Paul, 91, 125, 138

Lafuente Ferrari, Enrique, 49, 136
Lamb, Winifred, 8
Lambert, Élie, 24
Lambotte, Paul, 48
Lampérez y Romea, Vincente, 31
Lancour, Adlore H., 2
LANCRET, Nicolas, 107
Landsberger, Franz, 18
Lane, Arthur, 71
Lantier, Raymond, 20
Lapauze, Henry, 105, 107
Laprade, Jacques de, 130
Laran, Jean, 85, 122
Larkin, Oliver W., 25
Lasteyrie du Saillant, Robert C., 28
LA TOUR, Georges Dumésnil de, 107
LATOUR, Henri Fantin, see FANTIN-LATOUR, Henri
LA TOUR, Maurice Quentin de, 107
Lauer, Philippe, 61
Laufer, Berthold, 12, 71
Laughlin, Ledlie I., 76
LAURANA, Francesco, 107
Laurie, Arthur P., 40
Laurin, Carl G. J., 24
Lauts, Jan, 78, 97
Lavagnino, Emilio, 22
Lavallée, Pierre, 53, 56, 82, 91, 95, 117, 137
Lavedan, Pierre, 28
Laver, James, 56, 67, 138
Lawrence, Arnold W., 8
LAWRENCE, THOMAS, 107
Leach, Bernard, 71
Le Bas, Georges, 85
LE BRUN, Marie Louise Élisabeth Vigée, 107–108
Leclère, Tristan, 126
Lecomte, Georges C., 85
LE CORBUSIER (Charles Édouard Jeanneret-Gris), 108
Lees-Milne, James, 77
Lefrançois, Louise P., 20, 35
Léger, Charles, 89

LÉGER, Fernand, 108
Lehmann, Walter, 14
LEHMBRUCK, Wilhelm, 108
Lehnert, Georg H., 63
Lehrs, Max, 56
Leipnik, F. L., 57
Lejard, André, 65
LELY, Peter, 108
Lemann, Bernard, 90
Lemoisne, Paul A., 43, 91
Lemonnier, Camille, 113
Lemonnier, Henry, 20, 101
LE NAIN, Antoine, 108
LE NAIN, Louis, 108
LE NAIN, Mathieu, 108
LE NÔTRE, ANDRÉ, 108
LEONARDO DA VINCI, 109
Leporini, Heinrich, 57
Leroy, Alfred, 43, 103
LESCAZE, William, 109
Leslie, Charles R., 87
Lethaby, W. R., 16
Leurs, Stan, 22
Lewis, George G., 65
Leymarie, Jean, 81
Liebreich, Aenne, 131
Lieure, J., 84
Lilienfein, Heinrich, 89
Lindblom, Andreas A. F., 49
Lipman, Jean H., 51
LIPPI, Filippino, 109–110
LIPPI, Filippo, 110
Lippmann, Friedrich, 57, 93
Litchfield, Frederick, 69, 72
Little, Frances, 65
Lloyd, Nathaniel, 30
Lockwood, Luke V., 69
Locquin, Jean, 117
London, Kurt, 23
London, Royal Academy of Arts, 21, 22, 23
Long, Basil S., 76
Longhi, Roberto, 46, 95
Longhurst, Margaret H., 74

Loran, Erle, 86
Lorenz, Paul, 82
LORENZETTI, Pietro, 110
LOTTO, Lorenzo, 110
Lowrie, Walter, 16
Lozowick, Louis, 57
Lozoya, Juan C., 24
Lucas, Alfred, 6
LUCAS VAN LEYDEN, 110
Luckiesh, Matthew, 40
Lüthgen, Eugen, 36
Lugt, Frits, 2, 57
LUINI, Bernardino, 110
Lukomskii, Georgii K., 49, 136, 137
Lumsden, Ernest S., 57
Lurçat, Jean, 65
Luthmer, Ferdinand, 69
Lutze, Eberhard, 132

Mabbott, Maureen C., 109
Mabee, Carleton, 116
McCausland, Elizabeth, 105
McClellan, Elisabeth, 67
McClure, Abbot, 68
McComb, Arthur K., 46, 82
McCurdy, Edward, 109
Macdonald, George, 8
McInnes, Graham, 25
MACINTIRE, Samuel, 110
Mack, Gerstle, 86, 135
Mackail, John W., 116
McKay, William, 104
McKearin, George S., 73
McKearin, Helen, 73
Mackenzie, Donald A., 3
McKIM, Charles Follen, 110
McKinney, Roland J., 94
Maclagan, Eric R. D., 37
McMahon, Amos P., 25
Macquoid, Percy, 69
MADERNO, Carlo, 110–111
MAES, Nicolaes, 111
MAGNASCO, Alessandro, 111
Magni, Giulio, 18

Mahon, Denis, 18
Mahr, Adolf, 16
Maillard, Élisa, 104
MAILLOL, Aristide Joseph Bonaventure, 111
Maiocchi, Rodolfo, 95
Major, Howard, 32
Malaguzzi-Valeri, Francesco, 77, 124
Mâle, Émile, 3
Malingue, Maurice, 96, 105, 115
Mallett, Daniel T., 2
Malraux, André, 5, 99
Mancini, Girolamo, 77
Mander, Carel van, 48
MANET, Édouard, 111
MANSART, François, 111
MANSHIP, Paul, 112
MANTEGNA, Andrea, 112
Marceau, Henri, 128
March, Benjamin, 72
Marchini, Giuseppe, 129
Maret, Jacques, 90
Mariani, Valerio, 78
Marillier, Henry C., 127
MARIN, John, 112
Markham, Violet R., 20
Marle, Raimond van, 16, 47, 112
Marquand, Allan, 125–126
Marquet de Vasselot, Jean J., 65, 74
Martin, Fredrik R., 12, 65
Martin, Henry M. R., 61
Martin, Kurt, 78
Martin, Wilhelm, 92
MARTINI, Simone, 112
Marx, Roger, 123
Maryon, Herbert, 34
MASACCIO (Tommaso Guidi), 112
Masai, François, 61
Maskell, Alfred, 34, 74
MASOLINO DA PANICALE (Tommaso Fini), 112
Maspero, Gaston C. C., 6
Mather, Frank J., 25, 40, 47
MATISSE, Henri, 112–113

Matthey, Werner von, 23
Mattingly, Harold, 9
Mauclair, Camille, 100, 135
Mauricheau-Beaupré, Charles, 20
Maurois, André, 90
Maxwell, Herbert E., 126
Mayer, August L., 37, 49, 57, 99, 100, 116, 125, 136
Mayer, Ralph, 40
Mayne, Jonathan, 98
MAZZOLA, Francesco, see PARMIGIANINO
Meder, Joseph, 57, 93
Meier-Graefe, Julius, 19, 99, 124
Mellaart, J. H. J., 57
Meller, Simon, 137
Mellerio, André, 123
Mellquist, Jerome, 25
MELOZZO DA FORLI, 113
MEMLING, Hans, 113
MENDELSOHN, Erich, 113
Meng-Koehler, Mathilde, 139
Merin, Peter, 21
Merrifield, Mary P., 40
Mesnil, Jacques, 112
MEŠTROVIĆ, Ivan, 113
MEUNIER, Constantin, 113
Meyer, Franz S., 63
Michel, André, 5, 82, 122
Michel, Émile, 102, 124, 133
Michel, Paul H., 43
MICHELANGELO BUONARROTI, 113-114
Micheli, Geneviève L., 61
Middeldorf, Ulrich A., 122
MIES VAN DER ROHE, Ludwig, 114
Migeon, Gaston, 12, 65
MILLAIS, John Everett, 114
Millais, John G., 114
Millar, Eric G., 62
Miller, Alec, 34
Miller, Dorothy C., 51
MILLER, Kenneth Hayes, 114

Miller, Margaret, 106
MILLES, Carl, 114-115
Millet, Gabriel, 16
MILLET, Jean François, 115
Minamoto, Hoshu, 12
Minghetti, Aurelio, 72
Minns, Ellis H., 9
MINO DA FIESOLE, 115
Mireur, Hippolyte, 2
MIRÓ, Joán, 115
Mock, Elizabeth B., 32
MODIGLIANI, Amadeo, 115
Moes, Ernst W., 101
Moholy-Nagy, László, 19
Molinier, Émile, 63
Molmenti, Pompeo G., 84, 134
MONDRIAAN, Pieter Cornelis, 115
MONET, Claude, 115
Mongan, Agnes, 57
Monro, Isabel S., 67
Moore, Charles H., 26, 84, 110
Moore, Hannah H., 65, 73
MOORE, Henry Spencer, 115
Moore, Robert E., 102
Morassi, Antonio, 134
MOREAU, Jean Michel, 115
MOREAU, Louis Gabriel, 115
Moreau-Nélaton, Étienne, 87, 88, 89, 91, 105, 111, 115
Moreau-Vauthier, Charles, 97
MORETTO, Il (Alessandro Bonvicino), 116
Morey, Charles R., 16, 25, 74
Morgan, John H., 132, 133
MORISOT, Bertha (Mme. Eugène Manet), 116
Morley, Sylvanus G., 14
MORRIS, William, 116
Morrison, Hugh, 133
MORSE, Samuel Finley Breese, 116
Moschini, Vittorio, 79, 80
Moss, Henry St. L. B., 16
MOUNT, William Sidney, 116
Moureau, Adrien, 115

Muchall-Viebrook, Thomas W., 57
Müller, Hermann A., 2
Müntz, Eugène, 65
Mulk-Raj Anand, 12
Mumford, John K., 65
Mumford, Lewis, 25, 32
MUNCH, Edvard, 116
Muñoz, Antonio, 22, 80, 81, 111, 116, 136
Munro, Thomas, 5
Munsell, Albert H., 41
Muratov, Pavel, 16
MURILLO, Bartolomé Esteban, 116
Murray, Margaret A., 6
Murrell, William, 91
Myers, Bernard, 41

Nagel, Charles, 69
Nagler, George K., 2
NASH, John, 117
NASH, Paul, 117
NATTIER, Jean Marc, 117
Neilson, Katharine B., 109
Neugebauer, Rudolf, 65
Neuhaus, Eugen, 25
Neuweiler, Arnold, 49
New York, Museum of Modern Art, 26
Newcomb, Rexford, 26
Newton, Eric, 41
Nicholson, Alfred, 87
NICOLA D'APULIA, see PISANO, Nicola,
Nierendorf, Karl, 106
Nørlund, Poul, 24
Nolhac, Pierre de, 82, 95, 108, 117, 126
Nordensvan, Georg G., 24
Novotny, Fritz, 86
Nutting, Wallace, 69

Oakeshott, Walter F., 45
Odom, William M., 69
Oertel, Robert, 110

Østby, Leif, 49
Ojetti, Ugo, 47
Okakura Kakuzo, 12
O'KEEFE, Georgia (Mrs. Alfred Stieglitz), 117
Okkonen, Onni, 24
Old Master Drawings, 57
Oldenbourg, Rudolf, 128
Olmer, Pierre, 69
Omont, Henri A., 62
Oppé, Adolf P., 58, 102
ORCAGNA, Andrea (Andrea di Cione), 117
OROZCO, José Clemente, 117
ORPEN, William, 117
Ortolani, Sergio, 121
Osborn, Max, 18, 58
Osmaston, Francis P. B., 134
OSTADE, Adriaen van, 117
OSTADE, Isaac van, 117
Ostwald, Wilhelm, 41, 63
OUDRY, Jean Baptiste, 117

Pach, Walter, 19, 105, 124
PACHER, Michael, 118
PALLADIO, Andrea, 118
Palliser, Fanny M., 66
Pallucchini, Rodolfo, 47, 101, 119, 120, 136
PALMA, Giacomo (Palma Vecchio), 118
Pane, Roberto, 118
Panofsky, Erwin, 18, 36, 93, 109
Papadaki, Stamo, 108
Papini, Roberto, 96
Pariset, François G., 107
Park, Lawrence, 133
Parker, Barbara N., 88
Parker, Karl T., 58, 84, 103, 137
PARMIGIANO, Il (Francesco Mazzuoli), 118
Passavant, Johann D., 58
PATER, Jean Baptiste Joseph, 118
Pater, Walter, 18

Pauli, Gustav, 19
Pazaurek, Gustav E., 73
PEALE, Charles Willson, 118
Peet, Thomas E., 6
Peirce, Hayford, 16
Pelka, Otto, 74
Pendlebury, John D. S., 9
Pennell, Elizabeth R., 58, 138
Pepper, Stephen C., 5
Perls, Klaus G., 95, 137
PERRAULT, Claude, 118
PERUGINO (Pietro Vannucci), 118–119
PERUZZI, Baldassare, 119
PESELLINO (Francesco di Stefano Giuochi), 119
Pethebridge, Jeanette E., 66
Petrie, William M. F., 6
Pevsner, Nikolaus, 5, 27, 41
Peyre, Roger R., 133
Pfuhl, Ernst, 9
Phillips, John M., 76
PIAZZETTA, Giovanni Battista, 119
Picard, Charles, 9
PICASSO, Pablo (Pablo Ruiz y Picasso), 119
Picton, Harold W., 21
PIERO DELLA FRANCESCA, see FRANCESCHI, Pietro di Benedetto dei
PIERO DI COSIMO (Piero di Lorenzo), 119
Pietro, Filippo di, 79
PIGALLE, Jean Baptiste, 119
Pijoán, José, 5
Pilcher, Donald, 30
Pillement, Georges, 37, 125
PILON, Germain, 119–120
Pinder, Wilhelm, 21, 28–29, 36
PINTURRICCHIO (Bernardino Betti), 120
PIOMBO, Sebastiano Luciani, 120
PIRANESI, Giovanni Battista, 120

PISANELLO (Vittore Pisano), 120
PISANO, Andrea, 120
PISANO, Giovanni, 120
PISANO, Niccolò, 120–121
PISSARRO, Camille Jacob, 121
Pissarro, Ludovic R., 121
Pittaluga, Mary, 58, 110, 112, 134, 135
Place, Charles A., 83
Planché, James R., 67
Planiscig, Leo, 37, 76, 92, 97, 126, 136
Platz, Gustav A., 29
Plaut, James S., 106
Plenderleith, Harold J., 58
Plietzsch, Eduard, 133
Plon, Eugène, 85
Podreider, Fanny, 66
POLLAIUOLO, Antonio, 121
PONTORMO, Jacopo da (Jacopo Carrucci), 121
Pope, Arthur, 41
Pope, Arthur U., 12
Pope-Hennessy, John, 47, 92, 98, 130, 135
Popham, Arthur E., 58, 109
Popp, Hermann, 29
Porter, Arthur K., 27, 30, 34, 38
Pospisil, Maria, 111
Posse, Hans, 89
Post, Chandler R., 34, 49
POUSSIN, Nicolas, 121
PRENDERGAST, Maurice Brazil, 122
Price, Frederic N., 90, 128
Prideaux, Sarah T., 58
Priest, Alan, 66
PRIMATICCIO, Francesco, 122
Prior, Edward S., 30, 36
PRUD'HON, Pierre Paul, 122
PUGET, Pierre, 122
Puig y Cadafalch, José, 31
PUVIS DE CHAVANNES, Pierre, 122
Puyvelde, Leo van, 23, 48, 58, 128

QUERCIA, Jacopo Della, 122
Quintavalle, Armando O., 118

Racinet, Auguste, 63, 67
RAEBURN, Henry, 122
Ramsay, John, 72
Ramsdell, Roger, 68, 71
Randall-MacIver, David, 9
Ranke, Hermann, 6
RAPHAEL (Raffaelo Sanzio d'Urbino), 122–123
Raphael, Max, 6
Rathbun, Mary C., 41
Ratouis de Limay, Paul, 58
Rave, Paul O., 44
Rawlinson, William G., 135
Raynal, Maurice, 41, 78
Read, Helen A., 102
Read, Herbert E., 5, 19, 41, 73, 115, 117
Reath, Nancy A., 66
Réau, Louis, 20, 23, 42, 43, 62, 94, 104, 119, 137
Redgrave, Richard, 45
REDON, Odilon, 123
Redslob, Edwin, 31
REGNAULT, Henri, 123
Regteren Altena, Johan Q. van, 59
Reilly, Paul, 30
Reinach, Salmon, 5, 9, 41
Reis Santos, Luiz, 31
Reitlinger, Henry S., 59
REMBRANDT HERMANSZOON VAN RIJN, 123–124
Renders, Émile, 94, 138
RENI, Guido, 124
RENOIR, Pierre Auguste, 124
Répertoire d'Art et d'Archéologie, 2
Rewald, John, 43, 86, 91, 96, 111, 124, 130
Rey, Raymond, 16, 37
Rey, Robert, 98
Reymond, Marcel, 37, 126, 137
Reynolds, Graham, 59

REYNOLDS, Joshua, 124–125
Riat, Georges, 128
RIBERA, Jusepe de (Lo Spagnoletto), 125
Ricci, Corrado, 22, 30–31, 47, 80, 88, 120
Ricci, Elisa, 3, 66
Rice, David T., 16
Rice, Tamara A. T., 23
Rich, Daniel C., 117, 127, 130
Rich, Jack C., 34
Richards, James M., 27
Richardson, Albert E., 30
Richardson, Edgar P., 5, 51, 77
RICHARDSON, Henry Hobson, 125
Richter, George M., 85, 97
Richter, Gisela M. A., 9, 70
Richter, Irma A., 109
Richter, Jean P., 109
Ridder, André de, 86
RIEMENSCHNEIDER, Tilman, 125
Rijksbureau Voor Kunsthistorische Documentatie, 2
Rinaldis, Aldo de, 47, 112
Ring, Grete, 44
Ritchie, Andrew C., 41, 83, 91, 111
Rittich, Werner, 29
RIVERA, Diego, 125
Rivière, Georges, 124
Rivière, Henri, 91
Rivoira, Giovanni T., 9, 12, 31
Robaut, Alfred, 88, 91
Robb, David M., 5, 41
ROBBIA, Andrea Della, 125–126
ROBBIA, Giovanni Della, 125–126
ROBBIA, Luca Della, 125–126
ROBERT, Hubert, 126
Robert-Dumesnil, A. P. F., 59
Roberts, William, 104, 126
Robertson, Donald S., 9
Robinson, David M., 6
Rocheblave, Samuel, 20, 44, 119
Rodenwaldt, Gerhart, 9
RODIN, Auguste, 126

Roger-Marx, Claude, 105
Rogers, Frances, 73
ROGERS, John, 126
Rogers, Meyric R., 70, 114
Rolfs, Wilhelm, 107
ROMNEY, George, 126
Roos, Frank J., 5, 32
Rooses, Max, 23, 105, 128
Roosval, Johnny A. E., 24
ROSA, Salvatore, 126
Rosenberg, Adolf, 117, 122, 124, 133
Rosenberg, Jakob, 89, 124, 128, 130
Rosenberg, Marc, 76
Rosenthal, Leon, 59
Ross, Denman W., 41
Ross, Edward D., 6
ROSSELLINO, Antonio, 126
ROSSELLINO, Bernardo, 126
ROSSETTI, Dante Gabriel, 127
Rossetti, William M., 127
Rossi, Giovanni B., 16
ROSSO, Giovanni Battista, 127
Rothe, Hans, 100
Rothschild, Lincoln, 34
Rotonchamp, Jean de, 96
ROUAULT, Georges, 127
ROUBILIAC, Louis François, 127
Rouchès, Gabriel, 79, 85, 121, 123, 130
Rourke, Constance M., 25, 131
ROUSSEAU, Henri Julien Félix (Le Douanier), 127
Rousseau, Henry, 35
ROUSSEAU, Pierre Étienne Théodore, 127
Rowland, Benjamin, 104
Rowley, George, 12
RUBENS, Peter Paul, 128
Rubissow, Helen, 23
RUDE, François, 128
Rudrauf, Lucien, 91
RUSH, William, 128
Rushforth, Gordon M., 89
Ruskin, John, 5
Russell, Archibald G. B., 81, 101

RUYSDAEL, Jacob Isaacszoon van, 128
RYDER, Albert Pinkham, 128

SAARINEN, Eliel, 129
Sabatini, Attilio, 121
Sachs, Eleanor, 66
Sachs, Paul J., 57, 59
Saglio, André, 70
Saglio, Edmond, 8
SAINT-AUBIN, Gabriel Jacques de, 129
SAINT-GAUDENS, Augustus, 129
Salaman, Malcolm C., 59, 138
Saladin, Henri, 12
Salis, Arnold von, 18
Salmi, Mario, 37, 85, 95, 112
Salmon, André, 86
Salverte, François de, 70
Salvini, Roberto, 74, 87, 98
Sanford, Trent E., 33
SANGALLO, Antonio da, 129
SANGALLO, Giuliano da, 129
Sangiorgi, Giorgio, 66
SANO DI PIETRO, 129
SANSOVINO, Andrea, 129
SANSOVINO, Jacopo (Jacopo Tatti), 129
Sapori, Francesco, 129
SARGENT, John Singer, 129
SARTO, Andrea del, 129-130
SASSETTA (Stefano di Giovanni), 130
Saunders, O. Elfrida, 21, 62
Saxl, Fritz, 21
Schäfer, Heinrich, 12
Schapiro, Meyer, 99
Scharf, Alfred, 110
Schéfer, Gaston, 115
Schendel, Arthur F. E. van, 59
Scherer, Valentin, 93
Schiavo, Armando, 114
Schiefler, Gustav, 116
Schilling, Edmund, 59, 60, 103

Schleinitz, Otto J. W., 138
Schlosser, Julius, 2, 97
SCHLÜTER, Andreas, 130
Schmarsow, August, 94
Schmeckebier, Laurence E., 14, 47
Schmid, Heinrich A., 103
Schmidt, George, 50
Schmidt, Max, 14
Schmidt, Robert, 73
Schmidt-Degener, Frederik, 83, 132
Schmitt, Otto, 21
Schmitz, Hermann, 66, 70
Schneider, Édouard, 77
Schnier, Jacques P., 38
Schoeller, André, 88
Schoenberger, Guido, 101
Schöne, Wolfgang, 82
SCHONGAUER, Martin, 130
Schottmüller, Frida, 70, 76, 78
Schrade, Hubert, 125
Schubring, Paul, 22, 31, 47, 92
Schudt, Ludwig, 84
Schuette, Marie, 66
Schwabe, Randolph, 67
SCOREL, Jan van, 130
Scott, Geoffrey, 5
Scott, Robert G., 63
Séailles, Gabriel, 85
Sedgwick, Henry D., 24
Seeger, Georg, 137
Segard, Achille, 132
SEGHERS, Hercules Pietersz, 130
Seligman, Germain, 130
Sellers, Charles C., 118
Seltman, Charles T., 10
Sensier, Alfred, 115
Serra, Luigi, 92, 123
Sérullaz, Maurice, 88, 90
Servolini, Luigi, 78
SEURAT, Georges Pierre, 130
Seymour, Charles, 34
Shaw, James B., 101
SHEELER, Charles, 131
Sherman, Frederic F., 51, 128

Shirley, Andrew, 81, 87
Shoolman, Regina L., 59
SICKERT, Walter Richard, 131
SIGNAC, Paul, 131
SIGNORELLI, Luca, 131
Silcock, Arnold, 12
Silsby, Wilson, 59
Simmons, Pauline, 66
SIMONE MARTINI, see MARTINI, Simone
Simpson, Frederick M., 27
Singer, Hans W., 2, 59, 93, 124
Sinibaldi, Giulia, 110
Sirén, Osvald, 13, 98
Sizer, Theodore, 135
Sitwell, Sacheverell, 18, 21, 30
Slatkin, Charles E., 59
SLOAN, John, 131
SLUTER, Claus, 131
SMIBERT, John, 131
Smith, Chetwood, 126
Smith, Earl B., 7
Smith, George E. K., 29, 31
Smith, Harold C., 70
Smith, Robert C., 14
Smith, Solomon C. K., 88, 89
Smith, Vincent A., 13
Smith, William S., 7
SOANE, John, 131
Soares, Ernesto, 60
Sobotka, Georg, 35
Soby, James T., 41, 47, 51, 87, 89, 106, 115, 127
SODOMA, Il (Giovanni Antonio Bazzi), 132
Solon, Louis M. E., 72
Soper, Alexander C., 13
Spahn, Annemarie, 118
Spargo, John, 72
Speltz, Alexander, 63
Spinden, Herbert J., 14
SPINELLO ARETINO (Spinello di Luca Spinelli), 132
Springer, Jaro, 130

Stange, Alfred, 29, 44
Stapley, Mildred, 67, 74
Statham, Henry H., 27
Stauffer, David M., 60
Stechow, Wolfgang, 128
Steegmann, John, 21, 125
STEEN, Jan Havicksz, 132
Stein, Gertrude, 119
Steinbart, Kurt, 112
Steindorff, Georg, 7
Steinmann, Ernst, 97, 114, 120
Steinweg, Klara, 117
Sterling, Charles, 44
Sternberg Harry, 60
STEVENS, Alfred, 132
STEVENS, Alfred George, 132
Stevenson, Robert A. M., 128
Stewart, Cecil, 16
Stix, Alfred, 60
Stokes, Hugh, 100
Story, Sommerville, 126
STOSS, Veit, 132
Stout, George L., 40
Strange, Thomas A., 70
Stratton Arthur, 29
STRICKLAND, William, 132
Strong, Eugénie S., 10
Strzygowski, Josef, 16
STUART, Gilbert, 132–133
Sturgis, Russell, 27
Suida, Wilhelm, 109, 123
Sullivan, Edward, 60
SULLIVAN, Louis Henry, 133
SULLY, Thomas, 133
Summerson, John N., 30, 117
Supino, Igino B., 86
Sutton, Denys, 60
Swarbrick, John, 77
Swarzenski, Georg, 60, 121
Swarzenski, Hanns, 62
Sweeney, James J., 86, 90, 115
Swillens, P. T. A., 136
Swindler, Mary H., 7
Sydow, Eckart von, 7

Symonds, John A., 22

Tabarant, Adolphe, 111, 121, 135
Tabor, Margaret E., 3
Taft, Ada B., 133
TAFT, Lorado, 35, 38, 133
Taki, Sei-Ichi, 13
Tallmadge, Thomas E., 30, 32
Tarbell, Frank B., 10
Tatlock, Robert R., 24
Tattersall, C. E. C., 65
Taullard, Alfredo, 14, 70
Taut, Bruno, 27
Taylor, Henry O., 16
TENIERS, David, 133
TERBORCH, Gerard, 133
Tériade, E., 108
Terrasse, Charles, 44, 120
Testori, Gianni, 113
Thieme, Ulrich, 2
Thiery, A., 113
Thompson, Daniel V., 39, 41–42
Thomson, William G., 66
Thorn, C. Jordan, 72, 76
Thorpe, William A., 73
THORVALDSEN, Bertel, 133
TIEPOLO, Giovanni Battista, 134
Tietze, Hans, 60, 93, 134
Tietze-Conrat, Erika, 36, 60, 93
Tikkanen, Johan J., 24
TINO DA CAMAINO, 134
TINTORETTO, Il (Jacopo Robusti), 134
TITIAN (Tiziano Vecelli), 134
Toch, Maximilian, 42
Toda, Kenji, 13
Toesca, Elena, 121
Toesca, Ilaria, 120
Toesca, Pietro, 47, 112
Toft, Albert, 35
Tolnai, Charles de, see De Tolnay, Charles
Toor, Frances, 14
Tormo y Monzó, Elías, 24

Toscano, Salvador, 14
Totten, George O., 14
TOULOUSE-LAUTREC, Henri Marie Raymond de, 134–135
Toussaint, Manuel, 14
Tovell, Ruth M., 49
Towndrow, Kenneth R., 132
Trapier, Elizabeth du Gué, 100, 136
Treves, Marco, 4
Tristram, Ernest W., 45
Trivas, Numa S., 101
Trübner, Jörg, 129
TRUMBULL, John, 135
TURNER, Joseph Mallord William, 135
Tyler, Royall, 16, 25

UCCELLO, Paolo (Paolo di Dono), 135
Uhde, Wilhelm, 42, 99
Updike, Daniel B., 60
Upjohn, Everard M., 5, 135
UPJOHN, Richard, 135
Urlichs, Heinrich L., 8
UTRILLO, Maurice, 135

Vaillant, George C., 14
Valentiner, Wilhelm R., 23, 35, 101, 104, 106, 111, 124, 134
Valotaire, Marcel, 90
VANBRUGH, John, 135
Van Millingen, Alexander, 17
Vanzype, Gustave, 132
Varenne, Gaston, 82
Vasari, Giorgio, 47
Vasari Society, 60
Vaughan, Malcolm, 92
Vavalà, Evelyn S., 47
VELÁZQUEZ, Diego Rodríquez de Silva y, 135–136
Venturi, Adolfo, 22, 47, 120, 131, 136
Venturi, Lionello. 42, 50, 82, 84, 86, 127
Verga, Ettore, 109

VERMEER, Johannes (Jan Vermeer van Delft), 136
VERNET, Carle, 136
VERNET, Horace, 136
VERNET, Joseph, 136
Verneuil, Maurice P., 115
VERONESE, Paolo (Paolo Cagliari), 136
VERROCCHIO, Andrea del, 136–137
VIGNOLA (Giacomo Barozzi), 27, 137
Viollet-Le-Duc, Eugène E., 27, 28, 70
VISCHER, Peter, 137
Vito Battaglia, Silvia de, 88
Vitruvius Pollio, 27
Vitry, Paul, 35, 87, 99, 112
VLAMINCK, Maurice de, 137
Volbach, Wolfgang F., 17, 66, 74
Voll, Karl, 113
Vollard, Ambroise, 86, 91, 124
Voss, Hermann G. A., 47, 60
Voyce, Arthur, 31
Vries, Ary B. de, 136

Wackernagel, Martin, 29
Waern, Cecilia, 107
Waetzoldt, Wilhelm, 93, 103
Waldmann, Emil, 19, 77, 126
Waley, Arthur, 13
Walker, John, 51
Walpole, Horace, 45
Ward, Thomas H., 126
Ward, William H., 28
Warner, Langdon, 13
Wasmuths Lexikon der Baukunst, 27
Waterhouse, Ellis K., 48, 125
Waters, William G., 37
Watkins, Lura, 72, 73
Watson, Forbes, 85
WATTEAU, Jean Antoine, 137
WATTS, George Frederick, 138
Watts, Mary S., 138
Waugh, Evelyn, 127
Weale, William H. J., 94

WEBER, Max, 138
Webster, Thomas B. L., 10
Wedmore, Frederick, 60, 138
Wehle, Harry B., 76, 100
Weigelt, Curt H., 48, 92, 98
Weigert, Hans, 21
Weinberger, Martin, 60
Weisbach, Werner, 18, 25, 119
Weise, Georg, 32, 38
Weismann, Elizabeth W., 14, 38
Weitenkampf, Frank, 60
Weitzmann, Kurt, 62, 73
Weizsäcker, Heinrich, 94
Weller, Allen S., 96
Wenham, Edward, 76
Werth, Léon, 122
Wescher, Paul R., 50, 95
Westheim, Paul, 108
Wethey, Harold E., 33
Wettergren, Erik, 24
WEYDEN, Roger van der, 138
Wheatley, Henry B., 102
Wheeler, Anne B., 88
Wheeler, James R., 8
Wheeler, Monroe, 60, 127
Whinney, Margaret D., 22
WHISTLER, James Abbot McNeill, 138
Whistler, Laurence, 135
Whitaker-Wilson, Cecil, 139
Whitehill, Walter M., 32
Whitley, William T., 45, 96, 133
Whitman, Alfred, 60
Whittemore, Thomas, 17
Whittick, Arnold, 27, 113
Who's Who in American Art, 2
Who's Who in Art, 2
Wickhoff, Franz, 17
Wiele, Marguerite van de, 117
Wight, Frederick, 51
Wild, Angenitus M. de, 42
Wildenstein, Georges, 86, 107, 111, 115

Wilder, Elizabeth, see Weismann, Elizabeth W.
Wilenski, Reginald H., 19, 35, 44, 45, 49
Wiles, Bertha H., 37
Williams, Hermann W., 116
Williams, William C., 131
Williamson, George C., 76, 110, 119
Willich, Hans, 31, 137
Wilpert, Josef, 17
WILSON, Richard, 139
Winchester, Alice, 51
Wingert, Paul S., 139
Winkler, Friedrich, 45, 49, 61, 62, 93, 107, 138
Winzinger, Franz, 61
Wissler, Clark, 14
Wittgens, Fernanda, 95
Wittkower, Rudolf, 21, 31, 80, 114
WITZ, Konrad, 139
Wölfflin, Heinrich, 5, 22
Wolf, Georg J., 77
Wolfe, Bertram D., 125
Woltmann, Alfred F. G. A., 103
Wood, T. Martin, 84
Woodall, Mary, 96
Woodforde, Christopher, 73
Woolley, Charles L., 7
Worringer, Wilhelm, 7, 17, 45
WREN, Christopher, 139
WRIGHT, Frank Lloyd, 139
Wulff, Oskar K., 17, 23
Wurzbach, Alfred, 2
Wyler, Seymour B., 76

Yashiro, Yukio, 82
The Year's Art, 2
Yorke, Francis R. S., 27
Young, George F., 22

Zervos, Christian, 7, 10, 19, 93, 100, 113, 119
Zigrosser, Carl, 61, 106

Zimmer, Heinrich R., 13
Zimmermann, Ernst H., 62, 137
ZORACH, William, 139
ZORN, Anders Leonard, 140
Zucker, Paul, 42
ZURBARÁN, Francisco, 125, 140

Z
5931
L93
1952

MAR 21 1967